ROUTLEDGE LIBRARY EDITIONS:
THE GOLD STANDARD

Volume 4

T0299830

THE BATTLE FOR BRITAIN'S
GOLD STANDARD IN 1931

THE BATTLE FOR BRITAIN'S GOLD STANDARD IN 1931

DIANE B. KUNZ

LONDON AND NEW YORK

First published in 1987 by Croom Helm Ltd

This edition first published in 2018
by Routledge
2 Park Square, Milton Park, Abingdon, Oxon OX14 4RN

and by Routledge
711 Third Avenue, New York, NY 10017

Routledge is an imprint of the Taylor & Francis Group, an informa business

© 1987 Diane B. Kunz

All rights reserved. No part of this book may be reprinted or reproduced or utilised
in any form or by any electronic, mechanical, or other means, now known or
hereafter invented, including photocopying and recording, or in any information
storage or retrieval system, without permission in writing from the publishers.

Trademark notice: Product or corporate names may be trademarks or registered
trademarks, and are used only for identification and explanation without intent to
infringe.

British Library Cataloguing in Publication Data
A catalogue record for this book is available from the British Library

ISBN: 978-1-138-56184-7 (Set)
ISBN: 978-1-351-24702-3 (Set) (ebk)
ISBN: 978-1-138-57581-3 (Volume 4) (hbk)
ISBN: 978-1-138-57582-0 (Volume 4) (pbk)
ISBN: 978-1-351-27140-0 (Volume 4) (ebk)

Publisher's Note
The publisher has gone to great lengths to ensure the quality of this reprint but
points out that some imperfections in the original copies may be apparent.

Disclaimer
The publisher has made every effort to trace copyright holders and would welcome
correspondence from those they have been unable to trace.

THE BATTLE FOR BRITAIN'S GOLD STANDARD IN 1931

DIANE B. KUNZ

CROOM HELM
London • New York • Sydney

© 1987 Diane B. Kunz
Croom Helm Ltd, Provident House, Burrell Row,
Beckenham, Kent, BR3 1AT
Croom Helm Australia, 44-50 Waterloo Road,
North Ryde, 2113, New South Wales

British Library Cataloguing in Publication Data

Kunz, Diane B.
    The battle for Britain's gold standard
    in 1931.
    1. Gold standard — History
    I. Title
    332.4'52'09   HG297

    ISBN 0-7099-3120-4

Published in the USA by
Croom Helm
in association with Methuen, Inc.
29 West 35th Street
New York, NY 10001

Library of Congress Cataloging-in-Publication Data

Kunz, Diane B., 1952–

    The battle for Britain's gold standard in 1931.

    Bibliography: p.
    Includes index.
    1. Monetary policy — Great Britain — History. 2. Gold
standard — History. I. Title.
HG939.K85   1987   332.4'222'0941   87-9065
ISBN 0-7099-3120-4

Printed and bound in Great Britain by
Biddles Ltd, Guildford and King's Lynn

CONTENTS

For my husband Tom –
without whom this book could
not have been written.

PREFACE

This monograph grew out of an interest in international monetary relations which began during the seven years I spent working as a corporate lawyer on Wall Street. Participating in the sovereign debt struggles of the 1970's and early 1980's led me to an examination of how analagous events affected Great Britain and the world in 1931.

The transition from law to history which might have proved difficult has been a fulfilling one and for that I owe a great deal to various members of Oxford University. My thesis supervisor, Dr. R.A.C. Parker, was unfailingly helpful. He provided both encouragement and assistance in exactly the right proportions. Mr. Philip Waller was generous with time and critical advice on the art of historical writing. Dr. Stephen Stacey read the entire manuscript with great care and his suggestions proved of inestimable value.

This study was also read by Dr. Harold James of Cambridge University. For his comments, his support and for his continued willingness to discuss the events of 1931, I am very appreciative.

I was most fortunate in receiving invaluable assistance at various archives. Indeed, without the generous access to bankers' records which I received, a study of this kind would not have been possible. In particular, Mr. Henry Gillett, archivist at the Bank of England, was indefatigably helpful. Far from resenting the many days I spent in his office, he always remained willing to find yet another file. Mr. Carl Backlund, archivist of the Federal Reserve Bank of New York, was also of great assistance as were the archivists at the Herbert Hoover Presidential Library, West Branch, Iowa, the National Archives, Washington, D.C. and Sterling Memorial Library, Yale University, New Haven, Connecticut.

I was privileged to have been given full access to the archives of Morgan Grenfell Group PLC. Due to the kindness of Mr. Desmond Harney, Mr. Anthony Weighall and the staff of the Corporate Finance Files Department, perusing these crucial documents became a most pleasurable task.

Finally, Mary V. Roney and Joanne Parnes Shawhan deserve my thanks for their support and for always listening.

INTRODUCTION

TRANSACTIONS OF GREAT SATISFACTION

> 'You have been kind enough
> to refer in your letter to
> the assistance given by
> means of these credits
> during the crisis of last
> year. For our part, we
> look back upon these trans-
> actions with great satis-
> faction....'
>
> George Harrison to
> Montagu Norman
> 8 December 1932

Addressing the Anglo-American Conference of Historians in London on 13 July 1931, Ramsay MacDonald said:

> When the road is made and the facts are
> settled, the historian comes along in a
> charabanc, as it were, informing the world
> - when the roadmaker is dead or forgotten
> - whether the passage was smooth or
> bumpy. [1]

The Prime Minister's timing was flawless. The events about to unfold would be examined and debated not by coaches but by planeloads of historians fascinated by the British political and financial crisis of 1931.

While explanations of the departure of Great Britain from the gold standard were not long in coming (The Times was first into the field with a series of articles published in early October) the first scholarly treatments of the events of 1931 appeared in the 1950's and 1960's. They fall into two categories. The first, to which Reginald Bassett's 1931 and Robert Skidelsky's Politicians and the Slump were the most notable contributions, focused on the political events of the year. [2] Valuable as they are, works of this kind are inevitably incomplete since the battle to maintain the British gold standard was waged primarily by bankers and not by politicians.

In the second category are books on central banks. Chief amongst them are Henry Clay's biography of Montagu Norman, Governor of the Bank of

England, and <u>Central Bank Cooperation 1924-1931</u> by Stephen Clarke, followed by Robert Sayers' <u>The Bank of England 1891-1945</u>[3]. While providing much new information on the work of the Bank of England and the Federal Reserve Bank of New York ('FRBNY') both of which played crucial roles during 1931, these studies were not primarily focused on the British crisis and further did not cover the vital contributions made by private bankers to the attempt to rescue the pound. This same reservation applies to the treatments of the 1931 crisis published by economists such as Charles Kindleberger, Susan Howson and Sir Alec Cairncross and Barry Eichengreen[4].

The place of private bankers in the world monetary order has never received more attention than in the last ten years. Not since the 1930's were major money centre banks delegated so much authority, this time not to manage reparations but to recycle petrodollars. When the seemingly efficient international monetary order of the 1970's metamorphosed into the massive third world debt crisis of the 1980's, the actions taken by private banks and the supervisory monetary authorities who regulated their activities came under increasing scrutiny. Thus an examination of the role played by central and private bankers during the 1931 crisis and the underlying principles which governed the choices these men made is interesting as an historical question and also as a way of illuminating one of the major problems of our own time.[5]

The focus of this study, then, is on central bankers, especially Governor Montagu Norman and his colleagues at the Bank of England, and the merchant bankers of the House of Morgan since it is argued that a detailed examination of their actions is crucial to an understanding of the loss of the battle to keep Britain on the gold standard.[6]

A study of this kind demonstrates the ways in which central and merchant bankers exercised power and interacted with other interest groups notably the governments under whose jurisdiction they operated. No better topic than Britain's campaign to retain the gold standard in 1931 could be devised for this purpose. Given the historic role of sterling, the crisis itself was a paradigm of currency defence operations. Just as important, the events of 1931 marked not only the apogee of the bankers' power but also the beginning of its decline. Bankers, believing their calling to be above politics, achieved virtual autonomy during the

1920's. During 1931, however, the mounting economic crisis forced both Norman and Morgan's increasingly to look to governments to solve the problems with which they were faced. Simultaneously, unresolved monetary and fiscal problems compelled governments to begin the process of reclaiming control over financial matters. As bankers grew to accept that financial issues could not be addressed in a political vacuum, politicians grasped the basic point that by abdicating control over monetary issues, they had allowed the bankers' cart to pull their horse. The detailed chronological narrative herein is thus intended both to illuminate the battle for Britain's gold standard and to delineate the process by which bankers ceded power to politicians and civil servants.

Events pertaining to British governments - even the fall of the Labour Ministry - are examined only insofar as they relate to the struggle to keep sterling on the gold standard. For the same reason very little mention is made of members of the City community such as leading Clearing Bankers and Chairmen of Accepting Houses who, although prominent in financial circles, were of slight significance in the 1931 crisis.

As the pound had remained the currency franca, occupying the central position in world finance until the events of 1931, sterling's rise or fall was also a matter of great international importance. Other countries viewed the battle of Britain's gold standard as one in which they too had a stake. Indeed, the supranational aspects of the crisis were heightened by two developments. The first was Norman's espousal of the doctrine of central bank cooperation and the adoption of this goal by other central banks. Thus the major role played by the Bank of England's chief allies during the crisis, the Federal Reserve Bank of New York and the Bank of France, must be examined. The second factor was that to a significant extent the causes of Britain's departure from the gold standard were international in nature; the British struggle came after a series of banking crises had devastated the financial systems of Central Europe. Therefore the impact on Britain of catalytic events in Austria and Germany during the spring and early summer of 1931 forms an essential part of the analysis.

The year 1931 occupies a pivotal place in twentieth century British history because that year marked the conclusive failure of the widespread attempt made by financiers and politicians to return to the Edwardian Era. In Britain and elsewhere, a key component of the pre-war world was the role of sterling as the global currency and as the lynch pin of the gold standard which had been almost universally adopted in the thirty years prior to 1914. For this reason it became an accepted goal to return the pound, whose relationship to gold had been greatly eroded by wartime exigencies, to a gold bullion standard as soon as possible. That it was to be revalued at its pre-war dollar parity ($4.86 5/8) was virtually taken for granted, and for good reason. Britain's industrial supremacy had been steadily declining from the turn of the century. To compensate for this it was believed crucial to maintain the pre-eminent financial position of the City of London. The Bank of England, the City and various British governments, to the extent they focused on the issue, believed that this goal could be accomplished only by returning the pound to gold at a value which would ensure that confidence in sterling remained unshaken, namely $4.86 5/8. Furthermore a devaluation could have been read as a sign of the decline of British financial power, a statement that few in Britain were willing to make.

The pound was returned to the gold standard in April 1925 but instead of marking the culmination of post-war normalization, the return signalled the beginning of an increasingly difficult struggle for Norman and the Bank of England. The deteriorating British balance of payments coupled with the increasingly strong financial position of the United States and France kept the pound under constant pressure. Thus the first skirmishes of Britain's battle to retain the gold standard began in April 1925. Moreover, those in command of the battle had an insufficient understanding of how the pre-war gold standard worked. They viewed the mechanism as a self-correcting one which would automatically remain in balance through imports and exports of gold. This was an inaccurate depiction of the gold standard mechanism at its most efficient point and was even less applicable in the post-war world where, inter alia, countries deliberately sterilized gold flows.[7]

More importantly, the British believed the pre-war gold standard to be automatic because in large measure the adjustments necessary to keep the pound on gold had been unconscious. Before 1914 it largely suited the British economy to keep money cheap in London and to allow foreign issues easy access to the London financial market. This in turn helped to ensure a ready supply of capital in London with which to protect the pound. Given that there was no substitute for the pound, London's position as the world's financial capital was assured. But the centripetal forces which in combination had made the maintenance of the pre-war gold standard a relatively easy task switched direction during the 1920's. Then powerful centrifugal factors (such as the growth of alternative financial centres, the weakening of Britain's competitive position and the political force both of a Labour Party come of age and the newly enfranchised 'mass electorate') eroded the position of sterling and made its relationship to gold increasingly precarious. Faced with this situation, a determined effort involving financial sacrifices from all classes could have ensured the continuance of the gold standard. However, both politicians and many of their constituents thought the price was too high.

Yet the pound might have remained on the gold standard throughout the inter-war period (and with it many other currencies) but for one other factor. In a financial battle just as in a military confrontation a general cannot be victorious if he is not lucky. That fortune assuredly did not smile on Norman and the British helps explain the course of events between 1925-1931. Virtually all the economic predictions made prior to the return of gold proved wrong. Had they not been - particularly had there been the expected American inflation instead of a world wide depression with massive deflation - the course of monetary history could well have been different. Even so, 1931 might not have been the year of the gold standard's last stand had Britain not been dealt, within a three week period, a powerful triple blow. The German banking collapse of July 1931 was the first disaster to strike. Also in July came the publication of the Report of the Committee on Finance and Industry (known as the Macmillan Committee) which, at the worst possible time, revealed the large German exposure of British financial institutions. Finally on 1 August, the May Committee report exposed what was, for its era, a massive British budget deficit.

By the third week of July 1931 it began to be evident that the position of sterling was under serious threat and by the middle of August it had become obvious that the climax of the battle for Britain's gold standard had been reached. An examination of the months of intensive action - July, August and September - thus forms the core of the

5

analysis as the central banks of Britain, the U.S. and France, the three Morgan houses and, to a lesser extent, various governments, joined to save the British gold standard. The way in which these institutions acted during the emblematic monetary crisis of the inter-war period represented both the logical culmination of their activities during the preceding decade and also provided the last example of its type. Examining their actions during this time of trial illuminates both the institutions themselves and their larger role in British and world affairs. Furthermore it is possible to analyse the tactics used to defend the British gold standard, evaluate the effect the defeat had on Britain, and speculate on the answer to a question so many asked after 1931: had the battle been worth the candle?

Notwithstanding the concerted and sometimes heroic efforts of the Bank of England and its comrades in arms, the fight ended in surrender on 20 September 1931, in the process shattering forever the belief that sterling was as good as gold. This dénouement also fatally damaged the gold standard as it had been defined until then since the role of the pound in world monetary affairs was still such that its departure from gold caused most of the world's currencies to follow suit, culminating in the demise of the American gold standard in April 1933.

The fall of sterling brought many other changes in its wake. It helped to end the dominance of the Bank of England over the fate of the pound. Thereafter no senior Treasury official could say as did Sir Richard Hopkins in 1930: 'the control of the currency is exclusively a matter for the Bank of England. It is not a matter in which the Government intervenes....'[8] As the aura of omnipotence shielding the Bank's activities disintegrated, Government officials and Cabinet Ministers began to assume control over monetary matters. The decline in central bank cooperation greatly accelerated when, after the British collapse, the U.S. and France felt themselves increasingly threatened by the actions and inaction of their erstwhile ally. The power of merchant bankers, which had been invaluable to governments and central banks for centuries, was eclipsed as economists usurped their role as monetary magicians. None of these changes came about solely because of the demise of the British gold standard in 1931, but both the nature of the British decision and the way in which it was made accelerated these developments and therefore heavily influenced our own pattern of international monetary relations.

NOTES

1. The New York Times, 14 July 1931, p. 1.
2. R. Bassett, 1931 (Macmillan, London, 1958); R. Skidelsky, Politicians and the Slump (Macmillan, London, 1967).
3. H. Clay, Lord Norman (Macmillan, London, 1957); S.V.O. Clarke, Central Bank Cooperation 1924-1931 (Federal Reserve Bank of New York, New York, 1967); R.S. Sayers, The Bank of England 1891-1944 (Cambridge University Press, Cambridge, 1976).
4. C.P. Kindleberger, The World In Depression 1929-1939 (University of California Press, Berkeley, 1973); S. Howson, Domestic Monetary Management in Britain 1919-1938 (Cambridge University Press, Cambridge, 1975); A. Cairncross and B. Eichengreen, Sterling In Decline, (Basil Blackwell, Oxford, 1983).
5. Concerning the role of private bankers during August 1931 see also, P. Williamson, 'A Bankers' Ramp? Financiers and the British Political Crisis of August 1931', English Historical Review, xcix, October 1984.
6. The House of Morgan was composed of three inter-related banks: J.P. Morgan & Co. (New York), Morgan Grenfell & Co. (London) and Morgan et Cie. (Paris).
7. For a discussion of the ways in which pre-1914 gold standard was a managed rather than an automatic one, see, e.g., A.I. Bloomfield, Monetary Policy Under the International Gold Standard 1884-1914 (Federal Reserve Bank of New York, New York, 1959).
8. Evidence Before the Committee on Finance and Industry, Day 29, 16 May 1930.

Chapter One

BACKGROUND TO A CRISIS

1918-1930

'Could anything be more
heartening than for England
and America to lock hands
for honest money?'

Russell Leffingwell, 10
September 1923, advo-
cating an American
loan to help Britain
return to the gold
standard

i

Although Sir Edward Grey's celebrated remark
'the lamps are going out all over Europe' is
generally quoted in a political context, it is
equally applicable to international financial
relations. The pre-war monetary system based upon
the gold standard was another casualty of the
Great War. While it was neither as simple nor as
automatic as nostalgic retrospective accounts would
maintain, the financial order which had existed
prior to 1914 had functioned smoothly and, <u>inter
alia</u>, had allowed Great Britain without undue strain
on her resources to maintain the position of top
ranked player in the league table of nations. It is
thus not surprising that even before the war had
ended, in fact while Britain was still officially on
the gold standard[1], the Committee on Foreign
Exchanges After the War (known as the Cunliffe
Committee) declared:

In our opinion it is imperative that
after the war the conditions necessary
to the maintenance of an effective gold
standard should be restored without
delay. Unless the machinery which long
experience has shown to be the only
effective remedy for an adverse balance
of trade and an undue growth of credit
is once more brought into play, there
will be grave danger of a progressive
credit expansion which will result in a
foreign drain of gold menacing the

convertibility of our note issue and so
jeopardizing the international trade
position of the country.[2]

In its deliberations the Committee assumed that
when the pound was returned to gold its value would
be set at the pre-war dollar parity of $4.86 5/8.
Even when the pound, which had been pegged during
the war at $4.76 7/16, was released from its golden
moorings in 1919 and quickly plummeted to $3.40 by
February 1920, this assumption was not seriously
questioned by those studying currency matters. This
is not surprising if one remembers the concerted
attempt throughout the world, as American President
Warren G. Harding rather infelicitously termed it,
to 'return to normalcy'. A re-creation of the
status quo ante meant for Britain, among other
things, the safeguarding of her traditional financial primacy. In order to accomplish this the first
prerequisite, according to the City, the Bank of
England and the Treasury, was a strong and reliable
pound. Furthermore, particularly during the first
years after the war, the fact that Britain had been
victorious and indeed had greatly enlarged the
territory under her control through the acquisition
of League of Nations' mandates coupled with both the
need to vindicate Britain's role in the awesome
conflict and also the ephemeral promise of reparations resulted in a general lack of cognizance of
the enormous price the British had paid for
'victory'. Yet even the most sanguine observer
could not help but be daunted by a total war expenditure of £8,215 m over and above the expected
£1,000 m estimated as the total budget cost for the
years 1914-1918 had the war not taken place. As
only 10.7% of this amount had been paid by taxation
the result was an enormous increase in the national
debt.[3] A large percentage of this debt was held
abroad and, while Britain remained a net creditor in
1918, her financial strength had been greatly
eroded. For example, by 1918-1919, British privately held debt in the United States alone amounted to
$1,027.3m.[4] Simultaneously the war had caused a
great improvement in the economic position of
Britain's erstwhile ally. From a net debtor on
private account until 1916, the U.S. had emerged
from the war a net creditor with a surplus balance
of $3.5 billion and government debts owing to her in
excess of $10 billion.[5] This change in America's
financial situation was to have a significant effect
on her diplomacy and would boost the competitive

ability of New York bankers vis-à-vis the City of
London. It would also alter the nature of the
relationship between the U.S. and Britain.

The financial threat from the U.S., to the
extent that it was perceived by British financial
and political leaders between 1918 and 1925, un-
doubtedly served as incentive to return the pound to
gold as soon as possible. (That the emphasis which
was placed on the importance of the pound to the
British economy represented to a large extent a
reversal of cause and effect was not yet apparent).
One of the most influential advocates of this course
was Montagu Norman (1871-1950), Governor of the Bank
of England from 1920 to 1944. Norman, by virtue of
his enormous presence, air of mystery and unprece-
dentedly long tenure as Governor of the Bank of
England, has remained a figure of fascination.
Variously described as having the appearance of a
courtier in Queen Elizabeth's court or looking like
a band leader, his reign in Threadneedle Street
represented a coalescing of the man and the
moment.[6] Norman became Governor at the last time
that the Bank would possess full responsibility and
free discretion in currency matters. Unlike previous Governors, including his grandfather, who had
so served from 1885 to 1887, he did not hold an
important position at a City firm and thus was
prepared and even eager to devote all his energies
to the Bank and to the stabilization of the pound.
Moreover he was imbued with a Weltanshaûng which
would provide both a stable world financial system
and a central role for Norman and the Bank of
England.

This scheme for financial reconstruction,
formulated in memoranda prepared by the Bank in
connection with the international economic conference held in Genoa in April 1922, was based on
four principles which Norman hoped would be followed
by every central bank. The first was 'co-operation'
which represented the intention by central banks to
consult on matters of joint relevance. 'Exclusive-
ness' referred to technical banking relations .in
countries outside the central bank's own and
envisioned a commitment of the central bank to
maintain transactional relationships only with other
central banks and not with foreign commercial banks.
'Balances', the third principle, embodied the
willingness of the Bank of England and hopefully
other central banks to handle interest bearing
accounts for fellow central banks and also served as
a rubric for the legitimization of the gold exchange

standard. This offshoot of the traditional gold
standard allowed central banks who were still
considered to be on it to hold their reserves either
in gold or in the currency of a country on the gold
standard. While this was not a new development, it
only became accepted practice in the 1920's when
financial leaders were forced to cope with what was
generally perceived as a drastic shortage of monetary gold.[7] Adherence to the gold exchange
standard was seen as a way to economise the use of
gold and, it was believed, would strengthen the
position of the central banks which issued reserve
currency. That this created a two tier network of
countries was immediately apparent to the French and
Belgians whose opposition to the gold exchange
standard at Genoa led to a drastic watering down of
the Conference's resolutions. What was less obvious
was that a central bank which issued reserve
currency garnered prestige and a strong boost for
its currency only at a potentially very high price.
Its currency would increasingly be held by foreign
central banks and these institutions might choose to
use the power which they had thus achieved in ways
detrimental to the issuing central bank and the
economy it guarded. The fourth principle was that
of 'autonomy': central banks should be independent
in both form and substance.[8] Norman held banking
to be above politics and believed in the importance
of independent experts for the achievement of
financial stability.[9] His own bifurcation
mandated that the Bank of England should concern
itself with matters technical and financial while
the Government in general and the Chancellor of the
Exchequer in particular handled the political and
fiscal side.[10] Because he felt the creation of
central banks modelled upon his own institution to
be one of his most important tasks, Norman was ready
to send Bank of England advisers to any country
which requested them and urged governors of other
central banks to spend time at the Bank of England
with the aim of allowing his guests 'to share our
everyday life, just as it is and to feel that, in
some way, it expresses a generally human
reality.'[11] Norman's efforts resulted in the
creation of strong personal and institutional ties
between the Bank of England and central banks in the
dominions, in countries like Austria and Germany and
in many Eastern European countries. However it was
Norman's relationship with Benjamin Strong, first
Governor of the New York Federal Reserve Bank
('FRBNY') which provided Norman not only with a

personal relationship which he cherished but with an alliance of great importance for the future of the pound.

To say that the United States Federal Reserve System was in its infancy in the 1920's is no exaggeration; it was only created in 1913 and began operations the following year. Unlike previous attempts at an American central bank (the ill-fated Banks of the United States), it was not patterned after the Bank of England. Instead there had been created a financial institution which, mirroring the government it served, was notable for its separation of powers. The nation was divided into twelve federal reserve districts each with a federal reserve bank whose activities would be in part independent but would also be coordinated by an autonomous Federal Reserve Board in Washington. It was felt that this plan would dilute the influence of the Wall Street 'money trust' on the one hand and the Federal Government on the other. What its creators did not foresee was that their finely balanced equilibrium created a power vacuum which presented both the opportunity and the need for someone to provide leadership. From 1914 until 1928, when ill health caused his resignation and subsequent death, Benjamin Strong filled the gap, so much so that many British accounts of the inter-war period, both contemporaneous and historical, refer to the FRBNY as the American central bank. Strong was both a committed internationalist and a man who realised that the United States had interests separate from those of Europe. However, in his devotion to the gold standard and in his belief that Britain should return to it as soon as possible he was at one with Governor Norman whom he had met frequently since Strong's first war-time trip to London. [12]

Other influential Americans also wanted to aid the British return to gold. Most important among them were the partners of J.P. Morgan & Co. The 'house that Morgan built' was really three inter-related houses: J.P. Morgan & Co. (New York), Morgan Grenfell & Co. (London) and Morgan, Harjes et Cie., later Morgan et Cie. (Paris). [13] This financial empire was founded in London in 1838 by American expatriate George Peabody who grew successful by selling American securities to British investors. Junius Morgan became a partner in 1854 but it was his son J. Pierpont Morgan who was responsible for the House of Morgan's climb to the top of the Wall Street pyramid. Until his father's death in 1890,

Pierpont concentrated his efforts in the United
States and in so doing controlled by the turn of the
century the United States Steel Corporation, the
largest corporation in the nation, as well as a
majority of the country's railroads.[14] By 1901
the American satirist Peter Finley Dunne could write
that when Morgan was in the mood he could buy up
Europe and reorganize it on a paying basis by using
his small change.[15] The firm's British power base
had in fact been strengthened the previous year when
Morgan recruited as a partner Edward C. Grenfell,
future Conservative M.P. for the City of London and
member of the Court of Directors of the Bank of
England. Partly because of these London connections
and also because uniquely among major American
investment houses in the beginning of the twentieth
century it had no German connections, Morgan's
(N.Y.) was chosen to serve as the financial agent
for Great Britain during the First World War. Its
stalwart efforts on behalf of the Allies (the firm
also represented the French Government) and the
close relationship between Morgan's and the Bank of
England ensured them a firm place in the British
financial world after the war.[16]
    During the inter-war period the New York house
was led by a triumvirate of influential individuals.
The senior partner was J. Pierpont Morgan, Jr., who
had taken over at his father's death in 1913.[17]
J.P. was a confirmed anglophile who had lived in
Britain for many years and still spent between three
and six months a year in this country where he
maintained three homes. As he lacked the
overweening ambition of his father, Morgan did not
seek to maintain the House of Morgan's total
dominance of Wall Street which had existed prior to
the War. But he had inherited his father's view
that those possessing great wealth had the responsibility to use it rationally and constructively; this
was demonstrated by the House of Morgan's international lending activities during the two decades
after Morgan's succession. In recognition of his
firm's contribution to the British war effort and
also in gratitude for his gifts to the British
Museum, he was awarded an honorary Doctorate of
Civil Law by Oxford University in November 1930.[18]
    Thomas W. Lamont and Russell C. Leffingwell
made up the balance of the leadership of Morgan's
(N.Y.). Lamont, who had gone to Harvard on a
scholarship, joined Bankers Trust Company after a
stint as a newspaperman. Invited to be a Morgan
partner in 1911, he was the man responsible for

creating the face Morgan's presented to clients and to the general public. Conscious of the fact that the atmosphere of unbridled power created by Morgan, Senior had caused great problems for the firm, he made use of his background in journalism to cultivate good relations with reporters and editors. His efforts extended to clients and potential clients as well; for example, in 1927 he offered to arrange a special dinner for Ramsay MacDonald who was making a private tour of the United States, a gesture which led to the development of a personal relationship between the two men.[19]

Russell Leffingwell, wartime Undersecretary of the Treasury and Wall Street lawyer, joined Morgan's (N.Y.) in 1923. The acknowledged 'brain' of the firm, his role was to take apart and reassemble potential transactions to increase their viability and eliminate risks to the extent possible. His partners also grew to rely on his trenchant reading of political events and leaders. Together with Morgan and Lamont he shared a common outlook, one important part of which was a belief in the importance of the restoration of the gold standard for the world in general and Britain in particular.[20]

It was not only foreign bankers and the Bank of England who favoured the return to gold between 1919 and 1925, when the task was finally accomplished. The Treasury was behind this move as were many British industrialists who believed that price uncertainty was playing a large role in the decline of British exports.[21] The City of London was united in its support as were various politicians and economists. As one historian has said, 'the conflict was about means, not ends.'[22] Interestingly, what was true in 1918 remained unchanged in the early 'twenties: there was virtually no discussion about an alteration in the parity of the pound. Thus one of the most important milestones before Britain could return to the gold standard was a raising of the exchanges.

The other stumbling block which needed to be removed was the overwhelmingly large principal amount of British war debt owing to the United States which by Armistice Day existed in the form of a demand obligation to the United States in the amount of £978,000,000. In January 1923, Chancellor of the Exchequer Stanley Baldwin together with Montagu Norman journeyed to Washington to negotiate a settlement. Although Baldwin made a very good impression on the Americans, the resulting agreement which called for repayment over 62 years at a split interest rate of 3% for the first ten years and 3½% for the remaining life of the loan was only accepted grudgingly by the Bonar Law Cabinet and British opinion at large.[23] Yet it would have been naive to expect a settlement much better than that which the British obtained. It is true that nations who settled later received better terms but Britain's case was unique. The ambivalent nature of the Anglo-American relationship was composed of mutual admiration and suspicion, the desire to cooperate being mixed with the urge to compete. This created a tension that was apparent not only in the debt negotiations but at the various naval conferences held during the 1920's. Furthermore, Britain did not exhibit a humble attitude towards the U.S., either in general or specifically at the negotiating table. A continued belief that Britain remained the preeminent world power might have been the honest British view and it might also have been appropriate if Britain were to retain her financial leadership. However, it was ill-calculated to appeal favourably to the prevailing American sentiment best exemplified by President Calvin Coolidge's remark made in explanation of his opposition to a further reduction in war debts' payments: 'they hired the money, didn't they?'

ii

Once the debt settlement was history and particularly after the Conservatives returned to office in November 1924, the pound's steady appreciation convinced both the Bank of England and the Treasury that the time was approaching for Britain to return to the gold standard. That the Act prohibiting the free export of gold was due to expire at the end of 1925 provided a further impetus towards making a decision soon, notwithstanding the fact that hearings in front of the Chamberlain-Bradbury Committee on the amalgamation of the note issues had elicited a mixed bag of opinions as to the right time for this major step.[24] With the stabilization of Germany accomplished by the Dawes Plan, Treasury officials were convinced that 'the greatest danger is that London will be isolated in a gold standard world.'[25] During 1924 as well, Governor Strong, believing that American domestic conditions warranted such a move, brought down the Federal Reserve discount rate (the American equivalent to Bank rate) below the London Bank rate, thus strengthening the pound.[26] At the end of the

year Norman, accompanied by his deputy Sir Alan
Anderson, journeyed to New York in order to ascertain if Strong and Morgan's (N.Y.) believed that a
return to gold was feasible during 1925. According
to J.P. Morgan:

> The first question was whether in our
> opinion England should return to a free
> gold market at the end of this year when
> the export restriction law expires. To
> this, without hesitation, we replied in
> the affirmative. The next question was
> the method and amount of insurance against
> difficulty, which the British Government
> and the Bank of England should set up to
> protect themselves against undue flood of
> gold exports by speculators.... It would
> be really important to have the Federal
> Reserve Bank in it for as much as they
> could arrange with satisfaction to the
> Bank of England but as I told Norman, we
> could work up a bank credit here for
> $300,000,000 or for the whole
> $500,000,000.[27]

Strong also believed supporting credits were a
prerequisite. They were to be just as Morgan said,
insurance, the purpose of which was not only to stop
speculation but also to show potentially nervous
investors that Great Britain had the financial
resources to make the stablization of the pound
stick. With this raison d'être the credits had to
be of a high order of magnitude, thus Norman, Morgan
and Strong contemplated a figure of $500 m. The two
central bankers agreed with Morgan that part of the
money should take the form of a credit granted by
the FRBNY to the Bank of England with the remainder
to be in the form of a borrowing by the British
government from a syndicate of banks led by Morgan's
(N.Y.).

Simultaneously with these negotiations, senior
officials at the Treasury and the Bank convinced
Chancellor of the Exchequer Winston Churchill that
the gold standard was superior to a managed paper
currency. The gist of their argument was that it
was an overriding British interest that the pre-war
system should be restored. In response to the
Chancellor's concern over the domestic implications
of any Bank rate changes which might be necessary to
protect the pound, Churchill was told that the gold
standard could be defended by the other methods such

as the shipment of gold.[28] It is worth noting
that Churchill clearly foresaw that Bank rate and
the conflict between its international effect and
domestic ramifications would constitute the greatest
difficulty which would face Norman and the Bank of
England once the gold standard was re-established.
Nonetheless, Churchill acquiesced in the advice
offered him and on 28 April 1925 the decision to
return to gold was announced.[29] A $200 m credit
from the FRBNY had been obtained and a Morgan's
(N.Y.) managed credit, albeit for only $100 m, put
into place. The reduction in the latter's principal
amount had occurred in part because it was felt that
a total package of $300 m was sufficient but mainly
because the British Government baulked at paying a
commitment fee on the whole amount of the credit,
irrespective of whether it was used.[30] In the
event, the lesser amount proved ample, neither
credit was drawn down and the return to gold was
judged a success. It remained for Stanley Baldwin
to say:

> ...when I remember that the men responsi-
> ble in America for working with us in the
> restoration of the Gold Standard - which
> in itself is making a long step forward to
> the restoration of normal trade throughout
> the world - are Mr. Mellon, the Secretary
> of the Treasury, the Governor of Federal
> Reserve Bank and Messrs. Morgan I should
> like to say as my convinced opinion that
> in these men we are dealing with men [sic]
> than whom there are none higher for
> financial ability and moral rectitude. I
> would trust each and all of them no more
> and no less than I would trust the
> Governor of the Bank of England and those
> who have taken this matter in hand in our
> own country.[31]

His comparison of the American government, the
FRBNY and Morgan's with the Bank of England and the
British Government was an augury of the future - it
was precisely in these American entities that the
British would have to trust in the years ahead.

From May 1925 through 1926, the financial
waters were relatively tranquil but the first half
of 1927 proved otherwise as the Bank began to lose
sizeable amounts of gold. Partly in response to
this pressure Norman went to New York. There he not
only discussed financial and other matters with

Strong and with J.P. Morgan and his partners, Dwight
Morrow (future United States Ambassador to Mexico
and father-in-law of Charles Lindbergh) and Russell
Leffingwell, while cruising on Morgan's yacht the
Corsair, but participated in a conference of central
bankers held in Long Island in July, 1927. There
the projected French and Belgian stabilizations were
discussed and, more important to Norman, Strong
agreed to lower the FRBNY discount rate in order to
encourage funds to move out of New York and into
London.[32] For doing this Strong received both the
gratitude of Norman and the opprobrium of then
Secretary of Commerce Herbert Hoover. Calling
Strong a 'mental annex' of Europe, Hoover, not
alone, blamed Strong's action for triggering the
stock market boom which ended in Black Tuesday 26
months later.[33] This criticism illustrates yet
again the major problem the use of Bank rate could
cause for a nation's economy. Although it was the
traditional and still preferred method of protecting
a country's exchange position during the 1920's, the
domestic results of using this weapon were for the
first time examined and, particularly in Britain,
excoriated. Although it had long been realised that
a high Bank rate necessarily has a deflationary
effect, it was only after the First World War, when
unemployment and the decline in British industry
became major national concerns, that the tension
between the country's external and internal needs
became apparent. The domestic pressures against
raising Bank rate resulted in it being changed only
18 times or an average of three times a year during
the period May 1925 - September 1931 in contrast to
the six year period 1908-1914 when it was altered 39
times or an average of six times a year. Although
in 1929 Norman still felt sure enough of his authority to raise Bank rate without first consulting the
Chancellor of the Exchequer, there is no question
but that the Governor felt debarred from the unre-
stricted use of this device which his principles
would have seemed to mandate. No matter how firmly
he believed that Britain's international position
had the first priority, the state of British industry during the nineteen-twenties could not be
ignored, particularly when those who claimed that
high interest rates were destroying their hopes of
prosperity had articulate spokesmen such as John
Maynard Keynes and Reginald McKenna. Therefore,
during the difficult years 1928-1931 Norman increasingly utilized other weapons, primarily open
market operations, to protect the pound. He thus

shielded British industry from the full effect of the return to gold but also changed the nature of Bank rate from an everyday tool to a relatively drastic measure, a development which would have ramifications during the 1931 crisis.

Britain's problems in 1928 were largely a result of actions taken by two of her erstwhile allies. In New York the stock market boom drew money like a magnet from all over the world particularly after the FRBNY, partly in response to pressure from Washington, began to raise discount rates. American policy was also affected by Benjamin Strong's retirement in 1928 and his replacement by George Harrison. A personable man, Harrison was a lawyer by training but had no banking experience other than at Strong's side, first as Counsel and then, from 1920-1928, as Deputy Governor. His liabilities and strengths were summed up by Leffingwell who said in a letter to Edward Grenfell:

> George Harrison has been under the disadvantage of being young and new and a promoted subordinate and he has inherited all the antagonisms that poor Ben left behind him. But I have confidence in the soundness of his views and his ability to work out the situation ultimately.[34]

Unfortunately at a time of growing crisis the Federal Reserve System needed leadership and Harrison, although of sufficient standing to fight to a deadlock with the Governors of the Federal Reserve Board with whom he came into conflict (first Roy Young and then Eugene Meyer), did not have the strength to win. The resulting drift in United States monetary policy, best exemplified by the conflict over discount rates during 1929, had negative effects not only in the United States but throughout the world.[35]

The Bank of England's other problems were French in nature. France had officially restabilized the franc in June 1928 at the undervalued exchange rate of one-fifth of its pre-war level. This strengthened the franc's position and increasingly, foreign money was attracted to France. The Bank of France's firm resistance to a rise in the franc's value and its disinclination to follow Norman's suggestion and move to a gold exchange standard further resulted in the accumulation by France of gold reserves which by 1931 were second only to those of the United States. The success of the French stabilization had immediately placed a strain on Britain as large sums of French money which had flown from France in the years prior to 1928 were repatriated after June of that year. However, after this 'stabilization shock' had been assimilated there continued an irregular seasonal drain on the City caused by variations in the French money supply which affected London because, due to the undeveloped nature of the Paris money market, French banks and other institutions invested their short term funds in London. Of course such trans-actions were the lifeblood of the City, and indeed one of the impetuses for the return to gold had been to ensure that the pound would be considered a safe currency for investors. What was not foreseen was that the solid cushion of earnings from British overseas investment would decrease in size, that London would be robbed of the monopoly of inter-national money markets by the emergence of New York as an alternative center and that the financial bill, of which London was master, would become less important to international transactions due to the growth of wire transfers of money. The net result was that the British financial structure was far more vulnerable than before the war to the possible effects of sizable deposits and withdrawals beyond the control of the Bank of England. To the extent that this was perceived in Britain, there appeared to be little to be done except to cling tighter to the gold standard; financiers agreed with J.P. Morgan who had said that '[I] believe this step [the return to gold] the most important that has been taken since the war as showing how far Great Britain has gone on the road to recovery...'[36] Further no one offered a viable alternative to the gold standard; not even Keynes was yet ready for the brave new world of totally managed money.[37] The parlous state of British industry only encouraged this view for, to the extent that Britain had a positive balance of payments, it was due to the City whose financial health, according to contemporary wisdom, depended on the continuance of the gold standard, which therefore had to be protected.

British problems with the French were not limited to currency matters for personalities played their part. As Norman was a convinced francophobe, it was not surprising that his relations with the various governors of the Bank of France were the exception to his rule of close ties with other heads of central banks. Power politics contributed to this continual enmity, for men like Emile Moreau saw in the Bank of England's eager assistance to nations seeking to create a central bank an attempt to subvert France's traditional ties with Eastern Europe and a new form of British imperialism.[38] The continuing point of contention was reparations. Beginning with the negotiations at Versailles, Britain and France had been at odds over how much the Germans should be made to pay. The French had not forgiven the British for their lack of support over the Ruhr confrontation while the British, for their part, believed that the French insistence on Le Boche payera would only lead to the continued destabilization of Europe.

In 1929 the reparations controversy assumed the form of negotiations on and disputes concerning the Paris and Hague Conferences held to draw up what would become the Young Plan. Under the leadership of American industrialist Owen D. Young, a committee of experts gathered yet again to revise downward German obligations to the Allies. The American delegation (acting in their individual capacities, not as official representatives of the United States) included both J.P. Morgan and Thomas Lamont, choices dictated no doubt in part by the fact that the House of Morgan was now at the pinnacle of its international power and prestige. The war had played havoc with the various European currencies, and accordingly there was a pronounced need for a supranational banking institution to help accomplish the required stabilizations. The Bank of England, under Norman's leadership, provided advisors but was under pressure to conserve its own assets and limit the outflow of private British funds abroad. The House of Morgan, with three branches and ready access to plentiful American funds, willingly stepped into the breach. Not only were foreign transactions profitable but they satisfied the Morgan partners' sense of duty.

During the period 1919-1933 foreign issues sold by Morgan's approximated $1.350 billion. They helped draw up the Dawes and Young Plans and managed not only their American tranches but also organised the British credit and aided, among others, the governments of Austria, Belgium, France and Italy.[39] These loans provided the fuel to power the triangular flow of funds which transformed the nature of international financial relations during the nineteen-twenties; money was raised in the U.S. which enabled Germany to pay reparations to the Allies who made payments to the U.S. in respect of their war debts. This willingness to assume quasi-governmental responsibility illustrated by their international transactions and the participation by Morgan and Lamont in the Young negotiations was appreciated by the government in Washington which was maintaining the increasingly transparent fiction that reparations bore no relationship to war debts and further were of no interest to the U.S. That Morgan's (N.Y.) assumption of responsibility would cause problems when the interests of the American Government and Morgan's (N.Y.) diverged was not yet apparent.

Norman felt increasingly anxious about the position of the pound in 1929; by March it was only one-quarter of a cent above the gold point.[40] As he ascribed the 'increasing feeling of nervousness in London' to the situation in America,[41] Norman took the opportunity of a March visit to the Young conferees to complain to both Young and the Morgan partners:

> 1. While in Paris I protested ... to Owen D. Young against conditions in U.S. which have lasted long and which in spite of your [Harrison's] personal endeavours continue. For these conditions especially those of your credit position and money rates he as a Director cannot escape some responsibility. I pointed out that ignoring Berlin and Paris the whole exchange strain of Europe falls on London and that penal rates in London cannot fail to affect half-a-dozen European banks.
> 2. Similarly I protested to J.P. Morgan and T.W. Lamont generally as regards Europe and particularly as regards those countries which they assisted to stabilize on gold. I asked them whether under present conditions in U.S. it was proper for J.P. Morgan & Co. to watch without attempting to help the position of these stabilised European clients jeopardized by the present action or inaction of the System.[42]

Yet Harrison and the Board of Directors of the FRBNY had no choice but to continue pushing for ever higher discount rates as they made a futile attempt to contain the New York stock market boom, no matter what the effect on London. Norman's comments to Morgan and Lamont showed how the Governor, taking

them at their own valuation, expected Morgan's
(N.Y.) to act in a governmental fashion. He did not
appreciate the constraints which faced the New York
partners, for while their leadership may have been
recognized in Wall Street, it was shunned and
resented in other parts of the country, especially
the south and west, where the word 'Morgan' conjured
up the 1913 Pujo Committee hearings which had
attempted to expose a Money Trust supposedly led by
J.P. Morgan, Senior. These hearings had found not
an explicit illegal combination in restraint of
trade but instead revealed a network of control by
Morgan partners which encompassed seventy-two
directorships in forty-seven large financial corporations worth more than $10 billion.[43] A result of
these hearings was the establishment of the Federal
Reserve System and thus for Morgan's (N.Y.) to
attempt explicitly to pressure the FRBNY was something that even if they wished to do would have been
disastrous.

Norman had a further opportunity to continue
his conversations with Lamont in July 1929 when,
during a temporary breakdown in the Young negotiations, the latter came to Britain. He had lunch at
the Bank of England and met with Chancellor of the
Exchequer, Philip Snowden, who told him Britain
would bear the brunt of any problems caused by an
untimely termination of the reparations' revision
talks.[44] Norman went further; when Lamont, the
Governor and Prime Minister MacDonald conferred in
Scotland the following month, Norman said that the
consequences of a breakdown in negotiations would be
'the financial collapse of Germany followed by most
severe trouble in England and a possible abandonment
of the gold standard.'[45] During August as well
Norman and Harrison were discussing by cable the
purchase by Federal Reserve Banks of sterling bills
to help bolster the pound and Harrison even
suggested a credit to support the pound, an option
which Norman quickly dismissed.[46] Fortunately the
immediate cause of the strain on London, the high
New York discount rate, was soon removed. That the
cause, the Wall Street crash, was worse than the
disease would later be evident; initially the
feelings of most British bankers were voiced by
Keynes who said:

> We in Great Britain cannot help heaving a
> big sigh of relief at what seems like the
> removal of an incubus which has been lying
> heavily on the business life of the whole
> world outside America.[47]

The relief generated by easing conditions in New York did not solve London's problems; in fact as 1930 succeeded 1929, the situation seemed to worsen. The chief culprit in the minds of the British remained the French. Sir Otto Niemeyer, advisor to Norman, attributed a French unwillingness to conduct their gold transactions in London to a desire to weaken sterling, both to emasculate Britain's negotiating position at the Hague and to further the development of the nascent French money market.[48] Certainly the French wanted to improve the Paris market. According to Charles Rist, Professor of Finance and Director of the Bank of France, the short term market had to be reorganized so that it no longer compared unfavourably with that of London, New York or even Berlin.[49] The British found themselves with ambivalent feelings about their French competitor. As long as gold flowed from London to Paris the British longed for a French market which could absorb some of the demand. Indeed during 1929-31 they intermittently campaigned to encourage the growth of a putative Paris competitor.[50] When the gold drain ceased, the British desire for a preeminent London market with its prestige and power unchallenged overcame the fear of being forced off gold. Thus great importance was placed on this topic during the discussions between the British and French Treasuries detailed below.

The Bank continued to focus on French activity during the summer and autumn of 1930. An unsigned internal memorandum written at the end of July criticized French policy as selfish and mistaken but concluded:

> There is little doubt that they intend to pursue it relentlessly and so long as they do so we may expect the continuance and at times an increase of the gold drain to Paris.[51]

In December the Bank of England compiled statistics which showed that between May and November the Bank of France had taken £20.8 m gold from the Bank of England and £16.8 m gold from the London market.[52] Attempting to ameliorate this situation, British Treasury officials suggested that Norman approach his counterpart in Paris but, according to Sir Frederick Leith-Ross, 'The Governor always takes the line that it is contrary to the prestige of London to make any representations to the French about these gold movements.'[53] Perhaps spurred on by the fact that after November 1930 the Bank of England's net gold position began to deteriorate, Norman did go to Paris in December 1930. His discussions with Governor Clement Moret of the Bank of France achieved little because, according to a French diplomat, Norman appeared reluctant to enter any substantive discussions.[54]

In response to this failure, the British Treasury and the French Ministry of Finance agreed to hold discussions as soon as a new French government was constituted. When Norman was told of this he said that while discussions on monetary matters were all well and good, tariffs, war debts, cartels, etc. would all have to be brought into a comprehensive discussion.[55]

The Governor was correct in his view that given world conditions at the end of 1930, a purely monetary solution to Britain's problems did not exist. Though his statement showed an enormous leap from his earlier position which mandated an independent and autonomous place for monetary matters, Norman did not yet take the next logical step: if the state of the nation's currency could be considered only together with matters which were under government control, it followed that once the Government understood this, it would seek power over monetary affairs. Such a realization would be one of the results of the 1931 crisis.

NOTES

1. Britain was officially on the gold standard throughout the war but on 1 April 1919, coinciding with the end of official support measures for the pound, the export of gold was prohibited by regulations promulgated under the Defence of the Realm Act. The necessary regulations were combined in the Gold and Silver (Export Control) Act 1920 which was due to expire in December 1925.

2. Public Record Office, Kew, T208/17, Cunliffe Committee, 'First Interim Report', 15 August 1918, para. 47.

3. PRO, T208/41, R.G. Hawtrey, 'The Cost of the War', 12 August 1921.

4. K. Burk, Britain, America and the Sinews of War 1914-1918 (George Allen and Unwin, London, 1985), Appendix III.

5. M. Leffler, 'Expansionist Impulses and Domestic Constraints' in W. H. Becker and S. F. Wells, Jr., eds., Economics and World Power (Columbia University Press, New York, 1984), p. 227.

6.   _Time_, 19 August 1929, p. 52.
7.   Although the gold exchange standard as such was not followed before the war, foreign exchange holdings by central banks were accepted practice prior to 1914. See, _e.g._, Bloomfield, _op. cit._, pp. 55-6; K. W. Dam, _The Rules of the Game_ (University of Chicago Press, Chicago, 1982), pp. 31-4.
8.   R.S. Sayers, _op. cit._, pp. 157-9, Appendices 9 and 10.
9.   See, _e.g._, Bank of England Archives, London, ('B/E') G3/198, Norman to D.M. Mason, 5 November 1931, where Norman expounded on the Bank's complete impartiality towards all British governments and the related need for the Bank to remain above politics.
10.   B/E, G15/7, Note of a conversation between Norman and P. Snowden, 4 September 1929.
11.   B/E, G3/197, Norman to W. Wroblewski, 17 March 1930.
12.   L. Chandler, _Benjamin Strong, Central Banker_, (Brookings Institution, Washington, D.C., 1958), p. 94.
13.   J.P. Morgan & Co. held a partnership interest in both the London and Paris houses and thus the New York partners were partners in the foreign houses.
14.   A. Sinclair, _Corsair, The Life of J. Pierpont Morgan_ (Little Brown & Co., Boston, 1981), pp. 124-39.
15.   Peter Finley Dunne, _Mr. Dooley_, quoted in Sinclair, _op. cit._, p. 140.
16.   The term 'Morgan's' as used herein refers to the three houses as a whole while 'Morgan's (N.Y.)' refers specifically to the New York house.
17.   At his father's death, J.P. Morgan Jr. dropped the 'Jr.' and thus will be referred to herein without it.
18.   _The New York Times_, 24 November 1930, p. 14.
19.   Baker Library, Harvard University, Cambridge, Mass., T.W. Lamont Papers, 52-4, Lamont, to E.F. Wise, 28 February 1927.
20.   Leffingwell expounded this view often. In a penetrating eight page letter written on 10 September 1923 to Morgan he proceeded to enumerate the risks to Britain whichever decision was made and explained why he felt it was of overriding importance both to Britain and to the world for Britain to return to the gold standard, in the process demolishing the arguments of J.M. Keynes. (Morgan

Grenfell & Co., Limited, London, Morgan Grefell Papers, ('Morgan Grenfell'), R.C. Leffingwell, Bundle 252).

21. PRO, T173/46: Memorandum: 'Return to the Gold Standard', undated.

22. Howson, op. cit., p. 35.

23. Lamont Papers, 111-15, Lamont to E.C. Grenfell, 26 January 1923.

24. This Committee was set up to deal with the problems caused by the war-time issue of Treasury notes but at its wide ranging hearings considered the question of a return to gold at great length.

25. PRO, T208/54, Hawtrey, 'Sterling and the Gold Standard', 24 April 1924.

26. Chandler, op. cit., p. 305.

27. Morgan Grenfell, British Gold Credit - 1925, Morgan to Grenfell, 11 February 1925.

28. B/E, 95.04, Hawtrey, 'The Gold Standard', 2 February 1925.

29. The decision took the form of an announcement by Churchill that the Act of 1920 prohibiting the export of gold would be allowed to lapse.

30. Morgan Grenfell, British Gold Standard Gold Credit - 1925, Morgan to Grenfell, 7 March 1925.

31. Morgan Grenfell, British Gold Standard Gold Credit - 1925, Grenfell and Lamont to Morgan, 25/4615, 5 May 1925.

32. At this time each Federal Reserve Bank had the right to set its own discount rate although in practice they usually followed the FRBNY.

33. H. L. Hoover, The Memoirs of Herbert Hoover - The Great Depression (Macmillan, New York, 1952), p. 9.

34. Yale University, New Haven, Conn., R.C. Leffingwell Papers, I/3/69, Leffingwell to Grenfell, 29 May 1929.

35. See, e.g., B/E, G3/194, Norman to E. Moreau, 23 March 1929.

36. Morgan Grenfell, British Gold Standard Credit - 1925, Morgan to Baldwin, 30 April 1925.

37. In this connection, it is interesting to note that as late as November, 1931, Keynes was advocating instead of a system of totally managed money the linkage of the pound to a commodity-based index. (PRO, T188/48, Keynes, 'Notes on the Currency Question', 16 November 1931.)

38. Chandler, op. cit., p. 380.

39. Morgan Grenfell, JPM Miscellaneous, File 18/A, Statement of G. Whitney to the U.S. Senate Subcommittee on Banking and Currency, 25 May 1933.

40. B/E, G3/194, Norman to R.V.N. Hopkins, 4 March 1929.
41. B/E, G3/194, Norman to Moreau, 23 March 1929.
42. Morgan Grenfell, British Gold Standard Credit - 1925, Norman to Harrison, 12 March 1929.
43. Sinclair, op. cit., p. 223.
44. Lamont Papers, 173-1, Lamont Diaries, 29 July 1929.
45. Lamont Papers, 173-1, Lamont Diaries, 10 August 1929.
46. Columbia University, New York, N.Y., G. L. Harrison Papers, Binder 18, Harrison Memorandum to Files, 16 August 1928.
47. J.M. Keynes, The Collected Writings of John Maynard Keynes, Vol. XX - Activities 1929-1931, (Cambridge University Press for the Royal Economic Society, Cambridge, 1981), p. 1.
48. B/E, OV45/3, O.E. Niemeyer, 'French Exchange and the Gold Efflux', 24 February 1930.
49. B/E, OV45/3, C. Rist, 'The Paris Market Should Play an International Role', L'Europe Nouvelle, 11 January 1930.
50. Concerning the sometime British desire to see an expansion of the Paris market, see, e.g., a list of practical suggestions to curtail gold movements to France drawn up at a meeting of Sir F.W. Leith-Ross, S.D. Waley, O.M.W. Sprague and H.A. Siepmann, on 30 January 1931 (B/E, OV45/4).
51. B/E, OV45/3, Memorandum: 'The French Demand for Gold', 29 July 1930.
52. B/E, OV45/3, Memorandum: 'France - Estimate of Gold Movements - 1930', undated.
53. PRO, T208/148, Leith-Ross, 'Note of an interview with Monsieur Pouyanne on 16 December 1930', 17 December 1930.
54. Ibid.
55. PRO, T208/148, Hopkins postscript to above cited Note, 17 December 1930.

Chapter Two

STORM BEFORE THE CALM, CALM BEFORE THE STORM

January - May 1931

'Cooperation between the
United States and Great
Britain on monetary prob-
lems [is] called for.'

Ramsay MacDonald to
Thomas Lamont
9 May 1931

i

The New Year did not relieve the strain on
London caused by continued exports of gold to France
because the normal January improvement in the
exchanges did not occur. This lent a note of
urgency to the Anglo-French Treasury discussions
which began in Paris on 2 January 1931. Sir
Frederick Leith-Ross, senior British Treasury
representative at these meetings, felt that the
French had changed their attitude and were in
earnest about seeking to improve relations although
the only tangible result of these first meetings was
the decision to resume talks in London on 14
January.[1]
These unprecedented meetings attracted a great
deal of attention. American Ambassador to France
Walter Edge cabled Secretary of State Henry Stimson
that the purpose of the talks was to plan a conference on the question of gold movements and Edge
further reported that the French were offering the
British a credit to support sterling.[2] The French
press also carried the latter story but maintained
that British pride would not permit them to accept a
credit from France.[3]
Norman was not impressed by the joint Treasury
meetings, informing the Committee of Treasury of the
Court of Directors of the Bank of England (the group
of Directors who performed a quasi-governing
function) that the first round had produced no
tangible results and expressed doubt as to whether
there would even be a second encounter.[4] He added
that by mutual agreement the Bank of England and the
Bank of France had not participated in these
discussions, a statement which would indicate that
Norman was either uninformed about French views or

being disingenuous since according to Leith-Ross, the French wished the Bank of France to be involved.[5] At this same 7 January Committee of Treasury meeting Norman discussed the continued drain of gold and possible steps to be taken to protect the exchanges. Three options appeared to be open: raise Bank rate to induce funds to remain or return to London, convert foreign currency into earmarked gold which would obviate the necessity to ship gold from London and thus make the bank return look better, or to play a waiting game and hope the situation would improve. The last course of action was chosen.[6] A week later Norman explained his problems to Harrison in the following fashion:

> [A Bank rate increase] depends on gold movements. Firstly if exports continue making substantial reduction in our holding market may become nervous and notwithstanding shortage of bills may lift rates to a point which would force us to raise Bank rate. Secondly even although market rates failed to rise sufficiently to force us we may have to go up if continued drains were to reduce our gold holding to some total which I cannot now forecast....
>
> The above may seem indefinite but our actions must be governed by gold movements. We could not in any case remain passive indefinitely in face of continued losses of gold, especially taking into account our present fiscal and industrial position.[7]

Norman's dilemma was clear. Caught between the Scylla of Britain's domestic position and the Charybdis of international economic currents, his room for manoeuvre was very limited. One option Norman did have was to pressure the Government to try to take action to calm the market and he did not hesitate to read his cable to Harrison to Snowden and tell him that a flight from sterling could be caused by a loss of gold, budget problems or social- ist legislation and in any such eventuality a rise in Bank rate (then at 3%) would be necessary.[8] It should be noted that this enumeration indicates that the three elements underlying the summer crisis - gold movements caused by domestic and international problems, a British budgetary crisis and the dislike evidenced by the financial community within and without Britain of the dole and other 'socialist' accomplishments - were already present in January. They would remain important elements of the British financial and political scene, although their strength would ebb and flow, until August when the simultaneous reemergence in full force of all three factors would culminate in the crisis.

The joint Treasury discussions resumed as scheduled and the French submitted a memorandum designed to answer British charges that London's problems were due to a combination of weaknesses in the French money markets and deficiencies in the enabling legislation of the Bank of France which prevented it from engaging in open market operations or taking a major foreign currency position.[9] The French response, written by M. Escallier, ascribed the increase in the Bank of France's gold reserve to the French balance of payments surplus which began in 1926 and continued through 1930. Admitting that French investors deposited and withdrew large balances frequently from London, he pointed out the obvious fact that this was a chief function of the London market and then somewhat disingenuously complimented the London market on its fine handling of these transactions. Escallier did state that the French were planning to open up the French market to foreign issues (another British idea) and then suggested that if the British wished to end the gold drain they should 'allow free play to the whole of the factors which tend the whole time to bring the amount of the foreign liabilities of a country into due proportion with its foreign resources' which was to say the British should raise Bank rate and improve their export position. After criticizing the Bank of England's resort to open-market operations, Escallier, with what his opposite numbers must have considered a typically gallic twist of the knife, expressed the hope that his British colleagues would examine their own system 'in the same spirit' as the French had shown.[10]

The British dismissed the Escallier memorandum, the Treasury concluding it was wrong on every major point.[11] They missed the central fact - that their demand that the French Ministry of Finance and Bank of France mend their evil ways was exceedingly arrogant. Indeed one has only to imagine Montagu Norman's reaction if he had received a list of alterations to be made to the Bank of England's Charter. That under the circumstances the French not only prepared the Escallier memorandum thereby

showing a willingness at least to examine their
policy but also came to London to meet with Treasury
officials supports Leith-Ross's assessment that the
French were seeking to improve relations. This
conclusion is buttressed by the results of the
London meetings. The French agreed to minimize the
amount of idle balances at the Bank of France, said
they shared the British view that a resumption of
foreign lending by London, New York and Paris was
imperative, and promised to consider allowing the
League of Nations Gold Delegation (which had been
formed to examine the causes of the fluctuations in
the purchasing power of gold and their economic
effects) to publish its report - a step the British
were very much in favour of but one the French had
formerly opposed. Thus Leith-Ross's conclusion of
15 January that the value of the meetings should not
be underestimated is not surprising.[12] Another
sign of a continued pattern of French helpfulness
was the Bank of France's acquiescence in Governor
Norman's request that the Bank of England be allowed
to swap dollars it held in New York for francs held
by the Bank of France, which francs the Bank of
France would apply to purchases of sterling thereby
obviating the need for gold shipments from London to
Paris.[13]
      It is interesting to speculate on the reasons
for this change of attitude on the part of the
French. Partly no doubt it was a response to the
fact that the slump, which had been late in arriving
in France, had begun to affect the French economy by
late 1930.[14] This had the effect of altering the
French view that their excellent monetary policy had
rendered them immune to economic dislocation.
Secondly, conditions in Germany were clearly deteriorating; a British Treasury official writing in the
second half of January said: 'I feel that events in
Germany are moving slowly but inevitably to disaster.'[15] The French no doubt wanted to have the
British on their side if there was to be yet another
revision of reparations and this was far more likely
if monetary cooperation between Britain and France
was improved.
      The position of sterling, however, continued
very weak and the Daily Herald attributed this to 'a
very serious quarrel between powerful American and
British banking interests.' It further stated that
the American grievance resulted from resentment over
the loss of foreign business to London.[16] The
Herald's report was clearly erroneous; although it
was true that the principal amount of foreign

securities offered for sale in the U.S. in 1930 and early 1931 was far lower than in previous years, this had been caused not by successful competition from Great Britain but resulted from a decline in American interest in foreign securities growing out of the Wall Street crash and increased by a loss of confidence in European borrowers.[17] Far from gloating over the paucity of American loans to Europe, the British Treasury was clearly concerned about the American reluctance to lend abroad.[18] However, this article does illustrate a readiness among some members of the Labour party to ascribe British economic problems to American financiers – an uncanny foreshadowing of the famous Herald story of 25 August 1931 which ascribed the fall of the Labour government to a bankers' ramp led by George Harrison.

Yet American policy was not only the concern of the British left during early 1931; it was discussed as well when the Chairmen of the 'Big Five' clearing banks made their speeches at their banks' respective annual general meetings. According to Reginald McKenna, Chairman of Midland Bank Ltd., a fair percentage of British problems could be laid at the door of the late Wall Street speculative fever while F.C. Goodenough, head of Barclay's Bank Ltd., urged America to improve her own economy and that of the world by cancelling war debts.[19]

The Chancellor of the Exchequer took up the theme of the war debts and the American attitude towards them during his major speech on the budgetary situation delivered on 11 February. Presented against a back drop of the continuing drain of gold which had reached such an alarming level that Keynes wrote that for the first time in his memory there were open discussions about a devaluation of sterling and the abandonment of the gold standard,[20] Snowden said:

> We have the burden of the war debt. I do not wish to give offence to anybody when I make this statement, that when the history of the way in which that debt was incurred -- its recklessness, its extravagance, commitments being made which were altogether unnecessary in the circumstances at the time -- when that comes to be known I am afraid posterity will curse those who were responsible.[21]

Perhaps Snowden's main target was David Lloyd
George, leader of the Liberal Party and Prime Minister during the First World War, but he obviously had
no hesitation about attacking the U.S. in the process. The pendulum marking the British attitude
towards the U.S. appeared to have begun to swing to
a hostile position. At the same debate the Chancellor, faced with his own estimate of a budget deficit
for the 1931-2 fiscal year of £30 m and a projected
gap of £50 m for the following year, ended his
speech by saying that:

> If there were a well grounded fear that
> this country's budgeting was not sound, it
> might have very disastrous consequences,
> which would have their repercussions
> abroad. It is quite true that other
> countries are watching, and that there-
> fore, we must maintain our financial
> reputation and that we can do. [22]

Snowden was correct. Britain had to decrease its
budget deficit and rationalize its finances.
London's unique strength, her financial markets,
were more and more proving her Achilles heel and
concern about their condition would increasingly
burden the British government both domestically and
internationally.

As Snowden saw the budget as crucial, his
acquiescence in the Liberal amendment to a
Conservative motion which provided for a committee
to be appointed in order to propose government
economies was not surprising. With the creation of
what would become the May Committee, another of the
fires which would ignite the August crisis was now
laid.

The issue of war debts was also the subject of
discussions between France and Britain; Montagu
Norman reported to the Committee of Treasury that:

> The French government are anxious for all
> European nations concerned to agree
> beforehand to pursue a common policy
> concerning Debt payments. If Germany
> defaults on Reparations, France and Italy
> will claim a moratorium on War Debt
> payments.

According to the Committee's minutes, it was decided
that 'the matter should remain open for further
consideration in the light of the conditions ob-

taining if and when the need for a decision should arise.'[23] Thus the issue of war debts could force Britain to decide with whom to side: France or the U.S. The answer had obvious implications for the course of European history.

Norman also took this occasion to tell the Committee of Treasury that he had agreed to submit what would sometimes be known as the Norman Plan to the Bank for International Settlements for its consideration. This scheme, also called the Kindersley Plan after its architect Sir Robert Kindersley, Chairman of Lazard Brothers and a director of the Bank of England, called for the formation of an international corporation which would make loans to foreign countries and corporations. The capital of the corporation would be subscribed by France, the U.S. and Britain but it was to the 'surplus' gold supplies of France and the U.S. that Kindersley primarily looked for money which would be recycled into the hands of the debtor nations.[24] In January Norman had said he thought the plan not very practical and, although he had not changed his mind (he told Treasury officials in late February it would not work), he had obviously decided there was no harm in proposing the plan.[25]

It may be that Norman's increasingly pessimistic view of global financial conditions motivated this change of heart. He ascribed British problems 'to defects in our financial policy during the last few years and a consequent lack of confidence in British Government securities and sterling.' He even went so far as to say that the French were correct when they emphasized the importance of a loss of confidence in Britain to an understanding of the British plight, thus providing one of the very few instances when the Governor said the French were right about anything.[26] The Treasury was not as self critical, continuing to blame the French for causing an 'abnormal' gold drain from London to Paris.[27]

The Bank for International Settlements ("BIS") took up the Kindersley Plan at its monthly board meeting of 9 February 1931. An outgrowth of the Young Plan and designed with the main purpose of facilitating German reparations payments, this first supranational banking institution had begun operations in May 1930. The central banks of all major gold standard countries were founding members save for U.S. which refused to join because of the Bank's explicit connection with reparations. Instead Morgan's (N.Y.), The First National Bank of New York

and the First National Bank of Chicago subscribed to
the American shares which were subsequently sold to
the public. The FRBNY began a careful tightrope
walk between involvement and non-involvement, a task
not made easier by the selection of Gates McGarrah,
a former director of the FRBNY as the first President of the BIS, a choice determined by the need to
preserve neutrality between the French and the
Germans.

Norman quickly became disparaging about the
'World Bank' as the BIS was occasionally called. By
September 1930 he had stated that:

> It is common talk that the BIS is a menace
> to the international exchange market and
> judging by the way this [dollar] swap was
> proposed and is now commenced, this common
> talk is true.[28]

The next month he wrote to the Governor of South
Africa's central bank that:

> The BIS in its administration is dominated
> by American habits and by French ideas and
> these ideas include a good deal of adver-
> tisement and the seeking of conditions,
> profits and the like, which you and I have
> not been accustomed to associate with
> Central Banking.[29]

One reason for Norman's dislike of the BIS was his
recognition that the BIS, by creating a mechanism
for government to government transfers of money
outside the realm of central banks, was eroding the
theretofore total control of central banks over
foreign transfer payments. The Governor was concerned enough to note this change to the Committee
of Treasury:

> [The Governor] mentioned that the advent
> of the BIS had altered the time honoured
> relations between the Bank and the
> Treasury.... This fact necessitates
> frequent interviews and consultations
> between officials of the Treasury and the
> Bank with the result that the Governors
> are not and cannot be the sole connecting
> link. He viewed this situation with some
> disquiet....[30]

In fact the BIS not only encroached upon what Norman considered the Bank of England's prerogatives but took over some of Morgan's functions, specifically their provision of dollars for the British payment of its war debts to the U.S.[31] It thus represented one of the first steps in the shift of power from central banks and their merchant bank allies to governments which would be enshrined in post-Second World War creations such as the International Bank for Reconstruction and Development (also known as the World Bank) and the International Monetary Fund.

Notwithstanding his feelings Norman made a practice of attending the monthly BIS board meetings held at its Basle headquarters. If nothing else these gatherings of central bankers provided them with an opportunity to discuss their mounting problems in an informal and relatively private manner particularly at the Sunday night dinners which preceded the regular Monday board meetings. It was at such a dinner that Norman first learned that the Kindersley Plan was not receiving an enthusiastic reception from the French and the Americans, partly due to a suspicion that the Plan was designed to steal their well-earned gold reserves in order to redistribute them to countries who through their own profligacy had squandered the opportunity to amass comparable stocks. It is not difficult to see why they had bristled; the original summary of the Plan, later revised to soothe those nations' ruffled sensibilities, began by stating:

> Many Authorities are agreed that the mal-distribution of gold has in large measure contributed to the existing world crisis... and that world recovery will be impeded by the fact that the U.S. and France, instead of lending back to the world their surplus for a usable balance of payment, have been taking this surplus in the form of gold.[32]

This exposition reflected the British contention that not only did the U.S. and France possess an inequitable proportion of the world's monetary gold but that they had made matters worse by 'sterilizing' it; that is to say, refusing to allow imports of gold to have the inflationary effect on the American and French money supplies which the theory nominally adhered to by all nations on the gold standard would have mandated. There is no question but that the Americans and French were guilty as charged but what the British failed to recognize was that they were not in a position to throw stones; by increasing its tacit reliance on open-market operations in lieu of increases in Bank rate, the Bank of England was also deviating from the practices mandated by traditional gold standard theory. However, as the American and French actions were far more visible, it is not surprising that these countries bore the brunt of the Interim Report of the League of Nations Gold Delegation. This document, prepared in 1930-31, criticized the hoarding of gold by avaricious countries and without naming names pointed a finger at the U.S. and France.[33] Perhaps because of the discussions connected with the Kindersley Plan, it began to be rumoured that the BIS might expand on the work of the Gold Delegation, specifically by effecting a reduction in the proportion of gold reserves held by member nations' central banks, and indeed this possibility continued to be mooted at Basle over the next few months.[34]

During late February as the Kindersley Plan was being debated in financial capitals by central banks and merchant bankers (Lamont was sent a copy on 14 February), the British and the French Treasuries resumed their talks.[35] The background was still ominous, Kindersley writing that French investors, fearing that Britain might go off the gold standard at any moment, were loath to purchase British bills.[36] These discussions did not progress very far because the British baulked at the French deflationary remedy for their problems - an increase in Bank rate.[37] The French were equally reluctant to adopt any of the detailed suggestions the British had prepared for them; to be precise, ten 'bright ideas'.[38] Once more a suggestion of a British loan in Paris, this time in the form of the discounting by French banks of British bills, was discussed. According to Ambassador Edge, the French officials were unhappy with the British noncommittal attitude to this possible solution to British problems, a response attributed by an official of the Bank of France to:

> a hesitancy in accepting any arrangement that might eventually, even in some small degree lead to the transfer to Paris of world financing operations, in which London has hitherto played the leading role.[39]

While Leith-Ross retained his view that the French
sought to cooperate with their British counterparts,
his positive feelings about the French were not
shared by the Prime Minister Ramsay MacDonald.[40]
Speaking on the subject of naval negotiations, he
said: 'France plays her usual game of dishonest
construction on words and approaches. The sole
problem for Europe apparently is to be how to keep
France in her place.'[41] With a leader who had
formed such a negative view of the French and, given
that the Bank of England was consistently anti-
French, it is not surprising that the attempt at an
Anglo-French financial rapprochement did not succeed. Having thus turned away from Europe, the
issue for Great Britain was whether a working
relationship with the U.S. was possible.

MacDonald's counterpart in Washington was at
that time (21-22 February) contemplating the issue
of war debts in general and the British war debt in
particular. Herbert Hoover was America's 30th
President and almost certainly her unluckiest. A
native of middle America, born in very poor circumstances, he rapidly rose to fame as one of the
world's most successful mining engineers. Both as a
senior partner in Bewick, Moreing & Company, a
British firm, and head of his own firm of mining
consultants, he lived in London from 1907 to 1914
and it was his work organising facilities for
Americans stranded in Europe at the onset of the
First World War which led to his role as head of the
Commission for Relief in Belgium. (It should be
noted that the combination of his pre-war experience
in Britain and his battles with Asquith, Lloyd
George and Churchill over Belgian relief left him
with at least a slight anti-British bias.) As
Hoover's fame as 'The Great Humanitarian' soon
exceeded his reputation as the 'The Great Engineer',
he was the logical choice for U.S. Food Administra-
tor once the U.S. entered the War, in which capacity
he introduced 'victory sausage' and put the slogan
'Food Will Win the War' into the American vocabu-
lary.[42] In 1920, an amateurish attempt to run for
President having fizzled out in California, Hoover
campaigned for the Harding/Coolidge ticket and asked
for the position of Secretary of Commerce on the
condition that he be given responsibility for all
commercial activities including international
economic matters formerly under the supervision of
the Departments of State and Treasury.[43] His
terms were granted and Hoover ran the Commerce
Department for the next eight years, his tenure

being the only time in that department's history
when it attracted any attention. At Commerce,
Hoover attempted to implement his personal philosophy which consisted of an attempt to wed traditional
American ideology to the realities of twentieth
century life. He believed that science and ration-
alism would provide answers for most of the world's
problems and that, of all professionals, the engineer was the most important to modern life. As
Hoover considered that individual initiative was the
key to a nation's strength, he was against government intervention when there was any alternative,
particularly criticizing the dole.[44]

In 1928 Hoover ran for President and soundly
defeated Alfred E. Smith. While he did not coin the
slogan, 'a chicken in every pot', that was the
unsaid message; with Hoover the prosperity of the
1920's would continue. It was not to be. Barely
six months after taking his office came the Wall
Street crash and the beginning of what would common-
ly be called in the U.S. the 'Hoover Depression.'
Although he continued his very involved, 'hands-on'
Presidency (his style was very similar to that of
Neville Chamberlain and the contrast between Hoover
and his predecessor Calvin Coolidge analogous to
that of Chamberlain and Stanley Baldwin), Hoover
slowly turned bitter and isolated himself in the
White House. To Stimson meetings with the President
were like being in a bath of ink.[45] Initially
Hoover had believed that the depression was
temporary, isolated and home-grown but by December
1930 he had changed his mind, saying that 'in the
longer view the major forces of the depression now
lie outside of the United States.'[46]

Almost despite himself the President began
focusing on European problems and in particular the
war debts/reparations conundrum. Earlier he had not
been sympathetic to European complaints. In 1922
Lamont wrote Grenfell that 'Hoover, whose heart is
supposed to be melting with tenderness for Europe,
is the worst of the lot.'[47] In February 1931,
Hoover did not yet believe that the U.S. would make
any substantial contribution by postponing debt
payments; he told Stimson that a mere $250 m (the
total payments due to the U.S. in 1931) was too
small to have any effect on the world situation.
Furthermore nothing he did could aid Britain for,
thanks to the Balfour Note, any benefit derived from
a reduction in the amount of monies owing to the
U.S. by Britain would immediately be passed on to
her debtors.[48] It would take considerable pres-

sure - the failure of one country's major bank and the threat to a second nation's financial order - before Hoover would revise his thinking.[49]

As time passed and foreign demands for gold continued slowly but steadily to erode British reserves, R.H. Brand gloomily concluded: 'there is a great and growing lack of confidence, both here and abroad (which I think well justified) in our power to adjust ourselves to external conditions.'[50] Norman occupied himself by continuing to criticise the BIS, writing Harrison that 'the BIS is already slipping to the bottom of a ditch....'[51] His antagonism was probably not lessened by the fact that the BIS was at that time serving as a depositary for central banks which had converted sterling holdings into dollars.[52] At last, during the end of the first week of March, the pound had strengthened against the franc. However, sterling had weakened against the dollar and Norman reported that Snowden had said that he was always being told that no matter what he did, Britain would slide off the gold standard, to which the Governor had reassured the Chancellor that the Bank was prepared to take any steps that might be necessary, however drastic, to prevent that taking place. He had also informed the Chancellor that 'no financial position, however good, could be maintained indefinitely against worsening fiscal and industrial conditions.'[53] Again Norman had indicated the inextricability of financial conditions from other matters; the erosion of his original ivory tower conception of monetary matters was continuing apace.

In keeping with his usual custom and in order to discuss Britain's exchange position, Norman, together with Harvard Professor O.M.W. Sprague, who served as his advisor, made plans to visit the U.S. Leffingwell had offered him a home as had Parker Gilbert (former Agent-General for Reparations and now a Morgan partner) but on Harrison's advice Norman turned both men down and instead accepted the hospitality of the FRBNY's Governor.[54] Norman and Sprague embarked on 21 March and the Bank released a statement urging that no special significance be attached to his trip.[55]

The Governor was not yet aware that the last week in March marked the end of the first sterling crisis of 1931 - by the beginning of April the exchanges would turn definitely in Britain's favour where they would stay until mid-July. Ironically this earlier crisis, instead of serving as a warning, may have produced a false sense of security. For by standing fast Britain had weathered the storm. She had not made major concessions to anyone, nor had the Bank of England broken precedent and issued a public loan to shore up sterling. The truth of Sir Richard Hopkins' comment of a year earlier, that should an exchange crisis come there would always be plenty of time in which to handle it, appeared to have been borne out.[56]

ii

While Norman was en route, the Kindersley Plan returned to the forefront of international discussion; it was reported that J.P. Morgan had told Gates McGarrah that his bank was not interested in cooperating in its implementation.[57] This coincided with earlier intimations in Basle that the opposition of the Bank of France had doomed the Plan.[58] Yet on his arrival in New York on 28 March, Norman was immediately asked about it but, as usual, he refused to speak to the press, although he affably wished them 'better luck next time'.[59] Norman spent the first week of his trip in New York where he must have been cheered by the prevailing sentiment which was focused on the hope of an economic upturn. For example, the monthly First National Bank of New York Report said that there were continued improvements in the business situation [60] and Sullivan & Cromwell, a major Wall Street law firm, was under the impression that the German bond business would improve in the near future.[61] (The latter information confirmed British reports that the situation in Germany was getting better.[62]) Germany was in the forefront of the political news during this period; Foreign Offices and Treasury Departments 'were focusing on the Austro-German plan for a customs union. The U.S. State Department had difficulty deciding whether such a scheme would violate any existing treaties unlike the French who were sure it was illegal. Stimson's preliminary conclusion was that he should not allow himself to be quoted on the topic as the matter was bound to cause problems between France and Germany.[63]

Stimson began his direct involvement with the world of international finance when he visited the FRBNY in New York on 1 April. Until the previous month liaison with the FRBNY and the Federal Reserve Board in Washington had been handled by Harrison together with Undersecretary of State Joseph Cotton, but the latter's untimely death had left a vacuum which Stimson himself, at Harrison's suggestion, agreed to fill.[64] Thus when Norman arrived, an invitation to Stimson was extended and the latter travelled to the FRBNY's 33 Liberty Street headquarters to meet the British central banker. At their first meeting Norman apparently said very little but Harrison previously had reported that Norman believed that the key to the financial situation was the position of labour and that the depression would not be cured unless the price of labour was brought down to a par with other commodities.[65] Several days later, with sterling definitely improving, Norman journeyed to Washington where he met with President Hoover to whom he reiterated his views as to the necessity for the deflation of labour costs.[66] Stimson also had the pleasure of lunching with the Governor at Secretary of the Treasury Mellon's home and finally they had an extended discussion at the Secretary of State's office.[67] Norman, as was now usual for him, was very pessimistic about the general European situation. After excluding Belgium and France from consideration on the grounds that they were not badly affected by the slump, he singled out Poland, Czechoslovakia, Rumania and Yugoslavia as countries which Poincaré, by offering loans, had been trying to form into an anti-German block, thus mirroring the accusation Moreau had earlier levelled against Norman. The Governor put Germany and Britain in a category by themselves, being in very similar economic straits, and then proceeded to praise Germany and excoriate Russia as 'the very greatest of dangers.' Finally Norman spoke in very gloomy terms about the English predicament and the role of the Labour Party. While he had only the highest praise for Philip Snowden, calling him 'the best loved Chancellor of the Exchequer that England had had within his memory', the Governor said that the rank and file Labour party was socialistic and the leaders were tied to them and could not escape.[68]

Norman's comments are very revealing: he was obviously far more candid with the Americans than he was in Britain. One must conclude that his honesty did not aid the British cause during the next few months - having expressed a lack of confidence in the Government his Bank worked with, it was only logical that his audience came to share his misgivings. It is also interesting to consider the nature of his American reception. It would seem that Norman had reached the apogee of his success; he was received by the President, the Secretaries of

State and Treasury as well as by Harrison and various Morgan partners. Everyone was eager to hear what the Governor of the Bank of England thought about the world's problems. Perhaps if more constructive answers had been forthcoming, neither Norman's position nor that of the institution he represented would have declined in the years to come in the way that they did.

The American papers followed Norman's progress closely, not only speculating on possible results if the Kindersley Plan were adopted but publishing reports that a key purpose of his visit was to suggest an international parley on war debts.[69] French observers also watched carefully; according to an American diplomat, it was the secrecy and suddenness of Norman's trip which excited the interest Parisians obviously took.[70] Swiss reports were contrary to French comments which also emphasized a possible Anglo-American agreement on war debts; Basle gossip had it that Norman was seeking a reduction in the FRBNY discount rates, which was the only report seemingly borne out by future events.[71] At dockside on 14 April Norman again evaded questions save for one enquiry in response to which he said he did not believe that the fate of King Alfonse of Spain would have any effect on international finance.[72]

The Governor returned to London on 21 April and attended the Committee of Treasury meeting the next day. First Professor Sprague, summarizing the impressions he had garnered in his native land, opined that the hoped-for spring revival would not occur. The Governor then said that the attitude of the U.S. towards Britain specifically and the world generally had altered, that Americans believed that Britain either could not or would not adjust to present realities and that Germany was 'the outstanding country in Europe which possesses the foresight and courage necessary to deal with the problems of the present moment.'[73] What Norman appears to have done here is to quote himself back to the Committee of Treasury, attributing his sentiments to the Americans. This is clear when one examines what Stimson recorded Norman as saying specifically about the Germans:

she was the one country whose policy had been directed with manly courage ... they had got it to a point where the members of the employed class were ashamed not to be employed. They were ashamed to rest upon the dole....[74]

44

By emphasizing an American lack of respect for Britain, Norman may have hoped to force changes in her domestic monetary policy for this would not be the last time he misquoted others to suit his purposes. He was, however, right that Americans had at least perceived a shift in the balance of Anglo-American relations; for example, Stimson said in late April that Britain, instead of interfering in American diplomatic initiatives, now simply followed America's lead.[75] This alteration in the balance of power between the U.S. and Britain would obviously have ramifications on the events of the next few months.

Norman had much to occupy himself with upon his return. The sterling exchange continued to rise, an event which frankly puzzled the Governor.[76] A warning memorandum prepared by his central banking section was circulated in the Bank and shown to the Treasury. It predicted that in the summer the franc would strengthen and thus gold exports from London to Paris beginning in July until the middle of November must be expected.[77] Finally he surely paid attention to the budget which Snowden presented to Parliament on 27 April. Making use of the expedients for which he had so often condemned Churchill, Snowden balanced the budget chiefly by altering the timing of income tax payments.[78] While the ploy worked, no one doubted that the solution was purely temporary in nature.

By May even the American optimists had given up on a possible recovery; leading economist Irving Fisher told Stimson that the cause of the depression's continuing force was the failure of the FRBNY to purchase bonds on the open market and Fisher attributed Harrison's inaction to his being under the thumb of Russell Leffingwell.[79] Leffingwell's partners, J.P. Morgan and Thomas Lamont, were meanwhile journeying in opposite directions. Morgan, having left England where he had lunched with Norman at the end of April, was returning to New York while Lamont, after visiting Italy and France, arrived in Britain and immediately went to the Bank of England.[80] There he dined with Grenfell and Norman and the latter painted a dismal picture - finance was trying to keep on a steady course caught between the industrial crisis and political storms. According to the Governor:

> The Labour Government did not know where
> it was going - it had no fiscal policy
> that was settled.... England was not

> master in her own ship but the U.S. [was]
> blind and taking no steps to save the
> world and the gold standard.[81]

Putting this statement together with those he made
earlier, one can conclude that Norman, having
despaired of the pound's future, may have believed
that his chief hope was an American - sponsored
rescue.   Given his American ties (he had spent
several happy years there and had many friends in
the U.S.) and the support he had received from
Strong and Morgan's, such an attitude on his part
would not have been surprising.   It would also
explain why after Britain had gone off the gold
standard in September 1931, Norman was considered
the most likely originator of the destructive
rumours about the U.S. financial position which
caused her to suffer a massive gold drain.   If he
felt rejected by the country whose help he had
sought, he may have found a suitable revenge.[82]
     The exchanges remained favourable to Britain
and with call money rates in New York down to 1%,
their lowest rate since 1908, Norman felt justified
in cabling Harrison on 13 May that Bank rate would
be reduced to 2½% effective the next day.[83]   But
this development was not sufficient to overcome
Norman's depressed mood.   Firstly he was informed
that the report of the Macmillan Committee would
shortly be released and furthermore that it would
contain recommendations which would be embarassing
to the Bank.[84] Formally known as the Committee on
Finance and Industry, the Macmillan Committee had
been established in 1929 to investigate the position
of the City and its relationship with British
industry.
     More ominous at the time, the situation in
Austria was rapidly deteriorating.   The Bank of
England had maintained close ties with Austria,
aiding in her post-war reconstruction and helping to
create the Austrian National Bank while Britain had
been one of the guarantors of the various League of
Nations loans issued on Austria's behalf between
1922 and 1930.   Indeed, Norman's services were
appreciated by the Austrian government to the extent
that it decided to reward him; after some debate
between the propriety of a medal versus a piece of
art, he received the Grosse Goldene Ehrenzeichen am
Bande from Ambassador Baron von Franckenstein in
March 1931.[85]   In March as well, the negotiations
over the Austro-German customs union became public

knowledge and, as Norman's positive feelings about
this scheme were not shared by the French, tension
rose in Central Europe.[86] However, the general
feeling of apprehension over Austria's future was
replaced in early May by two specific worries. The
lesser was the release of information from the
Austrian Government budget office of figures which
indicated that notwithstanding various financial
sleights of hand, the Austrian budget had produced a
small deficit for the year 1930 and a very large
predicted deficit for 1931.[87] In the era when
what is now known as deficit financing was considered national bankruptcy, this was indeed
serious. The more present danger was represented by
a bank which has gone down in financial history as
the match which ignited the 1931 cataclysm - Credit
Anstalt. This bank was not only the largest bank in
Austria but controlled 40% of Austrian industry.[88]
After a somewhat halting start it had seemed that
this entity formed by merger three years earlier was
on solid footing but due to a witch's brew of
circumstances - the parlous state of the Austrian
economy, a general perception that the French were
withdrawing their funds out of anger over the
customs union plan and peculations at the Credit
Anstalt - by May the Credit Anstalt was on the verge
of closing its doors.[89] The problem was splashed
across front pages of newspapers in London, New York
and Paris on 11 May and by the end of that week the
Austrian government was urgently seeking new
financing. The government turned to Morgan's hoping
it would coordinate the loan but was told that
present conditions in London and New York prevented
their taking the kind of role the Austrian Government had envisioned.[90] By 18 May the major
central banks had become involved as they pondered a
BIS suggested credit of 100 m Schillings.[91]
Within the week both Norman and Harrison felt that
Austrian problems were so grave that it was imperative to involve their respective governments.
Therefore Norman went to Downing Street to report
about the crisis while Harrison called Stimson.[92]
During this period, and for the last time, Norman
and the Bank of England took the lead in organising
a rescue attempt, convening a Credit Anstalt credi-
tors' committee (including reluctant Morgan Grenfell
partner Charles Whigham) at the Bank of England and
supervising their deliberations.[93] In showing a
willingness to forget Great Britain's troubles in an
attempt to alleviate those of Austria, Norman was
motivated in part by his close ties with Austria but

47

more importantly by his belief that 'a monetary breakdown in Austria might quickly produce a similar result in several countries.'[94] Time would confirm his judgement.

NOTES

1. B/E, OV45/4, Leith-Ross, 'Note on Financial Discussions with the French Treasury', 5 January 1931.
2. National Archives of the United States, Washington, D.C., RG 59, 851.51/1663, W. Edge to H. Stimson, 7 January 1931.
3. NA, RG59, 851.51/1663, Edge to Stimson, 6 January 1931.
4. B/E, MB52, Committee of Treasury ("C/T") Minutes, 7 January 1931.
5. B/E, OV45/4, Leith-Ross, 'Note on Financial Discussions with the French Treasury', 5 January 1931.
6. B/E, MB52, C/T Minutes, 7 January 1931.
7. Federal Reserve Bank of New York Archives, New York, N.Y., C261, Norman to Harrison, 9/31, 13 January 1931.
8. B/E, MB52, C/T Minutes, 14 January 1931.
9. B/E, OV45/4, Hawtrey, 'French Gold', 26 January 1931.
10. B/E, OV45/4, Escallier Memorandum, 13 January 1931.
11. Hawtrey, op. cit., 26 January 1931.
12. PRO, T188/22, Leith-Ross, 'Memorandum Concerning Conversation with French Treasury Officials', 15 January 1931.
13. B/E, G3/198, Norman to C. Moret, 26 January 1931.
14. Bundesarchiv, Koblenz, Federal Republic of Germany, R 111/32, 'Operations of the Bank of France 1930', Bankers Trust Company Department of Foreign Relations - French Section, February 1931.
15. PRO, T188/24, Leith-Ross Memorandum, 20 January 1931.
16. The New York Times, 27 January 1931, p. 12.
17. W. Lippman and W.O. Scroggs, The United States In Foreign Affairs - 1931 (Harper & Brothers, New York, 1932) pp. 32-3.
18. See, e.g., Leith-Ross's comments in his 'Memorandum Concerning Conversations with French Treasury Officials', 15 January 1931, (PRO, T188/22).

19. NA, RG59, 841.516/80, R. Atherton to Stimson, 31 January 1931.
20. Keynes, op. cit., p. 485.
21. NA, RG59, 841.00/1145, Atherton to Stimson, 13 January 1931.
22. Ibid.
23. B/E, MB52, C/T Minutes, 4 February 1931.
24. NA, RG39, Box 104, M.H. Cochran to J. Cotton, 11 February 1931.
25. B/E, MB52, C/T Minutes, 7 January 1931; PRO, T208/149, Leith-Ross, 'Memorandum Concerning Conversation with Sir Richard Hopkins and Governor Norman', 17 February 1931.
26. Leith-Ross Memorandum, op. cit., 13 February 1931.
27. PRO, T208/149, Treasury Memorandum, 13 February 1931.
28. B/E, G3/197, Norman Memorandum, 19 September 1930.
29. B/E, G3/197, Norman to W.H. Clegg, 10 December 1930.
30. B/E, MB52, C/T Minutes, 17 September 1930.
31. Morgan Grenfell, British Government Loan in the U.S. - 5/3, Hopkins to Morgan Grenfell, 15 December 1930.
32. Cochran, op. cit., 11 February 1931.
33. NA, RG59, 851.51/1672, Edge to Stimson, 26 January 1931.
34. NA, RG39, Box 104, Cochran to Cotton, 6 February 1931.
35. Lamont Papers, 181-19; Lamont was sent a copy on 14 February 1931 by his Paris partner N.D. Jay who had received it from Gates McGarrah.
36. B/E, OV45/4, R. Kindersley Memorandum, 20 February 1931.
37. PRO, T188/22, Leith-Ross, 'Notes of a Meeting with French Treasury', 21 February 1931.
38. B/E, OV45/4, 'Notes of a Meeting of Leith-Ross, Waley, Sprague and Siepmann', 30 January 1931.
39. NA, RG59, 851.51/1684, Edge to Stimson, 26 February 1931.
40. Leith-Ross Memorandum, op. cit., 21 February 1931.
41. PRO, 30/69/1753, J. Ramsay MacDonald Diaries, 22 February 1931.
42. R.N. Smith, An Uncommon Man, The Triumph of Herbert Hoover (Simon and Schuster, New York, 1984), pp. 86, 89.
43. J.H. Wilson, Herbert Hoover: Forgotten Progressive (Little Brown and Co., Boston 1975), pp. 79-80.

44. *Ibid.*, pp. 149-51.
45. Yale University, Sterling Library, New Haven, Conn., H.L. Stimson Diaries, Vol. 3, Reel 16, 18 June 1931.
46. Lippman and Scroggs, *op. cit.*, p. 3.
47. Lamont Papers, 111-14, Lamont to Grenfell, 19 October 1922.
48. The Balfour Note of August 1922 announced that the British Government would collect only as much in debts owing to her from her former allies as was necessary to pay the U.S. in respect of British war debts. It failed to accomplish its purpose which was to influence the American government into cancelling or greatly reducing these obligations.
49. Stimson Diaries, Vol. 3, Reel 16, 21 February 1931.
50. Bodleian Library, Oxford, R.H. Brand Papers, 28.24, Brand to Hawtrey, 24 February 1931.
51. B/E, G3/198, Norman to Harrison, 3 March 1931.
52. N/A, RG39, Box 104, Cochran to Cotton, 26 February 1931.
53. B/E, MB 52, C/T Minutes, 4 March 1931.
54. FRBNY, C261, Norman to Harrison, 65/31, 4 March 1931; Harrison to Norman, 78/31, 9 March 1931.
55. B/E, C43/296, E.H.D. Skinner, to A.C. Grey, 21 March 1931.
56. PRO, T175/16, Hopkins Memorandum, May 1930.
57. NA, RG39, Box 104, Cochran to W.R. Castle, Jnr., 27 March 1931.
58. NA, RG39, Box 104, Cochran to Castle, 11 March 1931.
59. The New York Times, 28 March 1931, p. 6.
60. Bundesarchiv, R 111/23, Report of The First National Bank of New York, March 1931.
61. Bundesarchiv, R 111/23, E. Archdeacon to O.P. McComas, 14 March 1931.
62. PRO, T188/24, E. Rowe-Dutton to Leith-Ross, 6 March 1931.
63. Stimson Diaries, Reel 3, Vol. 15, 25 March 1931.
64. Stimson Diaries, Reel 3, Vol. 15, 26 March 1931.
65. Stimson Diaries, Reel 3, Vol. 15, 1 April 1931.
66. The New York Times, 6 April 1931, p. 34; Stimson Diaries, Reel 3, Vol. 15, 7 April 1931.
67. Stimson Diaries, Reel 3, Vol. 15, 7 April 1931.

68. Stimson Diaries, Reel 3, Vol. 15, 8 April 1931.

69. The New York Times, 12 April 1931, p. 25.

70. NA, RG59, 841.51/910, B. Thaw, Jnr. to Stimson, 14 April 1931.

71. NA, RG39, Box 104, Cochran to Castle, 21 April 1931.

72. The New York Times, 15 April 1931, p. 13.

73. B/E, MB53, C/T Minutes, 22 April 1931.

74. Stimson Diaries, Reel 3, Vol. 15, 8 April 1931.

75. Stimson Diaries, Reel 3, Vol. 16, 21 April 1931.

76. FRBNY, C261, Norman to Harrison, 31/113, 29 April 1931.

77. B/E, OV45/4, Memorandum: 'The Normal Rhythm of the French Balance of Payments', 27 April 1931.

78. The New York Times, 28 April 1931, p. 1.

79. Stimson Diaries, Reel 3, Vol. 16, 23 April 1931.

80. B/E, ADM20/20, Norman Diaries, 30 April 1931.

81. Lamont Papers, 173-3, Lamont Diaries, 8 May 1931.

82. Herbert Hoover Presidential Library, West Branch, Iowa, W.R. Castle Jnr. Papers, Castle to O. Mills, 29 October 1931.

83. The New York Times, 12 May 1931, p. 1; FRBNY, C261, Norman to Harrison, 130/31, 13 May 1931.

84. B/E, MB53, C/T Minutes, 13 May 1931.

85. B/E, G3/197, Norman to Baron von Franckenstein, 3 December 1930; B/E, G3/198, Norman to Otto Juch, 11 March 1931.

86. Stimson Diaries, Reel 3, Vol. 15, 8 April 1931.

87. Morgan Grenfell, Austrian Negotiation 1931 - Documents, Memorandum: 'Present Outlook for Austrian Budget', 6 May 1931.

88. The Credit Anstalt, whose full name was the Oesterreichische Credit-Anstalt für Handel und Gewerbe, had been formed when the Oesterreiche Credit Anstalt, a Rothschild controlled bank, was forced in 1928 by the Austrian Government to take over the Boden Kredit Anstalt which had failed.

89. Morgan Grenfell, Credit Anstalt 1, Morgan's (N.Y.) to Morgan Grenfell, 11 March 1931. Kindleberger, op. cit., pp. 149-50, makes a persuasive case for believing that the charge against the French was unjust.

90. Morgan Grenfell, Credit Anstalt 1, C.F. Whigham to Baron Wimmer, 19 May 1931.

91. Harrison Papers, Binder 2, BIS to FRBNY, 31/308, 18 May 1931; PRO 30/69/288, Note to Prime Minister, 25 May 1931.

92. Stimson Diaries, Reel 3, Vol. 16, 27 May 1931.

93. Morgan Grenfell, Credit Anstalt 1, Morgan Grenfell to Morgan's (N.Y.) 31/4768, 26 May 1931; B/E, ADM20/20, Norman Diaries, 26 May 1931; B/E, MB53, C/T Minutes, 27 May 1931.

94. Harrison Papers, Box 20, Norman to Harrison, 143/31, 25 May 1931.

Chapter Three

TODAY GERMANY, TOMORROW THE WORLD?

June-July 1931

'Generally speaking the
position of the world is
getting worse.'

Montagu Norman to
George Harrison
1 July 1931

i

The looming world financial crisis had now
arrived. As the Austrian financial situation
continued to descend into chaos, rumours were
already circulating that Germany would request a
reduction in reparations during the month of
June.[1] Not only was the German financial situation precarious per se but it was exacerbated both
by domestic popular opinion and internal political
events. In a democratic age the views and reactions, political and financial, of the home popula-
tion must be considered when contemplating the form
and substance of financial plans. In the case of
Germany the increasing political strength of the
Nazis led the Brüning government to search for a
victory to weaken the appeal of National Socialists
and their allies. The first two ideas, the Austro-
German customs union and the construction of further
pocket battleships, were wrecked on the shoals of
French opposition. This caused a greater emphasis
to be placed on the third German venture into the
use of foreign success for domestic ends - the
endeavour to end reparations. The Germans began
manouevring for changes in the current scheme, newly
revised by the Young Plan of 1930, in early 1931.
While their efforts in large measure helped to
motivate the Hoover Moratorium, they also had the
effect of frightening holders of marks both within
and without the country away from the currency, thus
in part causing the financial crisis. This domestic
factor was also to play a large role in determining
the response of the British government and the Bank
of England to their own financial time of trial, the
difference being that while in Germany the government and central bank were at one, in Britain the
Bank of England held a philosophy different from

53

most of the governing party. Thus part of the story to be told involves the way in which the Bank of England attempted to manouevre the Labour Government into accepting its views on what should be done to ameliorate the British predicament.

The possibility of a German initiative on reparations thus occupied the British Treasury and Foreign Office staff who were preparing for the visit to Britain by Chancellor Heinrich Brüning and Foreign Minister Dr. Julius Curtius. The British had to consider not only what their attitude was on the issue of reparations revision but whether, in the event of a reduction in German payments, they should follow what would surely be the French approach and demand a corresponding reduction in respect of their war debts to the U.S.[2] These questions came to the fore at a time when the effect of years of financial strain on the British was becoming apparent to interested observers. American economist Dr. Walter Stewart, sometime advisor to Governor Norman, commented to the American Counsul in Basle that:

> While before the war the British occupied such a position in world finance and power that Great Britain could always be depended upon to assume a cold but righteous standard on any international financial question, its position has changed since the war and with the rise of American prominence in international finance. That is, when a question arises in an international meeting or body, the English representative is more likely to be found leaning towards that which is truly for the benefit of Great Britain than heretofore. As a result the American representatives at international financial meetings are usually the only ones who are truly independent and neutral and must finally bear the responsibility for many decisions.[3]

Although for different reasons, during the summer of 1931 it would become obvious that neither the British nor, after the London Conference, the Americans were able to take an international point of view.

The credit granted to the Austrian National Bank in May having proved insufficient, the BIS enquired of the Bank of England if it would be willing to extend another credit. Norman informed McGarrah that his aid and probably that of the FRBNY was contingent on the appointment of a strong willed outsider to clean up the Augean stables of the Austrian National Bank and the Credit Anstalt. Norman's candidates for this position were Hjalmar Schacht, who having resigned as head of the Reichsbank, was occupying himself campaigning for an end to reparations, or Gijsbert Bruins. This immediately led to difficulties with the French who had never liked Schacht. Norman, in turn, became angry at McGarrah, blaming the latter's lack of discretion for the commotion.[4] The question of a new Austrian credit was thus held in abeyance as during the end of the first week of June, attention shifted to Germany on both sides of the Atlantic.

On 5 June Lamont called President Hoover in Washington in order to urge him to declare a holiday on debt payments which would be contingent on a postponement by European countries of the debts and reparation payments due to them for the same period. That Lamont made this move shows that Morgan's (N.Y.) believed that matters were desperate. For the President was not a partisan of Wall Street bankers in general nor of Morgan's (N.Y.) in particular. In the U.S. as opposed to Great Britain, France, Germany and other major nations, the financial and political capitals were in different locations which, inter alia, created in the U.S. a division between New York bankers and the rest of the nation. Hoover's pre-existing bias against New York bankers had been greatly exacerbated by the malignant effect of the Wall Street crash on his administration and it was in that connection that an encounter with Lamont had occurred which left the President with a rather low opinion of the banker. In October 1929 Hoover sent his unofficial advisor on banking and finance, Henry L. Robinson, head of the California-based Security National Bank to Lamont, as doyen of Wall Street, to discuss the speculative boom and its possible economic effects on the country. In an eighteen page letter written just ten days before the crash, Lamont dismissed the President's worries, concluding that no corrective intervention needed even to be contemplated at that time. Hoover's sardonic comment that 'this document is fairly amazing' scrawled on the top of the letter in 1931 summed up his view of Lamont's acumen.[5]

However, Lamont, perhaps realizing Hoover's feelings, constructed his appeal cleverly. He began by pointing out that under the debt agreements the European countries had the right under certain circumstances unilaterally to declare moratoria and, if Germany stopped paying reparations, this was the response the President could expect. Lamont countered Hoover's comment that Germany could always summon the Committee of Review provided for by the Young Plan with the observation that such an action would cause foreign lenders to pull out of Germany, almost certainly triggering a German collapse. Then Hoover made a remark important both in the context but also indicative of the concerns which would guide his actions throughout the months ahead:

> I will think about the matter, but politically it is quite impossible. Sitting in New York, as you do, you have no idea what the sentiment of the country at large is on these intergovernmental debts. Added to this, Congress sees France piling up loads of gold, increasing armaments and encouraging other European armaments among her Allies. I could not make any headway.

Yet Lamont persevered, replying that something had to be done and if the President took a courageous step, it would only help his chances in the 1932 Presidential election. Hoover ended the conversation in a non-committal fashion, agreeing to read the memorandum Lamont offered to send and acquiescing in Lamont's suggestion that their conversation should be kept confidential.[6]

Lamont's plea, however, had been addressed to a willing listener. Since early May when Frederick Sackett, U.S. Ambassador to Germany, had called Hoover to say that the German situation was deteriorating rapidly, Hoover had been considering a reduction in war debts.[7] Therefore it is not surprising that immediately after his conversation with Lamont he summoned Stimson, Secretary of the Treasury Andrew Mellon and Undersecretary of the Treasury Ogden Mills to the White House and discussed Lamont's ideas with them. Stimson was very impressed by Hoover's attitude and the way in which he ignored Mellon's lack of enthusiasm.[8]

The next day Stimson, upon hearing a rumour that Germany had declared a moratorium, called Sir Ronald Lindsay, British Ambassador to Washington, and asked that he tell MacDonald, at that moment meeting with the Germans at Chequers, that any such move would be disastrous because it would trigger a withdrawal of Germany's short-term bank credits.[9] Against this backdrop, the Chequers meetings of 4 to 6 June were played. The results unfortunately were equivocal. True, a large gesture towards the return to normal diplomatic status for Germany had been made (this was the first visit of German statesmen to Britain since the war) but Brüning, having come looking for new money and the revision of reparations, returned empty-handed. MacDonald, after recounting this to the American diplomat Ray Atherton, told the latter that he had two worries: the spectre of a revolution in Germany triggered by the economic stringency imposed by the financial crisis and the increasing shadow of French domination over Europe. MacDonald ended the conversation by quoting Norman's observation that matters were not as bad in Germany as the Germans had indicated and urging the Americans to consider, with the French, the idea of lending gold to Germany.[10]

The American President and his advisors, however, during the next ten days were too busy debating what would come to be known as the Hoover Plan to consider any new initiatives as the President alternatively blew hot and cold on this scheme. His big stumbling block was that the Plan involved making an explicit connection between debts and reparations, something American governments had scrupulously avoided for 13 years. Stimson tirelessly urged Hoover forward, pointing out that his action would, among other things, help Great Britain stay on the gold standard.[11] Experienced hands such as Dwight Morrow, now Senator from New Jersey, and Garrard Winston, Wall Street lawyer and former secretary of the various Debt Funding Commissions, were consulted as the Plan was debated in government circles.[12]

In the meantime Norman fought other fires. Hungary, not surprisingly, was affected by the Austrian crisis and appeared on the verge of collapse, while halfway across the world the problem of Indian finance was so acute that the Governor predicted that the outcome might well be insolvency.[13] Yet Norman fought on, working to convince British bankers not to withdraw credits from Germany and keeping in close touch with Reichsbank officials in order to monitor the situation.[14] The news was not encouraging. Withdrawals of gold and foreign exchange were clearly continuing.[15] Worse; there were now rumours that German's second largest bank, the Darmstadter und National ('Danat'), was in trouble and, while the Reichsbank dismissed this, the situation remained disquieting, especially taken in conjunction with the news that Rumania, Poland and Spain were verging on collapse.[16] In the light of this information, Norman decided that a German crisis was becoming more imminent, telling Charles Whigham on 13 June that the German position was becoming dangerous. Yet the Governor still believed that it was the Austrian debacle which was largely responsible for German problems and there-fore urged Whigham to use Morgan Grenfell's French connections to obtain French participation in a loan of 150 m Schillings (£4.5 m) for the Austrians which Norman believed was urgently needed.[17] It is interesting that Norman, having admitted to a German problem, erroneously attributed it to Austria; it would seem he was very reluctant to criticize the handling of the German economy over the past few years, perhaps because that would mean impugning the actions of his close friend, former Reichsbank Governor Schacht.

On the same 13 June, the Reichsbank, now under the leadership of Dr. Hans Luther, followed classi-cal banking theory by raising its discount rate, on this occasion from 5% to 7%. Meanwhile Norman, together with Sir Frederick Leith-Ross, arrived at Chequers to discuss the German situation which, according to Leith-Ross was getting steadily worse, so much so as to require the Young Plan to be revised.[18]

As Morgan Grenfell, attempting to comply with the Governor's requests, negotiated with the French Banque National de Paris et de Pays-Bas to organize an Austrian loan, the Hoover Plan continued to be at the center of American discussions.[19] Harrison's opinion was that a two year moratorium would be best while MacDonald called Stimson (with whom he had a fairly close relationship[20]) and told him that Norman had said this was the time for the President to move.[21] The Americans began to consider talking to the French so as not to present them with a fait accompli and drew up lists of influential Senators and Congressmen whose approval ought to be sought. (The moratorium was proposed as a Presiden-tial action which would need to be ratified by Congress when it reassembled the following Decem-ber.)

Attention in London, New York and Washington thus continued to oscillate between a German and Austrian focus. By 14 June Norman was convinced that Austria needed the new loan within 24 hours. Since Morgan's efforts to arrange French participa-

tion had so far failed, Norman decided unilaterally
to lend the entire 150 m Schillings.[22]   This was
accomplished on 16 June.   Austria thus received a
much needed respite at the price of incurring for
Norman and the British the enmity of the French who
had delayed the loan in the hope of being able to
extract political concessions from the situation.[23]   Norman, according to Atherton, believed
that there would have been a complete collapse were
it not for his loan.   Further the Governor said that
he had gone ahead with this credit although it was
not within the power of the Bank of England because
he believed, and the British government concurred,
that the rescue of Austria had to be accomplished,
come what may.[24]   Norman's action marked two
turning points.   It was the last time the Bank of
England would be in a position to intervene alone in
a major crisis and it was the last time a Governor
of the Bank would have the power to take such an
important decision during a crisis of this dimension
himself and then consult the Government.
     Norman and MacDonald now turned their attention
to entertaining Secretary Mellon who had arrived in
London en route to his planned Riviera holiday.
MacDonald shared with Mellon his view that the
Austrian loan was a splendid move but would be bound
to bring French revenge on Britain.[25]   Norman
reported to Harrison that he had told Mellon that
the world faced not only a financial crisis but also
a political and social one.[26]   The British Governor had apparently also tried to get Mellon to talk
to the French but the latter refused, determined to
go straight to Cap Ferrat.   MacDonald believed that
Norman's loan to the Austrian National Bank had
allowed Britain to score heavily in American eyes
and that Mellon was impressed by the Governor's
arguments in favour of a moratorium.[27]   Actually
the Hoover Plan was about to be made public: leaks
had already appeared in the press and thus the
President, convinced of the need for surprise,
decided to announce the plan on 20 June.   Unfortunately this meant that the French received a mere
twelve hours' official notice.   While in Washington
the French ambassador professed satisfaction at this
proposal for a one year suspension of all intergovernmental claims and obligations, his government
was not to take so sanguine a view.[28]
     British feelings on the Moratorium were mixed.
As the situation in Germany appeared now to be,
according to Norman, a matter of hours not days, any
move was welcomed.[29]   But the British received a

shock when they saw the text of the Hoover Plan
which was circulated on 20 June. They had planned a
postponement of European reparations and American
and European war debts not, as it turned out, of all
intergovernmental debts. In the case of Britain the
actual plan thus encompassed payments from the
dominions and various colonies, which would cost the
Exchequer far more than it had calculated, about
£11 m ($55 m) as compared with $250 m for the
Americans and $92 m for the French.[30] Still the
British felt it imperative to go along with the
American move; MacDonald wrote that he was very
pleased about the Moratorium, and went so far as to
take credit for it. The Prime Minister further made
the observation that the form of the announcement
showed the American lack of knowledge of European
details, something which would indeed be borne out
in the months to come.[31]

As the drain on German resources continued with
the Reichsbank losing between $12 m and $14 m in
gold and foreign exchange on 20 June, the focus was
on France and the question of her attitude towards
the Hoover Plan.[32] Hoover had been warned by
Morrow that the French should be privately approached well in advance of any public announcement
and, in the event, it was unfortunate that this step
had not been taken.[33] Too, the present French
government was a weak one which felt keenly the
difficulty of obtaining the approval of the Chamber
of Deputies for the Moratorium.[34] Still smarting
under the blow to their foreign policy dealt by
Norman's Austrian coup, the French were more determined than ever not to yield on Germany, a resolution bolstered by a belief that Germany was in large
part responsible for its own problems and by the
fact that at this point French banks had very little
German exposure. Mellon, persuaded it was vital
finally agreed to go to Paris to discuss the Moratorium with Premier Pierre Laval and Finance Minister
Pierre-Etienne Flandin[35] and Morgan's attempted to
do what it could to speed the process of French
acceptance. Morgan's (N.Y.) cabled Morgan at Cie.
that:

>...we are arguing not as a matter of
>principle but purely on the practical
>question of what is really going to
>happen. It seems to us to boil down to
>this. That if France is to gain her share
>of the benefit accruing to the whole world
>through this proposed action she must

respond in turn by being 'equally
generous'.... Otherwise, the repercussions
from the world disappointment will bring
about again the very crisis which the
world was facing last week and it might be
gravely intensified by reason of the
disappointment itself.[36]

The unconditional portion of the Young Plan
annuities proved a stumbling block, as all through
the last week of June, the Americans and French
attempted to resolve their differences while German
difficulties continued to grow in magnitude. Recent
historical research indicates that Harrison's view
that the crisis was triggered by domestic not
foreign flight from the mark was correct, but by the
second half of June American and British lenders
were clearly trying to disengage from Germany.[37]
With withdrawals of foreign currency continuing day
after day, it became very clear that the Reichsbank
needed a large credit. The problem was that the
theory of support credits developed largely by the
Bank of England during the previous decade called
for any such credit to be as international as
possible which meant including not only the FRBNY
and the Bank of England but the Bank of France as
well. Yet the Germans as well as Norman were loath
to approach the French.[38] To tide the Reichsbank
over Norman agreed on 23 June to advance it sufficient funds to maintain its required currency cover
of 40%, and then he set about trying to arrange the
necessary credit whose amount it was decided ought
to be £20 m ($100 m).[39] The Governor contacted
McGarrah who said the BIS would participate even
though he was clearly annoyed that the Germans had
turned to Norman and not to him.[40] Harrison was
willing to lend money but it remained necessary to
approach the French. (Norman was willing to depart
from his theory and split the credit with the FRBNY,
thus showing laudable generosity given the parlous
times but Harrison remained adamant that the French
be included.[41]) By 26 June the credit was
arranged; to run three weeks, it provided for each
of the B.I.S., FRBNY, Bank of England and Bank of
France to lend £5 M ($25 m).[42] To Norman, French
cooperation simply meant that the credit would be
more difficult to arrange and administer but the
Americans hoped that the French attitude represented
a signal that they would accept the Hoover Plan.[43]
However, according to the French financial attaché
in Washington the two situations were fundamentally

different although they both concerned Germany; it
was one thing to aid a central bank with cash flow
problems but quite another to expect the French to
deprive themselves voluntarily of their well de-
served reparations.[44]   This view was clearly in
evidence as the Franco-American negotiations dragged
on.   MacDonald called Stimson to urge him to stand
firm, stating that he viewed the possibility of any
departure from the Hoover Plan as alarming.   The
French had in fact put forth a counter proposal
involving the continued payment by Germany of the
unconditional annuities and their subsequent re-
lending to Germany through the BIS, which would
preserve the form of the Young Plan but MacDonald,
quoting Norman, informed the Americans that such a
compromise would ruin Germany's credit and cause a
collapse by 15 July, a prescient prediction.[45]
The Americans struggled on with the French to
produce an agreement - Mellon labouring together
with Ambassador Edge to achieve common ground with
Laval and Flandin.   Each night Mellon called Hoover,
Stimson and Mills; these conversations, together
with those between Stimson and MacDonald mark the
first time the telephone was regularly used as a
medium of diplomatic communication in a political
crisis.   This leap in communications technology
further signalled an alteration in the pace of world
events in which governments had hitherto lagged
behind private institutions.   Herbert Hoover was the
first President to have a telephone on his desk yet
investors and financiers had long been aware that
the telephone gave them the ability to take instant
advantage of news regarding financial and political
events.[46]   However, though Hoover and MacDonald
were now constantly using the telephone they, their
Governments and related central banks had not yet
come to terms with the fact that a major change in
the tempo of world financial relations had occurred.
     In the meantime Morgan's continued their
attempts to rescue the now floundering Hoover Plan.
According to Morgan et Cie., the French Treasury
thought it was doing all it could to negotiate a
settlement but was discouraged by what it perceived
as Washington's lack of recognition of its conciliatory attitude.[47]   Morgan's (N.Y.) replied that
Washington's attitude was really quite simple; if
the U.S. could give up $250 m, the French should be
willing to forego $92 m.[48]   In the hope of
breaking the stalemate it was decided that Secretary
Stimson who had previously scheduled a European
holiday would join the Paris negotiations.   Stimson

sailed 26 June and in his absence the acting Secretary of State, Undersecretary William Castle,
received a note from the British Treasury to the
effect that London was now financing the Reichsbank
but would be forced to withdraw its money if a
complete suspension of reparations was not immediately accomplished.[49] The motivation behind the
British message was, to quote Norman: 'to apply
pepper to the French and starch to the Americans in
order to maintain the sanctity of the Hoover
announcement.'[50] Norman, however, was continuing
to attempt to exert his influence behind the scenes.
Although he returned the telephone call he received
from Ogden Mills on 28 June, he told Leith-Ross that
the British Government should use Lindsay to communicate with the Americans, not him.[51] The Governor's rather out of character modus operandi would
continue in evidence as Norman faced what was
probably the most difficult time of his career.

ii

In Norman's colourful words; as the French and
Americans negotiated Berlin was being bled to
death.[52] The Governor continued to see the Prime
Minister almost every day as the Americans out of
frustration began to contemplate withdrawing their
offer from the French.[53] Matters were such that
Luther cabled Harrison and Norman on 4 July that the
delay in Paris had caused the Reichsbank to be in
the same position as if the Hoover Plan had not been
proposed nor the credit to the Reichsbank
granted.[54] Thus that the French and Americans
reached a compromise on 5 July was almost anti-
climatic, coming as it did too late to stop a German
debacle.[55] On 8 July Luther telephoned Norman to
say that 'the position was so critical that he
intended to come to London at once.'[56] His crisis
approach was echoed by Ambassador Sackett, an
example of an envoy who had begun to identify very
strongly with his host country, who urged the U.S.
to do more to stop the withdrawal of foreign
credits.[57] In response Castle called Harrison for
his reading of the situation. The latter stated
that the principal New York bankers were not withdrawing short term credits which led Castle to
conclude that the remedy for German problems would
seem to lie in Berlin rather than in New York.[58]
The Germans had formulated a self-help plan based on
the creation of a large guarantee fund but on 8 July
Norman called Harrison to say that Germany might

need a credit of £100-£200 m ($500 m - $1,000 m) and
the British Governor stated he would be willing to
participate providing the FRBNY and the Bank of
France did the same.[59] Harrison was aghast,
cabling Norman that it would be difficult if not
impossible for him to consider lending more money to
Germany until there was proof that the Reichsbank
had done everything it could to protect its
position.[60] On the same day, however, immediately
before leaving for Basle and the monthly BIS
meeting, Norman called Harrison to discuss the
German situation and curiously revealed that he had
apparently changed his mind on the question of a
credit; he told Harrison that no credit should be
granted because it would facilitate continued
payments of reparations to France, something Norman
(and also Harrison) wanted to avoid.[61] This
vacillation, a symptom perhaps of Norman's
approaching nervous collapse, would be in evidence
all month, serving not only to confuse the
politicians and financiers with whom Norman worked
but also contributing, at July's end, to the
dimensions of the British crisis itself.

Harrison continued to fight against a credit,
pointing out, among other things, that it made no
sense to provide central bank credits to enable
private banks to withdraw funds and Sackett's steady
stream of SOS messages did not alter his view.[62]
Morgan's (N.Y.) shared Harrison's opinion; the New
York house cabled Grenfell (for his own information
and for transmission to Norman at Basle) that they
did not see where the money was to come from as
neither private banks nor the FRBNY would participate in a proposal which was 'thoroughly unsound and
full of dangerous complications for the future, not
merely financial but also political.'[63]

The BIS board meeting was scheduled for Monday,
13 July but as usual the preliminary Sunday night
dinner was equally important. There Dr. Luther
presented Germany's case, saying that the German
economy was essentially sound, the budget balanced
and thus the present situation fundamentally
different from that which obtained in 1929.[64] His
speech illustrated that the Governor of the Reichsbank at least had realized that brinksmanship had
perhaps gone too far, a rather untimely discovery.
His listeners were not encouraged particularly as he
also said that the Reichsbank's cover based on its
own funds was only 20% and further that unless
unexpected events transpired, a German moratorium
would have to be declared within forty-eight hours.

In that event, McGarrah predicted, Austria, Hungary, Rumania and Yugoslavia (all of whom were in dire straits and receiving money from the Bank of England and the BIS) would follow suit.[65]

Norman left Basle, having concluded along with other central bankers that the world's problems were too big for the central banks and must be handled by the governments as there was nothing central banks could do now. He was also, according to Harrison, tired, disgruntled and discouraged, which is not surprising given the magnitude of the disasters of 13 July.[66] On that day, the Danat Bank closed its doors, triggering a general collapse of the German financial system as all German banks were closed and normal life ground to a halt.

On the same day the Macmillan Report (among whose witnesses had been Jacob Goldschmidt, head of the Danat Bank) was published. While the Report advocated the retention of the gold standard, it did so in such a half-hearted way that many observers were convinced that the British no longer possessed the necessary will to fight unflinchingly for the gold standard if such action were required. Just as damaging was the disclosure that Britain's short term debits exceeded credits by £267 m. This was especially worrying when a large percentage of British loans were frozen in Germany which meant that the imbalance was even worse than it appeared. These revelations together with the German crisis and the general apprehension prevalent during the summer brought on the same 13 July a realization that a run on sterling had begun the previous Friday sparked by withdrawals of French funds from London. Whether this was in anticipation of a prospective loan to Germany which would bring a higher rate of return than offered in London or whether, as Chancellor Snowden charged, it represented a French attempt to exert pressure on London to toe the French line on reparations (a charge the French denied), it was not a good portent of things to come.[67]

The central banks having thrown the German problem into the laps of the politicians, the latter began to try to find a solution or at least a path to one. The obvious answer was to have a meeting but that led to the further questions of who would attend, where it would be held and, most important, what would be discussed - the immediate crisis, as the Americans desired, or the entire framework of international payments, the goal of both Norman and the British Treasury.[68] By 15 July, MacDonald

decided that he should go to Berlin to try to solve
the German problems before the position of London
was undermined beyond salvage. His apprehensions
had not been lessened by a visit from a distraught
Norman who informed MacDonald that Britain might
have to declare a moratorium on its payments.[69]
That Norman would even broach this possibility is a
mark both of how seriously he was taking the yet
nascent drain of gold and how much he had suffered
from the strain he had been under for the past few
years. In January he had talked of 'the steady drip
of the unseen pressure on us' and, like water on a
rock, the result was a wearing away of the Governor's powers of resistance.[70] Norman, always of
nervous temperament, was thus not in a position to
handle smoothly the traumatic events of July. This
proved most unfortunate for Britain because banking
is to a large extent a matter of perception. A
determined face presented to the world by a nation
under threat will positively affect its chances of
withstanding a financial onslaught. The two major
symptoms Norman displayed during the next two weeks,
resort to dramatic overstatement and a vacillating
attitude towards possible courses of action, would
cause the drain of gold to continue to accelerate.

Secretary of State Stimson, now in Paris, met
with Foreign Secretary Henderson who was there to
discuss German problems with the French. When
Stimson called Hoover on 15 July he reported that
both Henderson and the French were considering a
joint loan to Germany guaranteed by the governments
of Britain, France and the United States. The
President said this was impossible for, among other
reasons, it would require Congressional approval
which would be unobtainable. A private loan,
however, appeared an option only if it received
priority over reparations, an improbability.
Henderson had told Stimson that Norman was over-
extended and was trying to withdraw Bank of England
commitments abroad. Hoover added that, according to
Henderson, Norman, believing the whole German
question was political, was advocating a conference
which would discuss the Treaty of Versailles,
reparations and debts, an approach unacceptable to
both Hoover and Stimson. Stimson then informed the
President that the French proposed to hold a conference in Paris and it was left that the Americans
(Stimson and Mellon) might attend if the agenda was
sufficiently narrow.[71]

As the Germans raised their discount rate from
7% to 10%, in Paris the British, French and Ameri-

cans debated courses of action. To the Americans and British the French were the villains. MacDonald said, 'France has been playing its usual small-minded and selfish games ... Its methods are those of the worst Jews.' while Ogden Mills castigated them for behaving with incredible stupidity.[72] However, the freedom of action of both countries to deal with the Laval government was circumscribed, in the case of Britain by the fear of a continued gold drain to Paris and on the part of the U.S., by its determination not to be saddled by the Europeans with the cost of German reconstruction.[73] The three-party discussions continued with their foci the questions of whether France would attend the Seven Power Conference which MacDonald with Hoover's encouragement had organized for Monday, 20 July in London, and the French proposal for a $500 m (£125 m) credit to Germany. Norman told Harrison that his government could not be a party to such a credit. His resistance was certainly influenced by his belief that the French were trying to box the Germans into a corner where they would have no recourse other than to agree to the credit although the French envisioned security provisions and political conditions which the Governor thought were demeaning.[74] When the Americans heard Norman's opinion they were unsure of how to interpret it because, knowing that Norman wanted a full blown reordering of the international financial structure, they were not sure if his views represented a realistic reading of the situation or an attempt to exacerbate the extant problems to force the more wide-ranging discussions they sought to avoid. Stimson and Mellon further resented what they saw as a British attempt to make them bear the onus of turning down the French plan when they knew the British were equally reluctant to lend new money.[75]

At this point Morgan's became involved in the imbroglio. Former Governor of the Bank of France Emile Moreau was in touch with Morgan et Cie. and, in order to advise their sometime clients the French Government and the Bank of France, the Paris house asked Morgan's (N.Y.) for their assessment. In response the New York partners stated on 17 July that 'the present German crisis must be solved without reliance upon getting fresh money from America to Germany.'[76] By the same day, the British and Americans had accepted that the French were determined to have a full blown conference of their own in Paris prior to the London conclave;

thus the schedule agreed upon was that the Germans would arrive in Paris on 17 July for talks with the French that day and for talks with anyone else who wished to participate the next day. Later on 19 July everyone would depart for London in order to reassemble on Monday, 20 July. This somewhat pointless jockeying for position exacerbated already wounded sensibilities but at least it ensured the French presence in London. During the period preceding the London Conference MacDonald and Stimson continued their telephone conversations, the Prime Minister revealing that Britain had had what he termed a financial crisis on the previous Wednesday, a reference to Norman's panicky 15 July. MacDonald also told the American that he had summoned Henderson back early Sunday so as to ensure the Sunday discussions were not lengthy.[77] At the same time Norman and MacDonald met daily as they prepared a proper agenda for Monday.[78] Sterling had shown a slight recovery but Norman was worried as he believed that the London Conference would be useless because it would not produce new money for Germany.[79] Again Norman had changed his mind on the necessity for a new credit.

As the transatlantic and transoceanic telephoning and cabling continued, it was becoming apparent that having called in their governments, the central banks of Britain and France were unable to agree with the politicians they respectively worked with on the proper approach to take towards the Germans and their problems. Norman, according to Lord Tyrell, British Ambassador to France, was determined to hold up any progress until the whole of European finance was reformed, an aim MacDonald did not share.[80] In the same way the Bank of France was apparently opposed to the plan which the French government had originated to grant Germany a credit. At this point, two equal power centres existed in both London and Paris but such marked disagreements would seem to indicate that in the not too distant future either the central banks would regain sovereignty over monetary issues or would yield it to their governments.

During the Paris negotiations the most upsetting revelation to Stimson came from an unexpected quarter. At a party held at the American Embassy on 17 July Stimson talked with N. Dean Jay, senior partner of Morgan et Cie. Jay showed him the Morgan's (N.Y.) cable which stated that no new American loans to Germany could be made. Notwithstanding that Morgan's (N.Y.) position was both reasonable and realistic, Stimson became furious because he felt that the Bank of France was holding back their support for the London Conference and that if they learned from Morgan's (N.Y.) that no American loan was possible, this could give the French an excuse to renege on their pledge to go to London.[81] Stimson, in fact, was so angry that when Hoover next called he said that if the President wished to contribute to the success of the London Conference he should call Lamont and tell him to stop interfering. Then the Secretary returned to Jay and told him, 'You have hit the London Conference right plumb in the eye and I want you to know it.'[82]

On Sunday, as Stimson prepared to leave for London, he called Hoover to discuss the American position at Monday's meeting. Conscious no doubt of the historic nature of his role as the first American governmental representative to participate in a conference on European financial matters since Versailles, Stimson's chief concern was that Morgan's had given the French the feeling that as the only nation to suggest a concrete plan to aid Germany, they held the trump card. The Secretary was still so upset at Morgan's that he took the opportunity to tell the President that Harrison and Federal Reserve Board Governor Meyer received their information from Morgan's implying it was therefore unreliable. Hoover told Stimson that the chief point to bear in mind was that as no American money could be forthcoming the American line should be that what was necessary was the stabilization of foreign credits in Germany, that is to say an agreement by the creditor nations that their banks would not withdraw their money from Germany.[83]

Prior to the opening of the London Conference, termed by The Times the most important gathering of its kind since the war, Stimson and Mellon met with Norman who reiterated his lack of optimism as to the outcome of the meeting.[84] Once the meeting began Stimson, at least, felt all participants were cordial although he was worried about the hostility of the French press. Stimson and Mellon pressed for agreement on the stabilization of German non-governmental credits which Hoover had wanted and which would come to be known as the Stillhaltung or standstill as they also tried to get the British to take responsibility for the defeat of the French plan.[85] Hoover continued to be much involved behind the scenes. During one of his talks he said that not only he but Harrison and Morgan partner

Today Germany, Tomorrow the World?

Parker Gilbert believed it was vital for Germany herself to take further measures, that is to say the maintenance of a high discount rate and exchange controls to stop the outflow of foreign exchange and gold.[86] Mills, a close ally of Hoover as well as Undersecretary of the Treasury, also called frequently and it was during one of his conversations with Mellon that the latter revealed that MacDonald had questioned whether Great Britain could maintain the present volume of its foreign credits, which illustrated that the Prime Minister shared the doubts of the world's investment community. During this same conversation Mills revealed that to ascertain the technical requirements of possible solutions he had called Norman for advice. Norman, however, said that the only way to make a stabilization program work would be to grant a suspension of reparations and war debt payments for three years.[87]

Norman was also the subject of a later phone call between Stimson and Hoover. Apparently MacDonald had suggested bringing Norman to the Conference sessions. Stimson, obviously horrified by this given Norman's depressed view of matters and his anti-French, pro-German bias, spiked MacDonald's guns by pointing out that if Norman attended it would only be fair that Clement Moret should as well. To the latter suggestion the French delegates revealingly objected with the result that the Conference was spared the presence of both central bankers. But before the meeting Norman had convinced MacDonald that the American approach would not work. Stimson, a shrewd observer, pointed out that not only was the Bank of England in a weak position but the Labour party, numbering few financial men among its members, had to rely very heavily on Norman. Yet the Secretary of State at this time reserved his strongest words for the British Treasury which had prepared a position paper based on the assumption that a full suspension of intergovernmental payments was a prerequisite to the solution of the German crisis.[88]

Stimson's gloom was not relieved the next morning when he met with MacDonald and Norman prior to the day's sessions and was informed that the British financial situation was worsening; according to MacDonald, Norman was 'frightened to death and scared.'[89] That Snowden continued to display his previous obstreperous attitude did not augur well for a speedy conclusion but finally a draft set of recommendations was arrived at. Adopted the next

70

day, 23 July, they embodied the Hoover approach and called for a renewal of the existing $100m (£20 m) central bank credit to the Reichsbank for a period of three months, the maintenance of foreign credits in Germany and the convening by the BIS of a committee of experts designated by central banks to enquire into the credit needs of Germany and the transformation of her short term credits into long term ones.

As the diplomats enjoyed themselves at a Buckingham Palace garden party and were presented to the King and Queen, Norman occupied himself with less pleasant matters.[90] The Conference had not accomplished the goals he had had in mind and the fact that Norman had to a great extent controlled the British politicians who were ostensibly in charge had not altered the outcome in the slightest. Furthermore the gold drain over the past ten days had taken £20m ($100m) from the Bank of England, which was equal to the total amount of gold gained by the Bank from April to mid-July. MacDonald on 23 July viewed the outlook as 'unpleasant'.[91] Carl Melchior, German financier and diplomat was even more pessimistic. Speaking to fellow negotiator Hans Schäffer about the proceedings of the London Conference he said:

> What I have just experienced means the end of a way of life, certainly for Germany and perhaps other countries as well. We have repealed the rules of the game that have regulated commerce between the nations of the world. The common vision of the future has been destroyed.[92]

NOTES

1. The New York Times, 28 May 1931, p. 1.
2. PRO, T188/16, Leith-Ross to Hopkins and Snowden, undated.
3. NA, RG39, Box 104, Cochran to Castle, 1 June 1931.
4. Harrison Papers, Box 20, Norman to Harrison, 31/155, 2 June 1931.
5. HHPL, Presidential - Personal Files - 1097, Lamont to Hoover, 19 October 1929.
6. Lamont Papers, 98-18, Lamont Memorandum, undated.
7. J.H. Wilson, American Business and Foreign Policy: 1920-1933 (Beacon Press, Boston, 1971), pp. 136-7.

8.   Stimson Diaries, Reel 3, Vol. 16, 5 June 1931.

9.   Stimson Diaries, Reel 3, Vol. 16, 6 June 1931; PRO 30/69/1753, MacDonald Diaries, 7 June 1931.

10. HHPL, Presidential Papers - Foreign Affairs - Financial ('FA-F'), Atherton to Stimson, 175, 8 June 1931; PRO 30/69/289, Memorandum: 'Meeting With the Germans At Chequers', 6 June 1931.

11. Stimson Diaries, Reel 3, Vol. 16, 8 June 1931.

12. HHPL, Presidential Papers, FA-F, Lamont to Hoover, 5 June 1931; Stimson Diaries, Reel 3, Vol. 16, 10 June and 11 June 1931.

13. B/E, G3/198, Norman to Hopkins, 8 June 1931; Harrison Papers, Binder 3, BIS to FRBNY, 477, 3 June 1931.

14. B/E, ADM 20/20, Norman Diaries, 10 June 1931.

15. See, e.g., B/E, OV 34/3, unsigned Memorandum concerning telephone conversation, 12 June 1931.

16. B/E, OV 34/3, E.R. Peacock to H.A. Siepmann, 12 June 1931.

17. Morgan Grenfell, Credit Anstalt 2, Morgan Grenfell to Morgan's (N.Y.), 31/4809, 13 June 1931.

18. B/E, ADM 20/20, Norman Diaries, 13 June 1931; PRO, T188/24, Leith-Ross to Sir R. Vansittart, 13 June 1931; B/E, OV 34/80, Reichsbank to Norman, 13 June 1931.

19. Morgan Grenfell, Austrian Crisis 1931, Morgan Grenfell to Morgan's (N.Y.), 31/2254, 14 June 1931.

20. MacDonald and Stimson shared an interest in disarmament and at the 1930 naval negotiations had begun to develop what both men believed was a good relationship.

21. Stimson Diaries, Reel 3, Vol. 16, 13 June 1931; FRBNY, 2013.1, Harrison to Mills, 10 June 1931.

22. Stimson Diaries, Reel 3, Vol. 16, 14 June 1931; Morgan Grenfell, Austrian Crisis 1931, Morgan's (N.Y.) to Morgan Grenfell, 31/2255, 15 June 1931; Morgan Grenfell to Morgan's (N.Y.), 31/4811, 15 June 1931; Morgan Grenfell, Austrian Negotiations 1931 - Documents, C.F. Whigham Memoranda I and II, 15 June 1931; B/E, ADM 20/20, Norman Diaries, 15 June 1931.

23. Morgan Grenfell, Austrian Crisis 1931, unsigned Memorandum (also circulated to Norman), 15 June 1931; Morgan Grenfell to Morgan's (N.Y.), 31/4815, 15 June 1931.

24. HHPL, Presidential Papers, FA-F, Atherton to Stimson, 196, 18 June 1931.

25. PRO, 30/69/1753, MacDonald Diaries, 17 June 1931; B/E, ADM 20/20, Norman Diaries, 18 June 1931.

26. NA, RG59, 462.00/R296/4040, Mills to Stimson, 18 June 1931.

27. PRO 30/69/1753, MacDonald Diaries, 18 June 1931.

28. Stimson Diaries, Reel 3, Vol. 16, 18 and 19 June 1931; The New York Times, 20 June 1931, p. 1.

29. FRBNY, 3115.2, Harrison Memorandum, 20 June 1931, concerning telephone conversation with Norman, 20 June 1931.

30. B/E, ADM 20/20, Norman Diaries, 20 June 1931; PRO, Cab35(31), 24 June 1931.

31. PRO 30/69/1753, MacDonald Diaries, 14 June and 21 June 1931.

32. The New York Times, 20 June 1931, p. 1.

33. Stimson Diaries, Reel 3, Vol. 16, 10 June 1931.

34. PRO 30/69/288, Memorandum of Conversation between Vansittart and A. de Fleuriau, 22 June 1931.

35. HHPL Presidential Papers, FA-F, Stimson to Mellon, 179, 22 June 1931.

36. HHPL, Presidential Papers, FA-F, Morgan's (N.Y.) to Morgan & Cie., 87514, 22 June 1931.

37. For the most comprehensive analysis of the German situation in 1931 see H. James, The Reichsbank and Public Finance in Germany 1924-1933: A Study of the Politics of Economics During the Great Depression (Fritz Knapp Verlag, Frankfurt Am Main, 1985), pp. 173-261.

38. B/E, OV 34/3, W. Layton to H.A. Siepmann, 23 June 1931.

39. B/E, MB53, C/T Minutes, 23 June 1931.

40. B/E, OV 34/3, Siepmann Memorandum concerning telephone conversation with McGarrah, 24 June 1931.

41. FRBNY, Harrison Papers, 3115.2, Harrison Memoranda concerning telephone conversations with Norman at 10:45 a.m. and 12:30, 24 June 1931.

42. Following the convention used at the time, all pound to dollar conversions have been computed at £1 = $5.

43. B/E, MB53, C/T Minutes, 24 June 1931.

44. NA, RG59, 462.00/R296/4323, Mills to Stimson, 23 June 1931.

45. PRO 30/69/1753, MacDonald Diaries, 25 June 1931; Stimson Diaries, Reel 3, Vol. 16, 25 June 1931.

46. G. Perrett, <u>America in the Twenties,</u> (Touchstone, Simon & Schuster, Inc., New York, 1982), p. 317.

47. HHPL, Presidential Papers, FA-F, Morgan & Cie., to Morgan's (N.Y.), 87540, 29 June 1931.

48. HHPL, Presidential Papers, FA-F, Morgan's (N.Y.), to Morgan & Cie., 66983, 29 June 1931.

49. HHPL, Presidential Papers, FA-F, Castle to Edge, 301, 28 June 1931.

50. B/E, G3/198, Norman to Vansittart, 26 June 1931.

51. B/E, ADM 20/20, Norman Diaries, 28 June 1931; PRO, T188/266, Leith-Ross to Hopkins, 29 June 1931.

52. FRBNY, Harrison Papers, 3115.2, Harrison Memorandum, 1 July 1931, concerning telephone conversation with Norman, 1 July 1931.

53. NA, RG59, 462.00/R296/4234, Stimson to Castle, 1 July 1931.

54. B/E, OV 34/3, Luther to Harrison, c.c. Norman, 4 July 1931.

55. The Franco-American agreement, signed on 6 July 1931, accepted the recycling of the unconditional annuities which would continue to be paid by Germany but would now be given to the BIS which would invest the monies in German railway bonds guaranteed by the German government. Thus a major part of the Hoover Moratorium had indeed been compromised for reparations would remain a first lien on a significant portion of German assets.

56. B/E, MB53, C/T Minutes, 9 July 1931.

57. Sackett had sent a continual stream of messages to Hoover and Stimson beginning in April. By July it was clear the President and Secretary were losing patience.

58. NA, RG59, 462.00/R296/4290, Castle to Sackett, 8 July 1931.

59. FRBNY, Harrison Papers, 3111.2, Harrison Memorandum, 9 July 1931, concerning telephone conversation with Norman, 8 July 1931.

60. Harrison Papers, Vol. 2, Harrison to McGarrah, 266, 8 July 1931, transmitting copy of cable sent to Norman, 8 July 1931.

61. FRBNY, Harrison Papers, 3115.2, Harrison Memorandum, 9 July 1931, concerning conversation with Norman, 9 July 1931.

62. Harrison Papers, Vol. 2, Harrison to McGarrah, 269, 10 July 1931; HHPL, Presidential Papers, FA-F, Castle to Sackett, 120, 11 July 1931.

63. Morgan Grenfell, German Crisis 1931, Morgan's (N.Y.) to Morgan Grenfell, 31/2312, 10 July 1931.
64. B/E, MB53, C/T Minutes, 15 July 1931.
65. NA, RG59, 462.00/R296/4436, Cochran to Castle, 12 July 1931.
66. FRBNY, Harrison Papers, 3115.2, Harrison Memorandum, 14 July 1931, concerning telephone conversation with Norman, 13 July 1931.
67. The New York Times, 12 July 1931, p. 1.
68. PRO, T188/26, Lindsay to Foreign Office, 14 July 1931.
69. PRO 30/69/1753, MacDonald Diaries, 15 July 1931; H. Dalton, Call Back Yesterday (Frederick Muller, London, 1953), p. 255.
70. B/E, G3/198, Norman to D. Fergusson, 27 January 1931.
71. Stimson Diaries, Reel 3, Vol. 17, 15 July 1931; HHPL, Presidential Papers, FA-F, Castle to Stimson, 15 July 1931.
72. PRO 30/69/1753, MacDonald Diaries, 5 July 1931; Library of Congress, Washington, D.C., Ogden L. Mills Papers, Container 109, Mills to G. Winston, 15 July 1931.
73. NA, RG59, 462.00/R296/4469, Castle to Stimson, 15 July 1931.
74. HHPL Presidential Papers, FA-F, Castle to Stimson, 362, 16 July 1931.
75. Stimson Diaries, Reel 3, Vol. 17, 15 July 1931.
76. Morgan Grenfell, German Crisis - 1931, Morgan et Cie. to Morgan's (N.Y.) 87572, 15 July 1931; Morgan's (N.Y.) to Morgan Grenfell, 31/2337, 17 July 1931.
77. Stimson Diaries, Reel 3, Vol. 17, 17 July 1931: Memorandum concerning telephone conversation with MacDonald, 17 July 1931.
78. B/E, ADM 20/20, Norman Diaries, 17, 18 and 20 July 1931; Morgan Grenfell, German Crisis 1931, Grenfell to Morgan, 20 July 1931.
79. Stimson Diaries, Reel 3, Vol. 17, 17 July 1931: Memorandum of Conference at the Ministry of the Interior at Office of Prime Minister Laval, 17 July 1931; Morgan Grenfell, German Crisis - 1931, Morgan Grenfell to Morgan's (N.Y.), 31/4880, 18 July 1931; Lamont Papers, 111-11, Grenfell to Lamont, 18 July 1931.
80. Stimson Diaries, Reel 3, Vol. 17, 17 July 1931: Memorandum concerning telephone conversation with Hoover, 17 July 1931.

81. NA, RG59, 462.00/R296/4600, Edge to Castle, 19 July 1931.
82. HHPL, Presidential Papers, FA-F, Transcript of telephone conversation between Stimson and Hoover, 17 July 1931; Stimson Diaries, Reel 3, Vol. 17, 17 July 1931.
83. Stimson Diaries, Reel 3, Vol. 17, 20 July 1931.
84. B/E, ADM 20/20, Norman Diaries, 20 July 1931; The Times, 20 July 1931, p. 13.
85. HHPL, Presidential Papers - FA-F, Transcript of telephone conversation between Stimson and Hoover, 20 July 1931.
86. HHPL, Presidential Papers - FA-F, Transcript of telephone conversation between Stimson and Hoover, 21 July 1931.
87. HHPL, Presidential Papers - FA-F, Transcript of telephone conversation between Mellon and Mills, 21 July 1931.
88. HHPL, Presidential Papers - FA-F, Transcript of telephone conversation between Stimson and Hoover, 21 July 1931.
89. HHPL, Presidential Papers - FA-F, Transcript of telephone conversation between Castle and Stimson, 22 July 1931; Stimson Diaries, Reel 3, Vol. 17, 22 July 1931.
90. Stimson Diaries, Reel 3, Vol. 17, 23 July 1931.
91. PRO 30/69/1753, MacDonald Diaries, 23 July 1931.
92. Bundesarchiv, NL Dietrich/303, Hans Schäffer Erinnerungen an Melchior (Supplied by Dr. William C. McNeil).

Chapter Four

SAVING THE POUND

July - August 1931

'...Norman felt that the
program was inadequate;
that we must not fool ourselves now, that any inadequate program would cause
trouble in a year or
so....'

George Harrison quoting
    Montagu Norman on the
    Government's economy
    programme
        23 August 1931.

i

On 15 July George Harrison cabled Governor
Norman to say, 'we are concerned and surprised at
sudden drop of sterling today. Can you throw any
light on this?'[1] Having gained reserves steadily
from April through the first week of July, the Bank
of England had suddenly come under heavy pressure.
Initial selling had appeared to be French in origin
with a variety of possible motives suggested to
account for this.[2] The British believed that the
French were selling sterling to pressure them into
supporting the French position on reparations, while
rumours were also current that the French were
increasing their liquidity in order to be able to
lend to Germany. However, it was evident that there
were underlying weaknesses in London's position
which clearly contributed to the pound's problems.
The first of these was the state of Britain's
balance of payments. Her visible position had been
in deficit in both 1929 and 1930 but each time a
surplus in invisible exports had been large enough
to allow a net surplus. In July 1931 that this was
not to be the case was known to many in Britain and
abroad.[3] Secondly: the City's position was
increasingly precarious. The usual summer strain
caused by French-generated seasonal pressure was
dwarfed by the problems caused by Germany.[4]
British accepting houses had extended large lines to
German businesses, having among other things on-lent
the funds they had received from French investors.

The German crisis therefore caused them to walk an increasingly precarious tightrope. Gossip about the solvency of major accepting houses was thick in Berlin and Paris and indeed Lazard Brothers had to be rescued by the Bank of England.

The publication of the Macmillan Report in July put further pressure on sterling. At a time when access to information was far more circumscribed than it is today, it being considered of vital importance to a currency's well-being to allow as little information about reserves etc. to be made public, the release of the Report had a most lamentable effect as it quantified British exposure and, notwithstanding the fact that German borrowings were not counted as frozen, pointed out that Britain had a negative net short term position which exceeded close to twice the total gold reserves of the Bank of England. The winds of panic, having swept through Austria to Germany, now reached London, creating an atmosphere where everyone, according to Walter Stewart, was 'frightened and paralyzed by fear.'[5] Finance and banking are to a great extent determined by perception - if a significant number of investors think a currency is undervalued or overvalued it will soon rise or fall, as the case may be. Prior to the First World War very rapid movements of money were not feasible. The post-war development of new modes of communication and transport, however, allowed investors to take quick advantage of events as was seen by the tumultuous movements which rocked all major money markets in 1931. Furthermore, the ability to transfer money quickly would not have been as advantageous as it was without the elevation of currencies other than the pound to the status of actual or potential reserve currencies. The virtual monopoly of international trade possessed by sterling before 1914 had been eroded by the strength of the dollar and, after 1928, the franc as well, giving those who wished to move out of sterling viable alternatives. Yet sterling had remained a very important reserve currency, particularly for those countries on the gold exchange standard. Norman had actively sought this role for sterling, believing it was important for the health of the world financial system and further that it increased the prestige of sterling. Now his efforts came back to haunt him for the sterling holdings of foreign central banks represented another threat to the position of the Bank of England.

It is thus understandable that from mid-July onwards Norman was increasingly anxious. On 15 July Norman told MacDonald that a moratorium on British payments might be necessary and the next day implied the same to Harrison, adding that the deteriorating situation was bringing matters to a head. The British Governor had considered raising Bank rate (currently at 2½%) but decided to postpone action until the London conference which Norman hoped would result in a fundamental readjustment of the world financial position.[6] At this early stage Norman's apocalyptic attitude was probably not warranted by the facts and was certainly ill chosen to reassure a nervous market. To inspire confidence one must be confident, a truism but one Montagu Norman would have done well to follow. (Dr. Pangloss does have his place in the world of international finance.) By maintaining a pessimistic attitude, in fact emphasizing it by continually making worst-case predictions, Norman was not serving his cause well, irrespective of whether his motivation was a genuine conviction in his Cassandra-like comments or a belief that brinkmanship would force the Government's hand.

During the meetings that made up the London Conference Norman continued to worry about sterling. On 21 July he called Harrison to announce that the gold drain had amounted to £10 m over the last three days and seemed likely to continue at the rate of £2 m per day if the exchanges stayed where they were. Although he increasingly believed he had no other option, Norman still hesitated to raise Bank rate and therefore asked Harrison for his advice.[7] Harrison was not slow in responding to this call for help; within two days it was agreed that the FRBNY and the Bank of England would cooperate by the former's purchase of sterling and the sale by the latter of dollars.[8] This represents the first financial assistance to Britain which was tendered by the U.S. during the battle. Harrison both initially and subsequently was eager to help the Bank of England, far more eager than he was to aid the Reichsbank, and his attitude would prove invaluable to Norman.

On 23 July the Bank of England also raised its Bank rate to 3½% which did not stop a further £5 m of gold being taken from London for Paris, Berlin and Amsterdam.[9] Norman now believed that with the London Conference having to his mind accomplished no useful purpose, the Bank of England was on its own. No doubt he took comfort from the fact that J.P.

Morgan, who had sailed from New York on 17 July, was
about to dock at Southampton, having already pen-
cilled in a visit to Norman.[10]

The Treasury was aware both that the Governor
and Morgan were scheduled to meet on Monday, 27 July
and that Norman's chief purpose was to ascertain
whether an American supporting credit for the pound
was obtainable. To Sir Richard Hopkins it was
imperative on Friday, 24 July to reiterate to the
government Norman's words of the previous day as to
the parlous state of the nation. Hopkins further
believed that with the May Report scheduled for
publication the following week and already a subject
of Parliamentary gossip the need for economy was
paramount.[11]

As the British awaited Morgan's arrival and
watched the exchanges to see if the Bank rate
increase would have the desired effect, various
Americans did what they could to help the British.
Jay E. Crane, Deputy Governor of the FRBNY, cabled
Moret to tell him of the American arrangement to
support sterling, a telegram motivated by Harrison's
belief that it was important to keep the French
advised of all developments.[12] More significantly, Stimson met with Premier Laval and the French
Ambassador to Britain, M. de Fleuriau, an old friend
of the Secretary of State. The French Premier,
according to Stimson, on his own accord offered to
exert all his influence to stop the Bank of France
and other French financial institutions from withdrawing gold from the Bank of England. Stimson was
very impressed both by this offer and by Laval's
conduct throughout the London Conference, con-
trasting the Frenchman's helpful attitude to that of
Snowden and Norman, the latter being described by
Stimson as nervous, greatly upset and having lost
his perspective decidedly.[13] President Hoover,
however, was less impressed by Laval, pointing out
when he talked with Stimson on that same 24 July
that the Bank of France had $700 m (£140 m) of gold
on deposit in New York which could easily be
switched to London where it could bolster the
British position.[14] This conversation is
revealing on two accounts. First: one can see the
very strong gold position of the United States; both
Hoover and Stimson were quite prepared to see a sum
equal to the whole of the Bank of England gold
reserves depart from the U.S. Second: during this
discussion - apparently the first by the President
of the British financial crisis - the American
government's desire not to become involved was

already clear. The Hoover Moratorium and the London Conference marked the highwater mark of inter-war American governmental participation in European affairs. At this juncture Hoover was not inclined to help Britain for he lacked the anglophile sentiments which would cause him to risk his increasingly frayed reputation on another European initiative nor was there public support for such a move. The deepening depression made those who favoured saving America first stand firm in their convictions and spurred on others to join them. The result was well depicted by a cartoon published in The New York Times on 26 July which showed a preoccupied Father Hoover talking on the telephone to Europe while trying to ignore crying children representing the farmers, the railroads and the miners.[15] Furthermore, far less American capital was tied up in Britain than in Germany and the position of Britain seemed far less acute than had that of Germany. Finally the element of rivalry, not present between the U.S. and Germany, dictated a less charitable attitude. Thus while those in Washington did not deter Harrison's efforts, they did nothing, neither in July nor later, to augment them.

French gold was again an important subject of discussion when representatives of the Bank of England and the Bank of France met the next day, Sir Robert Kindersley having journeyed to Paris to ask if the Bank of France would consider granting a credit.[16] The French thought the FRBNY not only knew about the British move but had already been asked for a credit themselves but in fact the telephone call to Crane by Robert Lacour-Gayet on 25 July was the first the Americans had heard of a credit.[17] In Harrison's absence, his deputy called Norman to confirm the French report. Norman said that the story was true but that the negotiations were still in the most tentative state and nothing at all would happen until Monday when he would have a meeting to decide the course of events. It is interesting to speculate as to which meeting Norman was referring to; the possibilities include the meeting with Morgan, a special meeting of the Committee of Treasury, a meeting with the clearing bankers or a conference with Sir Richard Hopkins. Another question is why the French were approached before the Americans. This is easier to answer. It made more sense to obtain French rather than American gold because the British reserves were flowing across the Channel not across the Atlantic. American funds would of course be of assistance but if they simply provided an increased fund for Continental investors to tap they would ultimately be useless.[18]

In the event Norman met Morgan earlier than scheduled at Cavendish Square on Sunday as soon as the latter arrived in London. At that meeting what was probably most important to Norman was the discussion of a possible credit to Britain. The Governor had in fact earlier prepared the ground by delineating the precariousness of the British situation in a very confidential cable in February and then raising the subject of a credit explicitly by means of a message delivered by Charles Whigham who went to New York in June. At that time the Morgan partners believed that such a credit operation was feasible.[19] However by 26 July the situation had changed – the now almost two-week-old gold drain and the attendant publicity had weakened Britain's position as a potential borrower. Although Morgan had left New York on 17 July, he was aware of the alteration in Britain's position which he viewed as primarily psychological. According to the American banker Norman was very upset because the Government ignored his continued warnings, apparently hoping to combine unbalanced budgets with short term borrowings. When asked about the feasibility of an American credit, Morgan continued:

> I said it seemed to me that before they could safely borrow in the USA, the Government would have to show at least some plan of restoration of financial stability and should at least have expressed the intention to reduce the expenditures to come within their means. This he [Norman] agreed was quite right and told me he had Snowden's permission to discuss the subject with me and report to him on the result.[20]

This was the first Anglo-American discussion about the British budgetary position and it displays the pattern which would be seen throughout. To be sure Morgan obviously felt a balanced budget was very important but he was only echoing the sentiments of Norman and Snowden.

By Monday word of Kindersley's trip had leaked to the press although The Times reported his purpose as merely the discussion of French withdrawals of gold.[21] On that same day the Committee of Treasury and Sir Richard Hopkins discussed the loan proposal. Norman related that Governor Moret was of the opinion that the British needed a French credit in the amount of £25 m ($125 m; 3,125 m F fr) to stop the gold withdrawals and in furtherance of this plan had called a meeting of Paris bankers the previous day who had agreed in principle to participate in such a transaction. Moret had further suggested that New York should provide a similar arrangement.[22] The French plan illustrated the three fundamental principles of support credits which had evolved during the preceding decade. First of all, such credits[23] should be, in Norman's words: 'as widely international as possible' with the aim that participation of a central bank would carry with it the support both of its related Government and the private financial institutions and investors of its country.[24] Second: it was necessary that the credit be large enough to convince nervous investors that it would be sufficient to accomplish its purpose which was the return of or maintenance of the borrower's currency on the gold standard. Thus in 1925 when Britain returned to gold credits of $500 m (£100 m) had been contemplated and $300 m (£60 m) arranged. The final axiom was the importance of speed. As delay bred rumours which further undermined the strength of a beleaguered currency, it was considered very important to accomplish a borrowing as soon as possible. Yet on 27 July it was clear that Norman was not following his own rules. He did point out at the Committee of Treasury meeting that he had told the Government that any borrowing would require the Bank to be protected by His Majesty's Government. Sir Richard Hopkins then joined the meeting and said that the Government took a contrary view: any such credit should be a purely banking arrangement and if credits could not be arranged and gold continued to be withdrawn, British banks should recall their loans from Germany which had been allowed to remain there under a standstill agreement. This last point may have been made in response to Norman's earlier comments that British exposure in Germany would necessitate a British moratorium but coming after the London conference it shows, to say the least, a certain naivete on Snowden's part for it would have been impossible for the British to obtain any significant repayment of their German loans at this time.

After this discussion, Norman and Deputy Governor Sir Ernest Harvey left the Committee of Treasury to attend a meeting of the clearing

bankers. The private bankers were opposed to the
idea of any credit but preferred that if a credit
were obtained it should be from New York not Paris.
They also urged the Bank of England to make use of
the traditional weapon of Bank rate. Upon hearing
this advice the Governor and his Deputy then
rejoined the Committee of Treasury meeting where it
was decided that Harvey should inform Kindersley
that no decision on a possible French credit would
be made yet and that the matter should be left
open. [25]

Before Norman left for a meeting with clearing
bankers Sir Harry Goschen and J.W. Beaumont Pease
where the question of the suspension of the gold
standard was discussed, he took the opportunity to
tell Hopkins that the clearing bankers doubted the
efficacy of Bank rate and were thus in favour of a
credit. [26] This was obviously the opposite of what
the bankers had said and was not the last occasion
where an official of the Bank of England would
mislead the Government. Norman also cabled Harrison
to say that the Bank's attitude to a credit was
quite undetermined. [27] But the next day Norman
declared the arrangement for the credit in abeyance
because there was a split between those who favoured
self-help at home and others who advocated foreign
borrowings. The former school was in the ascendant
for the time being because Norman predicted a 1%
rise in Bank rate on Thursday. [28] Norman gave no
hint of his own attitude which may fairly be said to
be the same one of vacillation he had displayed over
the German credit. Again it had a bad effect, as it
not only delayed ameliorative action but served to
confuse those who were attempting to help his
institution weather the storm. But this was not
surprising as Norman, whose increasingly distraught
state had been commented upon all summer, had now
spent what was to be his last full day at the Bank
until after the crisis was over. He left Threadneedle Street early on 29 July having felt 'queer'
and, save for a brief appearance on 3 August, did
not return until 28 September. [29] Leffingwell
later fittingly observed that: 'There was a certain
poetic justice in the coincidence of his [Norman's]
physical collapse with the collapse of the
pound.' [30]

Norman's place at the Bank was taken by his
deputy, Sir Ernest Harvey. The first person to rise
from the ranks to become Deputy Governor, Harvey had
occupied his present post for the past two years.
His most pressing matter now was to decide what to

do about the credits. As a stop gap, he wrote to Moret to ask him to consider reviving the dollar/franc swap arrangement which had worked so well in February.[31] Then at the Committee of Treasury meeting on 29 July the rise in Bank rate to 4½% which Norman had predicted was recommended and it was agreed to continue to discuss the French credit rather than to enter into it immediately. Finally:

> The Committee realized the impossibility in the time available of obtaining any guarantee that His Majesty's Government will take effective action to secure a balanced Budget: they agree, however, that the Chancellor be informed that while the Bank would recommend the acceptance of such credits in order to allow the Government time in which to formulate plans for balancing the Budget, the proposed credits would, in their opinion, be of no permanent avail unless followed by such action by the Government.[32]

It would seem that the Bank may have been playing for time, hoping that a rise in Bank rate would be sufficient to stem the gold efflux but further, the continued delay in obtaining credits showed a deep-seated feeling against any such borrowing. The Bank of England's reluctance was two fold. First, both the Bank of England and the Treasury believed that the British budgetary position, with its large imbalance, was at the very least an important cause of the gold drain. The May Report, which would be officially published on 1 August, predicted a budget deficit of £120 m ($600 m). The Treasury and the Bank considered that this report would wreak havoc on the money markets if swift governmental action were not taken to balance the budget. As the quote from the Committee of Treasury minutes makes clear, they despaired of MacDonald's willingness to take the necessary action, and thus feared that any credits would serve to give the Government an excuse to avoid the admittedly unpleasant task of cutting the budget.
Another motive for wishing to refuse French help was the Bank's distaste at the idea of borrowing from the French. Not only was this viewed as demeaning but the British believed that the French offer of help was motivated by, in Neville Chamberlain's words, a desire to have a hand on the British throat.[33] Finally there was the pressure - at

least implicit but perhaps explicit - to be expected from the French who wanted cooperation on both financial and political matters.

Clearly the British rarely ascribed charitable motives to the French, supporting Stimson's observation that the British attitude towards the French was one of coldness, constant suspicion and hostility.[34] This was never more true than during the July discussions on the German problem, yet it would seem that the British were somewhat unfair to their erstwhile allies. As early as 14 July the Bank of France was reported to be concerned about the recent appreciations of the franc against sterling and according to Dean Jay, Governor Moret was both capable and eager to cooperate with the Bank of England.[35] As this coincides with the cooperative attitude the Bank of France had demonstrated all year and with the conversation Stimson had had with Laval, there is little reason to doubt this evidence. It was, after all, in the French interest to aid the British; as of 29 July the French Treasury and the Bank of France had approximately £8 m ($40 m) and £75 m ($375 m) respectively in London; if the pound went off gold they stood to lose a great deal as did the French investors who had large deposits in London.[36] Furthermore the French realized that the advantageous position they had secured vis-à-vis the British by the relative undervaluation of the franc as against the pound would be destroyed by a devaluation of sterling. Finally it was clear to the French that it was imperative for the stability of both Germany and for Europe as a whole for British banks to retain their investments in Germany; yet if the pound were severely threatened, the British might try to pull their lines. Therefore it seems clear that the French sincerely desired to help the British, a view Sir Robert Kindersley obviously shared. He had been sent to negotiate with them because of his well known francophile sympathies but by 28 July he was quite angry, feeling he should not have been sent to negotiate a French credit if the Government meant to veto the idea.[37] Later on, in fact, Kindersley would tell the American Ambassador to London, Charles Dawes, that the hostile attitude towards France of Norman and Snowden and their foolish statements represented a great danger to the British position and an important cause of the drain of gold.[38]

However, Kindersley's mission to Paris proved not to have been undertaken in vain. After the

Committee of Treasury meeting on the 29th, Harvey called Harrison to say that the Bank of England had revived the question of a credit. Harrison was very surprised, telling the Deputy Governor that Norman had led him to believe that the British did not want a credit. As this discussion constituted the first official request by the British that the Americans consider a credit, Harrison told Harvey that he could not tell him what attitude the FRBNY would take until he consulted with his Board of Directors the next day. After talking with Harvey, Harrison called Lacour-Gayet to tell him of his conversation, surprising the French official who thought the issue was not if, but when, there would be a credit.[39] Obviously Kindersley had decided not to be very explicit about the Bank's waffling attitude.

Simultaneous with the central bank discussions, Morgan's was considering the question of a British credit. Morgan's (N.Y.) cabled J.P. Morgan to brief him on American sentiment. It was their belief that the rumours current on the 'Street' about the necessity for a British credit, which apparently stemmed from British banking sources, were pernicious and would only lead to American withdrawals from Britain. They attributed dire consequences to Norman's and Snowden's gloomy forecasts and opined that if only the British would sound more confident, matters might right themselves. Furthermore, if a credit were desired it would not be an easy matter to accomplish because both the German crisis and the British attitude had made American banks eager to avoid further foreign entanglements. Therefore the New York partners believed that Morgan should be wary of committing himself until the American banking community could be sounded out and prepared for the operation.[40]

Morgan responded the same day, cabling that he agreed that it would be best if Morgan's did not undertake a credit operation and thus believed that no discussion should be had with the American banks because such talk would be taken as a sign that Morgan's and the Bank of England were alarmed at Britain's situation. Finally Morgan observed that Norman had shown the effects of the great strain he had been under and that the situation in Britain was very confused.[41]

It was thus clear that at this point, if there were to be credits, they would be from the central banks. Harrison, as promised, called Harvey informing him that the directors of the FRBNY had authorized him to proceed with a credit of £25 m

($125 m) to take the form of an agreement to pur-
chase for a period of three months' prime commercial
bills of British banks bearing two signatures and
guaranteed by the Bank of England. He added that he
believed that the FRBNY credit should be mirrored by
a similar commitment on the part of the Bank of
France, and Harvey concurred. The two central
bankers then discussed further terms, e.g., that the
credits should be repayable in gold and that each
credit would be twice renewable albeit on the basis
of a gentleman's agreement. Harrison next stated
his preference that the Bank of France take the
entire French credit itself rather than sharing it
with various French banks as had been proposed. As
Harvey concurred, Harrison said he would raise the
matter with Lacour-Gayet that evening. Finally
Harrison mentioned the possibility of the British
undertaking a conversion operation involving the
whole or part of the British Government's massive
First World War public debt. That a later private
operation might take this form was Harrison's idea;
apparently he had previously discussed the question
with Norman.[42] The New York Governor's opinion
was echoed by the words of Eugene Meyer, Governor of
the Federal Reserve Board, who said it was his
opinion that Britain's difficulties were too severe
to be cured by a central bank loan; only a British
Government loan issued in New York which could be
for a much larger amount would do.[43]

By this time other Washington officials were
aware of the proposed operation. Undersecretary of
the Treasury Ogden Mills called Harrison to ask
about the status of the negotiations and was given a
progress report. Harrison further said that he
wanted to ask Mills, as Acting Secretary, if he had
any objections to a FRBNY credit although Harrison,
eager to safeguard his institution's independence,
made it clear that he was interested more in informing Washington as to the FRBNY's activities than
in asking for Treasury approval. Mills said that
both he and the President heartily agreed with this
step.[44] Across the Atlantic, the British Treasury
had also been kept informed of the progress of the
negotiations, in part because of Government approval
and further because it felt an increase in the
fiduciary issue might be necessary and that required
Government approval.[45] MacDonald no doubt preferred considering the question of a credit to
contemplating his Parliamentary position. The House
of Commons session on 30 July was the last before
the summer recess and if The Times description was a

bit overdone (the leader called the occasion 'as solemn and as critical as has ever been called.'[46]) there is no question that the position was not a comfortable one. The May Report was the proverbial political firecracker. To deal with the problem - or rather to postpone dealing with it - MacDonald proposed the appointing of a Cabinet Economy Committee to consider the May Report's suggested cuts and to propose others, the Committee to report in October when Parliament reconvened. This was a typical MacDonald gesture; to avoid trouble he had previously appointed a committee on the state of unemployment insurance and had acquiesced in the original appointment of the May Committee. This time the gambit would not prove successful.

Ramsay MacDonald was now aged 65 and in less than robust health, facing the most difficult period of his career. Secretary of the Labour Representation Committee since 1900 and leader of the Labour Party from 1911 to 1914 and from 1922 until the present, he was the man who had done the most to make Labour respectable. Now in his second term as Prime Minister he found his Government increasingly buffeted by financial crises both at home and abroad. Stalemated domestically, he sought and won the confidence of the Americans and the Germans but spurned the French whom he blamed for the First World War which MacDonald had always opposed. But it was the domestic crisis triggered by the run on the pound which would cast his fate.

On 31 July MacDonald and Stimson met, the latter saying that the important thing for Britain was to keep calm and that Snowden's talk about a possible moratorium had done great harm. MacDonald agreed, adding that Henderson was guilty in conversations with Laval of the same offence.[47] On the same day the FRBNY and the Bank of France reached agreement with the Bank of England on the credits, Harrison having successfully convinced the Bank of France to fund the entire French credit itself. The New York Governor appeared elated, telling Lacour-Gayet that their institutions' actions would have an electrifying effect.[48] The Bank of England had received assurances from the Treasury that the Government would take all necessary measures to help the Bank meet its commitments under the credit agreements and that the Treasury would place no obstacle in the way of any export of gold by the Bank of England pursuant to the terms of the credits.[49] The credit agreements were formally agreed upon the next day, Harrison writing to Harvey that he was very happy to have participated in this operation which he wished to be seen as evidence of the FRBNY's desire to be of assistance to the Bank of England in its present predicament and to restore confidence in the world economic situation.[50] Harvey for his part, writing to Lord Cullen, expressed the hope that the credits would restore the world's faith in sterling.[51] It was not to be.

ii

Simultaneous with the signing of the credit agreements, the Bank of England made a statutory request of the Chancellor of the Exchequer asking for the fiduciary issue to be increased from £260 m to £275 m for a period of three weeks.[52] The Currency and Bank Note Act of 1928, which fixed the fiduciary issue at £260, also permitted the Bank of England to request the Chancellor of the Exchequer to allow temporary increases in the fiduciary issue if the Bank thought it advisable. While it was envisaged that the mechanism would be availed of from time to time, depending on seasonal variations in money supply needs (and indeed the Bank had considered asking for an increase in 1929) this was the first time the Bank of England had made such a request.[53] Harvey, with the support of the Committee of Treasury, took this action ostensibly to obtain the increased flexibility that an extra £15 M in 'free' gold reserves would provide. Unfortunately the financial markets interpreted this as a sign of weakness because it looked as if the British were willing to wander from the path of financial orthodoxy.[54] That this reaction was predictable leads to the question of whether it was anticipated by the Bank of England. If the answer is affirmative it is not surprising that the action was nonetheless taken. For the Bank was both concerned that the Government realize the seriousness of the situation and also afraid that the acquisition of the credits would create a false impression of security. Thus Harvey and his associates may have believed that raising the fiduciary issue would serve a second salutory purpose by partly dissipating the positive impression created by the French and American credits and the rise in Bank rate.

Yet the credits did initially have a bolstering effect. Not only had Britain acquired a significant reserve, that is to say credits two and a half times larger than the Reichsbank had received, but the leading central banks had shown their solidarity. Although it was widely expected that, as in 1925, the credits would never be used, it was felt that they would be sufficient to maintain foreign confidence until October when Parliament would reconvene to discuss the May Report and the Budget.[55] The politicians dispersed on their holidays, MacDonald to Lossiemouth, Neville Chamberlain to Dalhousie, Stanley Baldwin to Aix-les-Bains while J.P. Morgan cabled his office on 4 August that all was quiet.[56]

The next day, however, proved the opposite as the Paris exchanges slipped drastically, the pound falling below the gold point against both the dollar and the franc. The explanation given by both the Bank of England and the Treasury was that it was due to a technical misunderstanding between the Bank of England and the Bank of France concerning the method of supporting the pound.[57] While the Foreign Office ascribed the problem to an inability on the part of Bank of England officials to understand French, the truth was somewhat more complicated.[58] The Bank of England had entered into the credits as a measure of insurance with the hope that it would be unnecessary to utilize them.[59] Therefore the Bank on 5 August allowed gold to be withdrawn rather than make use of the French credit and not only because gold exports to Paris were to be expected during the summer. The Bank of England was of the opinion that the lack of confidence in sterling was due to the British budgetary problems. As balancing the Budget was nothing if not unpalatable, the conclusion of the Bank (perhaps in part due to the failure of the markets to react 'sufficiently' to the increase in the fiduciary issue) was that the Government needed to be pushed into action and the most effective prod would be a loss of gold.[60]

Moret was frankly appalled at this manoeuvre. Obviously miffed that the British would take such action without consulting him, particularly as the Frenchman believed there was an understanding that the Bank of England would use the credits before losing any more gold, he further believed that the British had misjudged the strength of their position; to his way of thinking any further loss of sterling would have dire consequences.[61] The Bank of England, however, did not like the position the

French had placed them in as, among other things, it felt that the French wanted them to borrow under the credit to ensure British subordination to France. Yet they found themselves in a corner because it was clear that they could not do without French support. For that reason it was decided not to raise Bank rate on 6 August, the French having strongly advised against it, and instead the Deputy Governor was charged with informing the Chancellor about the Bank's financial position.[62]

Harvey wrote to Snowden the same day. After ascribing the 5 August debacle to a 'misunderstanding', again showing a certain lack of veracity, he got down to the main point of his letter which was to say that the position was very bad:

> No matter how black the Governor may have painted the picture in his discussions with you, his picture cannot have been more black than theirs [the Committee of Treasury and Court of Directors] today.

As had been agreed at the Committee of Treasury meeting, Harvey requested in conclusion that the Bank of England be allowed to communicate the situation to the leaders of the Opposition.[63] Snowden immediately wrote to MacDonald, enclosing Harvey's letter and noting that according to the Bank of England foreigners believed that the unsound budgetary position was causing sterling's difficulties. To Snowden it was clear that the previously agreed schedule which provided for the first meeting of the Cabinet Economy Committee on 25 August would not do; the Chancellor concluded his letter by saying: 'The collapse is certain to come before then if we delay.'[64]

MacDonald was not home to receive Snowden's letter; he was at Ben Armin, Scotland visiting Stimson who had rented a glen for the month of August. There they discussed many issues, most importantly, disarmament which interested both statesmen, but apparently did not touch on the British financial crisis.[65] This omission was certainly rectified when MacDonald arrived back in Lossiemouth and found Snowden's message awaiting him. In reply he offered to go to London whenever Snowden thought it proper and they agreed to meet on 11 August.[66]

The atmosphere of the metropolis MacDonald was returning to was quite different from the typical silly season; in Morgan's words, 'things have not

92

been very holiday-ish here.'[67] According to
Atherton much talk centered around the possibility
of a National Government; The Times concurred,
stating in a leader that fresh advocacy of such a
possibility (which had been the subject of speculation in July) had been the chief result of the May
Report.[68]

In New York, Harrison was very worried because
the 5 August manoeuvre, which had resulted in a loss
of £2 m, had badly frightened the Americans. After
some discussion he and Harvey agreed that the
British would draw down the whole of the French
credit for use as and when required and that the
British would take all necessary measures to keep
the exchanges above the gold point and avoid the
loss of any further amounts of gold.[69] More and
more the Bank of England's options were shrinking.
All it could do now was to use the credits, admittedly itself a sign of weakness, and help the
Government see where its duty lay. At this point
balancing the budget was indeed imperative if the
pound was to retain the confidence of the money
markets whose view was articulated by Morgan:·

> The fact is that this Government has so
> blithely gone along increasing, and
> threatening a continuance of the increase,
> of the deficit of the Budget, that the
> world in general having seen the results
> of such action in other countries, be-
> lieves that England requires a certain
> pulling-up before it gets too far along
> the downward path.[70]

The irony is that Britain was not the only
country with a budget deficit; indeed for the
1930-31 fiscal year the American deficit was $903 m
(£180 m). The New York Times ascribed to the
British a special interest in balanced budgets but
of course what concerned the markets was whether
Britain would stay on the gold standard.[71] By
August 1931 it was clear that this accomplishment
was no longer automatic, if ever it had been, but
instead required concerted action. Therefore the
budget took on a symbolic importance as it was
believed that if the Government did not have the
grit to cut the dole and other social measures which
were costly and to many financiers per se pernicious, Britain would not long remain on the gold
standard. H.D. Henderson, Secretary of the Economic
Advisory Council understood this point; in his

report on the May Report he said that although the British financial position as depicted in the May Report was in many respects misleading, the Government would have to make a great many budget cuts unless the gold standard was to be abandoned.[72]

As the Bank of England and the British Government attempted to deal with the budget issue, Harrison, now increasingly alarmed, discussed with Morgan's (N.Y.) the possibility of a British Government credit. The reply he received was that while the firm was eager to help the British to the best of their ability, in their opinion only an operation good for British credit should be considered and at the present time that criterion probably could not be met. In fact the 'Corner' believed that even raising the question of a credit would be harmful, for within one week to follow credits of $250 m by the organization of further loans would serve to exacerbate already existing fears about the European situation.[73] This answer, which Harrison said he would communicate to Harvey, cannot have comforted the Deputy Governor, beleaguered as he was by the failure of sterling to stabilize. Moret continued to lament the British action of 5 August which was of course not solely to blame for the British predicament.[74]

One interesting question is the identity of the sellers of sterling. Notwithstanding official British comments to the contrary, the British themselves were rushing to get out of sterling. Another large portion of sterling sales were German inspired; the investors of that nation, who had bought sterling in June and July, now moved into other currencies.[75] French sales continued, though not by the Bank of France, and a large percentage were unrelated to the crisis. It was the U.S. whose investors proved to possess the most faith in sterling - there seem to have been few American sales during July and August.[76]

MacDonald had left for London with a heavy heart, writing to Stimson that 'things are not at all good, and there appears to be no doubt but that certain interests are making dead set against us.'[77] On 11 August he saw Sir Clive Wigram, Private Secretary to King George V; and then together with Snowden met with Harvey and Edward (later Sir Edward) Peacock, the man designated by the Committee of Treasury to accompany Harvey to all his meetings with politicians. Peacock was a very interesting selection, being unique in his combination of international and domestic expertise; for

example, he was very involved in both Argentine
finances and the organization and management of
BIDCo, Norman's vehicle for the rationalization of
British industry. He also had close ties with
Conservative politicians (Chamberlain, a Unionist,
described him as someone who had a great reputation
for wisdom and sanity) and was one of Norman's
closest friends in the City.[78] When Norman took
sick, Peacock often as not handled his travel and
personal arrangements and was of such stature that
Grenfell could say in the summer of 1931 that he was
the most important man in the City, a sentiment
echoed at the same time by Jay Crane, who was in
London during August and early September 1931.[79]

Peacock and Harvey had only bad tidings for the
Ministers they met, telling MacDonald and Snowden
that it might be hopeless to try and keep the pound
on gold unless the Government took action.[80]
Again it should be noted that the bankers' approach
was one which emphasized the weaknesses in the
situation. Possessing a fundamental mistrust of
politicians, they acted on the belief that only the
most drastic statements could convince the government to make the needed budget cuts.[81] Their task
was made easier by the Government's (including the
Treasury's) complete reliance on the Bank for
information on the nation's financial situation.
Not only was the collection of economic statistics
in its infancy (the Bank's economic statistical
section did not begin operations until 1925) and the
prevailing theory one which emphasized the importance of secrecy and obstructed the publication of
information, but the Bank closely guarded what
information it had even from the Government: for
example it was not till late September that the Bank
began sending the Treasury weekly reports of its
foreign exchange holdings.[82] The consequent need
to rely on the Bank made it more unlikely that
MacDonald or Snowden would take independent action.
Yet they did not appear unhappy at their predicament, at least not in August. Snowden's highly
orthodox attitude towards finance had brought him
Norman's approbation, while one searches in vain
through the Prime Minister's papers for any sign of
rebellion against the Bank's leadership until after
the crisis was over. To be sure MacDonald was faced
with a dearth of alternative advice. During this
period, the last time when financiers rather than
economists acted as the leading experts on financial
and monetary matters, MacDonald was remarkable in
having established close links with economists

particularly through the creation of the Economic Advisory Council in 1930. But for the duration of the crisis he found little solace from either H.D. Henderson or J.M. Keynes. The former acquiesced in the conventional wisdom offered the Prime Minister while Keynes was simply not consistent. Keynes did write on 5 August that in his opinion a policy of 'deflation à l'outrance' was ill-advised but that letter was a weak reed to lean on as it appeared to link going off gold with an international conference.[83] The latter was obviously a chimera at this point; did that mean the former was as well? On 12 August Keynes wrote again but his advice was even more equivocal:

> I believe that it is still possible for us to keep on the gold standard if we deliberately decide to do so but if this is the case, we should have to conform our whole policy accordingly. Personally I should support for the time being whichever decision we made, provided the decision was accompanied by action sufficiently drastic to make it effective.[84]

No wonder MacDonald, who had just been briefed on the current depressing state of sterling by Harvey and Peacock, advocated taking the bankers' advice when the first meeting of the Cabinet Economy Committee took place.[85] Therefore it was decided at the second meeting of the Committee held the next day (13 August) that a report of suggested economies would be prepared for submission to the Cabinet in five days time.[86]

Between 12 and 18 August the Bank of England played for time. Harvey and Peacock had met with Conservative and Liberal leaders who were now more informed about the situation than the Labour Cabinet save for MacDonald and Snowden. Interestingly, this frequent contact did not result in a heightened sense of respect on the part of the Conservative leaders for the Bank of England. Sir Samuel Hoare, who accompanied Chamberlain to most of his August meetings, recounted that while the Conservatives were impressed by Harvey's personality:

> We were equally impressed by the ignorance of the Bank and the City as to what was likely to happen. The Bank seemed to have no means of obtaining accurate statistics as to the course of the flow of gold and

Harvey could make no estimates of what was
likely to happen on the following day.[87]

Of course, given the nature of the City-Conservative
links, the Tories had been fully aware of the
pound's predicament as it developed: Grenfell, for
instance, was not only a Director of the Bank of
England but also Conservative M.P. for the City of
London and Chamberlain was consulting Peacock about
the economy in July. These official connections
were supplemented by a host of informal ones.
Clubs, residential areas and 'old boy' associations
all provided meeting grounds for bankers and Opposition politicians. Furthermore their shared background produced a common outlook far removed from
that held by most Labour politicians. This resulted
not in an anti-Labour conspiracy (which actually
would have been far easier to combat) but in a
jointly held set of reflexes which automatically
operated against Socialist priorities. Thus the
bankers and both the Conservatives and the Liberals
could be relied upon to keep the pressure on the
Government, something which surely had been the
motive behind the Committee of Treasury's decision
to seek permission to communicate officially with
the Opposition.

Harvey also worked through the Treasury to keep
hammering the Bank's point across. Writing to Sir
Richard Hopkins he reiterated his fears about what
he termed the present unsatisfactory budgetary
position.[88] The international atmosphere further
engendered a feeling of concern. The Wiggin Committee, created in the wake of the London Conference to
draft a plan for the handling of Germany's short-
term debts, was meeting at Basle. With financial
luminaries such as Sir Walter Layton, editor of The
Economist, the Chase Manhattan Bank President,
Albert Wiggin, and the former Bank of France Governor, Emile Moreau representing respectively Britain,
the United States and France, it is no wonder that
rumours flew, mostly concentrated on the British
situation. Thus on 11 August, McGarrah cabled
Harrison to tell him that the Wiggin Committee
members were very concerned about talk that the Bank
of England was planning to reduce its gold reserve
substantially while the following week Francis Rodd
(later Lord Rennell of Rodd), seconded to the BIS
from the Bank of England and a future partner of
Morgan Grenfell, wrote that certain Germans seemed
to think the pound would be devalued.[89]

Saving the Pound

The French were still attempting to cooperate with the British to form a common currency protection front. On 11 August Leith-Ross met with French Treasury representatives at the latter's request. The French told the British that in their view sterling's problems were caused by the theories advocated by British economists and writers coupled with the budgetary problems and the ramifications of the German crisis including the panicked predictions of Snowden, Henderson and Norman as to the possible effects of a German moratorium on the pound's position. As a solution, M. Bizot advocated a loan to the British Government issued in Paris to which Leith-Ross suggested that as an alternative, France might consider early repayment of her outstanding First World War debts to Britain. Certainly the existence of these debts, which had been funded in 1926 on terms very advantageous to France, was a constant source of irritation to the British. Unfortunately most borrowers neither voluntarily prepay debts nor do they pay more than they are legally bound to pay.[90]

The Bank of England had in fact debated the possibility of a short term issue raised in France, but its unenthusiastic conclusion was that such a borrowing would be only a temporary palliative.[91] On the following day Siepmann produced the Bank's first written consideration of the merits of remaining on the gold standard. His approach can best be described as damning the gold standard with faint praise although he advocated protective measures to restore confidence in sterling.[92]

While the Government was pondering its fate, J.P. Morgan was shooting grouse in Scotland. However he remained in touch with Grenfell who sent him a steady stream of letters and cables. According to the British banker the problem with MacDonald was that 'he was so conceited and fluffy headed that it will be difficult to keep him up to the scratch.' Grenfell also mentioned that Montagu Norman, although well enough to meet with Stanley Baldwin on 7 August, had not rallied and would go on a rest cruise on 15 August.[93] Norman in fact sailed on the Duchess of York for Canada with his intended designation being Bar Harbor, Maine and the home of his old friend Mrs. Markoe, having turned down Morgan's offer of the use of the Corsair.[94]

Harvey, at the request of the Treasury, was now officially exploring with Harrison the possibility of a further borrowing in the U.S.[95] Feeling perhaps that Crane could speak more openly to the

98

FRBNY than he could, he asked the New Yorker to ascertain Harrison's advice on three points: whether a foreign loan should be arranged as soon as a programme of budget cuts was announced, would it be feasible to float a British loan in New York, and should Paris be asked to arrange a loan as well.[96] It was Harrison's view that a Government credit could indeed be quickly obtained and that it should be a joint New York-Paris operation. Harrison urged however that a 'very convincing budget' was a prerequisite for a successful operation.[97]

It was of course statements like this that provided the basis of the various 'bankers' ramp' legends. But rather than being a harbinger of the nefarious American governmental pressure on Britain alleged by the Daily Herald in its famous 25 August article, it is clear that Harrison was only echoing the sentiments of the Bank of England as well as of the Conservative and certain elements of the Liberal Parties. It was first Norman and then Harvey and Peacock who tried to use the sterling exchange situation as a club to beat the budget back to a state of balance. But was this a conspiracy to victimize the majority of Britons for the benefit of a few rapacious bankers? Further, did the bankers intend to use the crisis to force the Labour Party out of office? On the latter question the evidence is clear that both the Bank of England and Morgan's wanted Labour to stay in office because they believed that not only should the Government pay the price of its 'profligacy' but that the cuts would be more acceptable to Labour Party members if made by their leaders.[98]

As for the former charge, there is no question but that the bankers, both central and merchant, believed that expenditure on social services should be cut. Bankers are not original thinkers; as practitioners of the art of the possible they tend to adhere to financial orthodoxy. Prevailing sentiment in 1931 held an unbalanced budget to be both morally and financially pernicious. Furthermore the largest expenditures amenable to cuts were the sinking fund provisions and the unemployment and transitional benefits. Obviously the former could not be cut while the Bank was trying to convince financiers to keep and extend their British investments. Moreover to these men cutting the dole would end its unwholesome effect on the British character and would improve the competitiveness of British exports in world markets. The logical end result of this line of reasoning was a conclusion that eliminating or sharply curtailing the benefits in question, although painful, would be beneficial to the British people. Yet the Bank of England, the Bank of France and the FRBNY as well as financiers throughout the world and the governments of France and the U.S., all of whom shared this outlook, did not ignore the welfare of their poorer citizens. Rather they honestly believed that the course they advocated represented the surest guarantee for a better future. That it also benefitted their private interests does not derogate from most of these individuals' genuine conviction that they were advocating a course that was the best for Britain as a whole. As a borrower must ultimately acquiesce in its lenders' views if it is to get the loan it is requesting, it is true the British Government had no alternative but to balance its budget. But it must be emphasized that a belief in the desirability of a balanced budget was not forced on the British by external pressure but was rather a conviction shared by the Bank of England, the City, most of industry, the Treasury, the Chancellor and perhaps the Prime Minister as well as the Conservatives and a great many Liberals.[99]

The Opposition was placed in a difficult position. Although not wishing to be unpatriotic they were loath to give up the advantages that would accrue to them if, in Stanley Baldwin's words, 'Labour had to look after their own chickens as they came home to roost.'[100] Furthermore many of the Conservatives wished to use the crisis not only to force the Government to balance the Budget but to push through a tariff. Interestingly, one of the people they were relying on to accomplish this was Edward Peacock.[101]

18 August was a key day in the history of the financial crisis. In Basle the Layton Report on the state of German finance was released. It revealed that German short term debt was in excess of 7.4 billion RM, pointed out that of Germany's long term debt of 9.5 million RM, about 15% was British in origin and recommended the standstill arrangement be continued. All this boded ill for Britain for it revealed that her German exposure was greater than had been previously estimated and ensured that it was now to be basically permanently illiquid.[102] On the same day the Committee of Treasury, having realized that half the credits had been expended, authorized Dr. O.M.W. Sprague, Harvard Professor and advisor to the Governor of the Bank of England, to consider the possible effects of a departure from

the gold standard. At the same time as the Committee took this momentous step they authorized Dr. Sprague to invite Keynes to the Bank to discuss the situation with the hope that the revelation of 'the true facts' would convince him to change the tone of the articles he was writing on the financial crisis.[103] Finally the Cabinet Economy Committee completed their list of suggested economy cuts. Already acrimonious words had been exchanged between Henderson and MacDonald leading the latter to conclude that 'heavy is our just complaint against Providence.'[104] The report began with the basic assumption that the budget must be balanced, and went on to suggest departmental economies, increased taxation and a cut of £20 m in the transitional benefit. It was decided to submit it to the full Cabinet the next day.[105]

The members of the Cabinet who met on 19 August to consider the Economy Committee Report were in an unenviable position. They faced a Chancellor who had been told the previous day that there was an atmosphere of nervous hesitancy surrounding sterling, making it of paramount importance that the Government deliver an early announcement of its proposals for only then would the possibility of a sudden break in sterling be avoided, yet the Cabinet had no independent access to information.[106] They were battered by pressure from newspapers, e.g., The Times' leader of that day, not mincing words, said: 'It is necessary to insist again and again on the extreme urgency of the situation. The Budget must be balanced immediately.'[107] MacDonald was convinced that an American loan would solve his Government's problems and therefore desperately wanted budget cuts. As he had to cope with colleagues like F.W. Pethwick-Lawrence, who believed that Bank and City policy, not an imbalanced budget, had caused the crisis, his road was clearly not to be an easy one.[108] Thus it is not surprising that the Cabinet, although accepting the basic assumption of the Economy Committee report could not agree on how to accomplish its task. It took the now habitual route - a subcommittee was set up to consider the question of a cut in the transitional benefit and the Cabinet adjourned, to meet again on Friday, 21 August.[109]

On Thursday the 20th, MacDonald and Snowden had a crucial meeting with the General Council of the Trade Union Congress. Its leaders, Ernest Bevin and Walter Citrine, sceptical about the financial crisis, were unwilling to acquiesce in the Govern-

ment's planned economies. What is interesting is
that the TUC did not produce alternatives of their
own. Bevin, a member of the Macmillan Committee,
had signed a dissent in which he stated his belief
in the desirability of jettisoning the gold standard, although he had accepted the views of the
majority that the gold standard was necessary to
maintain Britain's position in the world.[110]   As
Britain was clearly losing her standing anyway, one
must ask why Bevin did not on 20 August advocate a
departure from gold as he was to do on 7-8 September
at the T.U.C. Congress. Had he followed such a
course MacDonald would have had a viable alternative
to the policy he was following at the behest of the
bankers, the Treasury and the Opposition. As it
was, MacDonald was justified in saying that nothing
the General Council representatives had put forward
addressed the basic problem which confronted the
Government.[111]
          While the financial world awaited a British
Government announcement, sterling fluctuated.   In
New York the Morgan partners considered at Grenfell's request the question of a British credit.
Their response was that an operation of the type
mooted (a long term loan) was difficult to undertake
because of the present market conditions and the
absence of so many bankers on holiday. They further
pointed out that sentiment having continued to
deteriorate, in their opinion it would be best to
wait till budget reforms had been accomplished
before attempting such an operation. However they
did believe a short term credit might be possible
and thus asked for specific information as to the
Government's timetable, the drawings under the
central bank credits and the withdrawals of short
term balances.[112]   Grenfell replied that the
Government had no timetable, that the answer to the
second question was confidential and that no one
knew the answer to the third question. He added
that MacDonald did not appear able to control his
colleagues and that the situation was becoming
increasingly unpleasant.[113] On Friday afternoon
Grenfell cabled New York again. Realizing the
weekend would be crucial, he asked the Morgan
partners to stand by.[114]
          Simultaneously the Cabinet met and decided to
consider various economies notwithstanding the
attitude of the T.U.C. A consensus was reached on
cuts of £56 m, a far cry from the May recommendations of £120 m which Snowden had revealed was
itself £50 m less than the latest estimated budget

deficit. In the meantime the Conservative and Liberal leaders anxiously awaited the Cabinet's decision, Lord Swinton writing to his wife that no one (including the Prime Minister) could tell from hour to hour what would happen.[115] But when Chamberlain, Liberal politician Sir Herbert Samuel and their respective associates saw MacDonald and heard his proposal, they told him that if the cuts remained as described they would turn him out as soon as Parliament reconvened. After a time MacDonald proposed submitting to Harrison through Harvey the program of £56 m of cuts together with an additional 10% cut in the dole for a total package of about £68 m. Harvey agreed to this although, according to Chamberlain, he was aghast at MacDonald's insistence that he should not disclose the true projected deficit.[116]

When the Deputy Governor cabled Harrison the next day he ignored MacDonald's suggestion and explained that the estimated deficit of £170 m would be corrected by cuts of £70 m, increases in taxation of £50 m and the balance from non-contractual sinking fund deductions.[117] Harrison replied that if the suggested program was approved by all three parties it would form a possible basis for a British Government credit but any decision was a matter for the partners of Morgan's (N.Y.) who would be meeting the next day. He concluded by reiterating his earlier suggestion that the French be approached as soon as possible.[118]

The Bank of England followed this advice and on the same day began to prepare the ground for French and American credits in line with MacDonald's request that they ascertain if the outlined program would be sufficient for its intended purpose. One should note that MacDonald was still apparently unaware that Morgan's not the FRBNY would be furnishing any credit but the former was not being left out of the discussions. Various partners had met with Harrison on 22 August and after hearing the British proposals the New York partners called Grenfell to give their reactions. They questioned whether the amount mentioned, £40 M ($200 m) each in Paris and New York, was not a bit optimistic and suggested that perhaps a total credit of half that amount was a more suitable goal. Next they enquired whether Parliamentary action was not necessary for balancing the budget and for the issuance of the contemplated tax-exempt dollar obligations. If this were the case Morgan's (N.Y.) believed that the only possible operation was a private banking operation

which they themselves had not yet really contemplated. This would not be easy for, as the New York
bankers said:

> We think you will realize that the public
> generally including the banks and banking
> houses have for a time looked with great
> apprehension upon the continued neglect of
> the present Government to establish sound
> fiscal policies and it is going to take a
> great deal more than simply the joint
> declaration of three Party leaders to
> convince the investment and the banking
> public here that real amendment has been
> undertaken and that the Government is in a
> position to command heavy foreign credit
> favours.

> You will realize too the same public looks
> upon the whole European situation as in a
> bad mess and will not be too ready to
> undertake to bail out any one part of the
> situation... these constitute another
> reason why a certain amount of time is
> necessary to educate our public and
> therefore why any too urgent operation
> should be avoided. [119]

Finally they suggested that Grenfell ask J.P.
Morgan to return to London and repeated that they
would be in Long Island awaiting his message on
Sunday.

When the Morgan partners assembled with George
Harrison at the house of F.D. Bartow they found a
request from the Bank of England transmitted through
Grenfell asking whether a proposal' basically in the
form outlined the previous day would be a satisfactory basis for a credit operation. MacDonald, now
realizing who his putative lenders were, asked
Harvey to find out if Morgan's (N.Y.) would consider
arranging the credit without committing itself so he
could tell the Cabinet that he had positive indica-
tions from foreign bankers and thereby obtain
Cabinet approval for the cuts. If the answer from
New York was negative, Grenfell stated that in his
opinion the Prime Minister would probably resign. [120] Although they had been requested to give
their reply by 7:00 p.m. London time, it was not
until two hours later that it arrived. Immediately
taken from the Bank of England to 10 Downing Street,
the Morgan's (N.Y.) cable was basically a restate-

ment of its position on the previous day. The cable
was phrased in a tentative fashion and well hedged
but the Morgan's (N.Y.) partners indicated that a
private credit of $100-150 m (£20-25 m) was possi-
ble, assuming that the French market provided an
equivalent amount. The cable concluded with the
question: were Morgan's (N.Y.) right in assuming
that the Government's programme had the sincere
approval and support of the Bank of England and the
City in general, for a positive response on the part
of the British public was crucial to the success of
the operation.[121]

Although Morgan's (N.Y.) had indicated, despite
their better judgement, that they would lead an
American syndicate, no American magic wand had
waived away MacDonald's problems. He walked into
the Cabinet room and announced that, if the programme of £70 m cuts were adopted, Harvey had said a
credit was obtainable. (It is unclear if MacDonald
told the Cabinet that Harrison had been the
initiator of the American response; certainly his
biographer only refers to the New York Governor, and
Morgan's (N.Y.) had deliberately not signed their
cable.)[122] After discussion, a vote on the cuts
was taken and the Cabinet split eleven to nine.
Thus, as what Geoffrey Dawson called 'the worst
night we have ever spent' ended, the future of the
British Government was unclear. The next morning
the King, who had returned from Sandringham the
previous day to meet with MacDonald and the Opposition leaders, again summoned them.[123] By the
afternoon of Monday, 24 August, MacDonald, together
with Conservatives and Liberals, had agreed to form
a National Government whose raison d'être was to
guide the nation through the financial crisis.[124]
It had the blessing of the Bank of England, the
Committee of Treasury concluding that this was the
best possible arrangement.[125] However, financial
markets adopted a 'wait and see' attitude. Thus
several weeks would be needed before the outcome of
the battle to save Britain's gold standard was
revealed.[126]

NOTES

    1. Harrison Papers, Box 20, Harrison to
Norman, 228/31, 15 July 1931.
    2. The New York Times, 12 July 1931, p. 1.
    3. See, e.g., B/E, SMT 5/3, Clay Memoranda,
15 August and 25 August 1931.
    4. B/E, OV 45/4, Memorandum: 'The Paris
Market', 23 July 1931.

5. Harrison Papers, Binder 45, Harrison Memorandum concerning telephone conversation with Stewart, 2 July 1931.

6. FRBNY, Harrison Papers, 3115.2, Harrison Memorandum, 21 July 1931, concerning telephone conversations with Norman on 15 July and 16 July 1931.

7. FRBNY, C261, Norman to Harrison, 231/31, 21 July 1931.

8. FRBNY, C261, Harrison to Norman, 243/31, 23 July 1931; Harrison Papers, Binder 59, Harrison Memorandum concerning telephone conversation with Eugene Meyer, 24 July 1931; Cable, Crane to all Federal Reserve Banks, 24 July 1931.

9. The New York Times, 24 July 1931, p. 10.

10. Morgan Grenfell, German Crisis 1931, Grenfell to Morgan, 204, 23 July 1931; Morgan to Grenfell, 103, 24 July 1931.

11. B/E, ADM 20/20, Norman Diary, 23 July 1931; PRO, T175/51, Hopkins to Snowden, 24 July 1931.

12. Harrison Papers, Binder 29, J. Crane to Moret, 103, 24 July 1931.

13. Stimson Diaries, Reel 3, Vol. 17: Memorandum of Conversation with P. Laval, 24 July 1931.

14. HHPL, Presidential Papers, FA-F, Transcript of telephone conversation between Hoover, Stimson and Castle, 24 July 1931.

15. The New York Times, 26 July 1931, p. 35.

16. According to Ambassador Edge, Moret had requested that Kindersley represent the British.

17. FRBNY, C261, Crane Memorandum concerning telephone conversation with Lacour-Gayet, 12:30 p.m., 25 July 1931.

18. The New York Times, 27 July 1931, p. 1.

19. B/E, G1/143, Norman to Mórgan, 2 February 1931; G3/198, Norman to Whigham, 30 June 1931; B/E, ADM 20/20, Norman Diaries, 26 July 1931.

20. Morgan Grenfell, German Crisis 1931, Morgan to Morgan's (N.Y.), 31/4894, 29 July 1931.

21. The Times, 27 July 1931, p. 10.

22. The Committee of Treasury generally had weekly Wednesday meetings but during the crisis met far more frequently.

23. In the inter-war period a distinction was often made between credits and loans. The former term covered private bank borrowings while the term 'loan' was used to refer to publicly sold debt issues.

24. B/E, G3/193, Norman to E.C. Riddle, 23 February 1928.

25. B/E, MB53, C/T Minutes, 27 July 1931.

26. B/E, ADM 20/20, Norman Diaries, 24 July 1931; PRO, T175/151, Hopkins to Snowden, 27 July 1931.

27. FRBNY, C261.1, Norman to Harrison, 245/31, 27 July 1931.

28. FRBNY, C261.1, Norman to Harrison, 247/31, 28 July 1931.

29. B/E, ADM 20/20, Norman Diaries, 29 July 1931; concerning Norman's mental state see, e.g., Leffingwell's letter to Morgan of 28 July 1931 (Leffingwell Papers I/6/127) where he says, 'Can't he [Norman] be persuaded to quit his panicky talk...' and Stimson's many comments.

30. Morgan Grenfell, R.C. Leffingwell, Leffingwell to A. Sanchez, 2 October 1931.

31. B/E, G3/210, Harvey to Moret, 28 July 1931.

32. B/E, MB53, C/T Minutes, 29 July 1931.

33. Birmingham University, Birmingham, Neville Chamberlain Papers, 2-22, Chamberlain Diaries, 22 August 1931.

34. NA, RG59, 841.51/928, J.T. Marriner to Stimson, 31 July 1931; Stimson Diaries, Reel 3, Vol. 17: Memorandum of Meeting with Laval, 24 July 1931.

35. Morgan Grenfell, German Crisis 1931, Morgan et Cie. to Morgan's (N.Y.), 87.570, 14 July 1931; Grenfell to N. D. Jay, 28 July 1931.

36. Morgan Grenfell, German Crisis 1931, Jay to Grenfell, 29 July 1931.

37. FRBNY, C261.1, McGarrah to Harrison, 27, 28 July 1931.

38. NA, RG59, 462.00/R296/4760, Dawes to Hoover, 30 July 1931.

39. FRBNY, Harrison Papers, 3125.2, Harrison Memorandum, 31 July 1931, concerning telephone conversation with R. Lacour-Gayet, 29 July 1931.

40. Morgan Grenfell, German Crisis 1931, Morgan's (N.Y.) to J.P. Morgan, 31/2350, 29 July 1931.

41. Morgan Grenfell, German Crisis 1931, Morgan to Morgan's (N.Y.), 31/4894, 29 July 1931.

42. FRBNY, Harrison Papers, 3117.1, Harrison Memorandum concerning telephone conversation with Harvey, 30 July 1931. For an account of British discussions in 1931 on the possibility of a conversion operation see Howson, op. cit., pp. 71-4 and also Sayers, op. cit., pp. 433-6.

43. Harrison Papers, Binder 21, Memorandum of Board of Directors, FRBNY, 30 July 1931.

44. FRBNY, Harrison Papers, 2013.1, Harrison Memorandum, 31 July 1931, concerning telephone conversation with Mills, 30 July 1931.

45. See, e.g., PRO, T175/56, Hopkins Memoranda, 28 July and 30 July 1931.

46. The Times, 30 July 1931, p. 13.

47. Stimson Diaries, Reel 3, Vol. 17: Memorandum of conversation with MacDonald, 31 July 1931.

48. Harrison Papers, Binder 59, Harrison Memorandum, 31 July 1931, concerning telephone conversation with Lacour-Gayet, 30 July 1931.

49. PRO, T160/444, Bank of England to Treasury, 1 August 1931, approved by Snowden, 31 July 1931; Hopkins to Bank of England, 1 August 1931, approved by Snowden, 31 July 1931; Harrison Papers, Binder 45, Harrison Memorandum, 3 August 1931, concerning telephone conversation with Harvey, 31 July 1931.

50. FRBNY, C261.1, Harrison to Harvey, 262/31, 31 July 1931.

51. B/E, G3/210, Harvey to Lord Cullen of Ashbourne, 1 August 1931.

52. The fiduciary issue represented that portion of the currency which was not covered pound for pound by gold.

53. B/E, Colleagues AB-Bi, B. Blackett to Norman, 5 September 1929.

54. The Commercial and Financial Chronicle, 8 August 1931, p. 841; Ibid., 15 August 1931, p. 1005.

55. B/E, G3/210, Harvey to Lord Cullen of Ashbourne, 1 August 1931; The New York Times, 2 August 1931, p. 1.

56. Morgan Papers, Morgan to H.S. Morgan, 4 August 1931.

57. PRO 30/69/260, Hopkins to MacDonald, 5 August 1931; HHPL, Presidential Papers, FA-F, Dawes to Hoover, 6 August 1931.

58. PRO, FO 37/15192, Minute of O.E. Sargent, 17 August 1931.

59. B/E, C43/298, Siepmann Memorandum concerning telephone conversation with Moret, 5 August 1931.

60. Ibid; Harrison papers, Binder 59, Harrison Memorandum, 8 August 1931, concerning telephone conversation with Lacour-Gayet, 6 August 1931.

61. B/E, C43/298, Siepmann Note concerning conversation with Moret, 7 August 1931.

62. B/E, MB 53, C/T Minutes, 6 August 1931.

63. PRO 30/69/260, Snowden to MacDonald, 7 August 1931.

64. PRO 30/69/260, Snowden to MacDonald, 7 August 1931.

65. Stimson Diaries, Reel 3. Vol. 17, 7 August 1931; The Times, 7 August 1931, p. 10.

66. PRO 30/69/1753, MacDonald Diaries, 11 August 1931.

67. Lamont Papers, 108-75, Morgan to Lamont, 7 August 1931.

68. NA, RG59, 841.51/931, Ray Atherton to Stimson, 7 August 1931; The Times, 7 August 1931.

69. FRBNY, C261.1, Harvey to Harrison, 280/31, 7 August 1931; B/E, OV/32, Harvey Memorandum concerning telephone conversation with Harrison, 7 August 1931; Harrison Papers, Binder 59, Harrison Memorandum, 8 August 1931, concerning telephone conversation with Lacour-Gayet, 7 August 1931.

70. Morgan Grenfell, British Government ('BG') Credit 1931, Morgan to Morgan's (N.Y.), 31/4904, 6 August 1931.

71. The New York Times, 13 August 1931, p. 18.

72. PRO 30/69/260, H.D. Henderson, Report on May Report, 7 August 1931.

73. Morgan Grenfell, BG Credit 1931, Morgan's (N.Y.) to J.P. Morgan, 31/2371, 8 August 1931; Morgan to Morgan's (N.Y.), 31/4913, 8 August 1931.

74. He apparently talked often with the partners of Morgan et Cie. emphasizing the importance of better relations between the central banks of Britain and France.

75. B/E, S74, 'GF' to Peacock; 9 August 1931; Harvey to Lord Bradbury, 17 August 1931; FRBNY, Crane Trip, Crane to Harrison, 4 August 1931.

76. The New York Times, 20 September 1931, p. 7.

77. Yale University, New Haven, Conn., Sterling Library, Henry L. Stimson Papers, Reel 81, MacDonald to Stimson, 9 August 1931.

78. Peacock's background was quite unusual. Born in poor circumstances in Canada, he had left his original profession of school mastering for the tough world of corporate reorganization. He came to the attention of the City of London because of his work on South American railroads and by the war was living in Britain. Norman invited him onto the Court of Directors where he served from 1921 to 1924 and 1929 to 1946.

79. Morgan Grenfell, BG Credit 1931, Grenfell to Morgan, 12 August 1931, FRBNY, Crane Trip, Crane, 'Note on Visit to England', 16 September 1931.

80. PRO 30/69/260, Harvey to MacDonald, 12 August 1931.

81. See B/E, MB53, C/T Minutes, 11 August 1931, where the fears of the Bank that Snowden was willing to leave the gold standard were articulated.
82. PRO, T160/385/F.10830/1, Waterfield to Lefeaux, 11 October 1931.
83. PRO 30/69/260, Keynes to MacDonald, 5 August 1931.
84. PRO 30/69/260, Keynes to MacDonald, 12 August 1931.
85. PRO 30/69/1316, Memorandum: 'The Financial Crisis', undated.
86. The Committee consisted of MacDonald, Snowden, Foreign Secretary Arthur Henderson, Colonial Secretary J.H. Thomas and William Graham who was President of the Board of Trade.
87. Cambridge University Library, Cambridge, Templewood Papers, Box Vll-1, 'The First National Government', undated.
88. B/E, G3/210, Harvey to Hopkins, 10 August 1931.
89. FRBNY, C261.1, McGarrah to Harrison, 484, 11 August 1931; B/E, S74, F. Rodd to Harvey, 17 August 1931.
90. PRO, T188/21, Leith-Ross Memorandum, 13 August 1931, concerning a discussion with French Treasury officials, 11 August, 1931.
91. B/E, OV 45/4, Memorandum: 'British Issue in France', 13 August 1931.
92. B/E, S74, Siepmann Memorandum, 14 August 1931.
93. Morgan Grenfell, BG Credit 1931, Grenfell to Morgan, 12 August and 14 August 1931.
94. Harrison Papers, Box 13, Peacock to Harrison, 14 August 1931; Morgan Grenfell, BG Credit 1931, Grenfell to Norman, 18 August 1931; B/E, Governor's Secretary's Correspondence, E.D.N. Skinner to Atherton, 14 August 1931.
95. B/E, MB53, C/T Minutes, 14 August 1931.
96. FRBNY, CF Crane Trip, Crane to Burgess, 14 August 1931.
97. FRBNY, 261.1, W.R. Burgess Memorandum concerning telephone conversation with Crane, 14 August 1931.
98. See e.g., FRBNY, C261.1, Harvey to Harrison, 343/31, 22 August 1931.
99. Thus the situation was quite different from that which has obtained in more recent years where countries, chiefly in response to the International Monetary Fund's policy of conditionality, institute deflationary measures in order to receive first, IMF loans and second, credits from

private banks which often make the receipt of new IMF funds a prerequisite to their own funding.

100. Chamberlain Papers, 7/11/24-1, Baldwin to Chamberlain, 15 August 1931.

101. See, e.g., B/E, SMT 5/3, Clay to Harvey, 17 September 1931.

102. Report of the Committee Appointed on the Recommendation of the London Conference 1931, 18 August 1931.

103. B/E, MB53, C/T Minutes, 19 August 1931.

104. PRO, 30/60/1753, MacDonald Diaries, 17 August 1931.

105. PRO, Cab 23/67, 19 August 1931.

106. B/E, G3/210, Harvey to Snowden, 18 August 1931.

107. The Times, 19 August 1931, p. 11.

108. PRO, 30/69/20, F.W. Pethwick-Lawrence to MacDonald, 19 August 1931.

109. PRO, Cab 23/67, 19 August 1931.

110. Cmd 3897, Report of the Committee on Finance and Industry, 1931, pp. 230-41.

111. Churchill College, Cambridge University, Cambridge, Ernest L. Bevin Papers, II 7/8, Meeting of Trades Union Congress General Council Subcommittee and Cabinet Subcommittee, 20 August 1931.

112. Morgan Grenfell, BG Credit 1931, Morgan's (N.Y.) to Grenfell, 31/2378, 21 August 1931.

113. Morgan Grenfell, BG Credit 1931, Grenfell to Morgan, 21 August 1931.

114. Ibid.

115. Churchill College, Cambridge University, Cambridge, Lord Swinton Papers, III-115, Swinton to Lady Swinton, 21 August 1931.

116. Chamberlain Papers, 2/22, Chamberlain Diaries, 22 August 1931.

117. FRBNY, C261.1, Harvey to Harrison, 343/31, 22 August 1931.

118. B/E, MB53, C/T Minutes, 22 August 1931.

119. Morgan Grenfell, BG Credit 1931, Morgan's (N.Y.) to Morgan Grenfell, 31/2380, 22 August 1931.

120. Morgan Grenfell, BG Credit 1931, Morgan Grenfell to Morgan's (N.Y.), 31/4929, 31/4930, 23 August 1931.

121. Morgan Grenfell, BG Credit 1931, Morgan's (N.Y.) to Morgan Grenfell, 31/2383, 23 August 1931.

122. D. Marquand, Ramsay MacDonald, (Jonathan Cape, London, 1977) pp. 633-4. It should be noted that the official memorandum on the crisis (PRO 30/69/1316: 'The Financial Crisis') makes the same error.

123. The King also dined with Peacock on Sunday evening, 23 August 1931.

124. PRO, Cab 23/67, 23 August 1931; Bodleian Library, Oxford University, Oxford, Geoffrey Dawson Papers, 35, Dawson Diaries, 23 August 1931; Marquand, op. cit., pp. 634-6, Kenneth Rose, King George (Weidenfeld and Nicolson, London, 1983), pp. 374-84.

125. B/E, MB 53, C/T Minutes, 24 August 1931.

126. See, e.g., FRBNY, Crane Trip, Crane to Harrison 15, 24 August 1931.

Chapter Five

NOBODY TOLD US WE COULD DO THAT

August - September 1931

'When England went off gold
it was like the end of the
world....'

Jackson E. Reynolds, Presi-
dent, The First
National Bank of New
York

i

On 24 August, even as Ramsay MacDonald began
the task of forming a National Government, it was
clear that it would not have a smooth passage. For
on the same day The Times' leader stated that the
central bank credits were almost exhausted.[1] Representing the first published indication of the Bank
of England's utilization of its borrowed funds, this
revelation had a negative effect on foreign exchange
markets and caused the Bank to lose more foreign
currency than on any previous day.[2] The acquisition of new credits thus continued to be the Government's first priority; therefore Morgan Grenfell, at
the request of the Bank of England, formally reiterated to Morgan's (N.Y.) the request of the British
Government for a short term credit, adding that the
Government was simultaneously approaching Paris. As
a stopgap measure the Treasury placed at the
disposal of the Bank of England dollar securities
amounting to some £28 m ($140 m) held for its
account by Morgan's (N.Y.).[3] Morgan's (N.Y.)
agreed to form a syndicate to provide the credit but
as their offer would not remain open indefinitely,
the New York house stressed the importance of
concluding the transaction as soon as possible,
emphasizing that it was of vital importance to
arrange the French half of the transaction.[4]
Negotiations in Paris had in fact begun with
the arrival of H.A. Siepmann on 24 August. However,
he took the approach that the question of a credit
was not a top priority matter, a rather surprising
position in the circumstances and one that not only
confused Governor Moret but diverged totally from
the viewpoint held by Morgan's (N.Y.) and Harrison.[5] The Americans were motivated by their

113

precise knowledge of the extent to which the Bank had supported sterling and by a belief that any delay increased the likelihood of failure for a stabilization operation. Their sense of urgency was also influenced by the mixed reaction of the foreign press to the new British Government. The New York partners believed very strongly that the Government's program must be seen to be widely supported by the British people, yet it was immediately and publicly evident that this was not to be the case. For example, The New York Times on 25 August reported that the trade union group of the Labour Party had declared war on Ramsay MacDonald and that Arthur Henderson now had an opportunity to become the Prime Minister.[6] But political concerns did not form the whole picture. In particular, various American financial publications focussed on underlying British financial weaknesses. Thus the Whaley-Eaton Service's Foreign Letter of 25 August stated that 'the British difficulty is too aggravated to be cured by a mere balancing of the Budget.'[7]

Negotiations for the American credit were conducted by Grenfell on behalf of his New York partners and by Harvey and Peacock for the British Government. They did not progress as smoothly as might have been expected. The stumbling block was not the amount of the credit, which was now envisioned to be at least $150 m and, with luck, $200 m, but rather was the cost of this financing to the British. The opening commission of 1% plus ⅛%, the same as in 1925, was not controversial. What was under discussion was Morgan's proposal that advances under the credit bear a rate of 4½% which was equal to Bank rate at the time. It is true that often the Bank rate or discount rate applicable to the borrower is used as the basis on which interest is calculated but in this case the borrower felt that with money cheap all over the world, particularly in the U.S. where the discount rate was 1½%, a rate of three times that was exorbitant.[8] The British were unhappy enough for MacDonald himself to complain to Stimson who had arrived in London en route to the U.S. In turn the Secretary of State called on J.P. Morgan to remonstrate with him but was told that the American banks, not appreciating the gravity of the situation, thought the proposed interest rate was very low because it was not higher than that charged in 1925.[9] In fact although Morgan's (N.Y.) previous reluctance to arrange a credit showed an awareness of the prevailing mood of

114

the American financial institutions, it was surprised by the hitherto unheard-of number of refusals
received in reply to its offer cable. As one turned
down such an invitation at the peril of being
excluded from future loan syndicates, that this
reaction was so common showed the depth of American
feeling in August 1931 against foreign credits.[10]
Therefore, the firm felt it would be impossible to
offer their participants any less than the terms
previously communicated to the British Government.
The British, who would ultimately capitulate, were
left with an increased resentment of American power
which had already begun to develop because of a
belief that the massive American hoarding of gold
was responsible for their problems. To Sir
Frederick Leith-Ross: 'American banks, finding
themselves tied on the Continent, recoup themselves
at our expense.'[11] As his comment indicated, for
at least some Britons the goal of Anglo-American
monetary cooperation was fast becoming a chimera not
worth the sacrifice of any British interest.[12]
    Morgan's had been insistent that no American
credit would be obtainable until a French credit for
an equal amount had at a minimum been agreed upon.
On 26 August, Anglo-French negotiations began in
earnest. Leith-Ross, who took his first aeroplane
ride in order to reach France in good time, was
joined by S.D. Waley and Siepmann for this meeting
between British and French Treasury officials.[13]
The British received a warm reception as the French
credit enjoyed the blessing of Premier Laval, the
French leader telling American diplomat Theodore
Marriner that the Governor of the Bank of France had
concurred in the decision that France together with
the United States should do its full share to help
the British.[14] Moret still believed that the
British goal ought to be a long term credit but
understood and supported the British request for a
short term credit.
    The two main subjects under negotiation were
the form the French credit should take and the
question of taxation. Moret believed that if the
French market was to provide the same amount as the
American tranche, now fixed at $200 m (£40 m), it
was necessary for the borrowing to be divided into
two parts, half to be provided as a bank credit and
the other half to take the form of a public subscription for one year British Treasury bills. The
British were not happy with the latter proposal both
because they believed that the French wished to
advertise British penury and French strength

publicly and also because it forced them to borrow
the entire amount of the public offering at once
instead of, like the bank borrowing, as and when
needed.[15] Yet once more the British had no choice
but to acquiesce in the French proposals. On the
taxation question, the French Treasury accommodated
itself by a piece of financial legerdemain to the
understandable British desire to pay as little tax
as possible (transaction taxes customarily are for
the account of the borrower).[16]

As negotiations continued the British fear that
the French would use this opportunity to pressure
them into changing their position on reparations was
shown to have been well-founded. During the most
crucial stage of negotiations Flandin took the
opportunity to bring up the German financial situation and state his Government's opposition to any
further conferences or meetings on the subject. He
sought to ascertain the British position and in
response Leith-Ross enquired whether Flandin was
deliberately linking reparations with the British
credit. Flandin disingenuously answered that he was
simply taking advantage of Leith-Ross' presence for
an exchange of personal opinions.[17]

By the following day, 27 August, discussions
had progressed far enough for Leith-Ross to meet
with representatives of the Paris banks. At the end
of the day the British received Treasury clearance
for the public issue notwithstanding the strong fear
that it carried with it the risk that the subscription would cause a drain of French funds from London
thus rendering the whole exercise pointless. The
only unsettled question was the interest rate for
the British borrowings.[18] Snowden and Morgan
discussed the same issue in London on 28 August.
Morgan carried with him a cable from Morgan's (N.Y.)
to be shown to the Chancellor. It stated that:

> In reference to the proposed interest rate
> in America we may emphasize further that
> there is not a single institution in our
> whole banking community which actually
> desires the British Treasury Notes on any
> terms either as to commission or interest.
> If they go into the matter it will be
> because of their becoming convinced that
> it is important and necessary for the
> whole banking community here to co-operate
> in the support of sterling....Every insti-
> tution is probably making strenuous
> endeavours to get its position more

liquid. At the cost of interest account the banks are allowing maturities to run off and are rejecting customer's loans which in normal times they would be glad to have. It is for this reason that quoted interest rates in this market by no means represent the actual state of affairs.[19]

The next day the British Government conceded and, Morgan's (N.Y.) having learned that an agreement in principle with the French had been reached at a cost to the British equal to that of the American credit, the agreement pertaining to the Morgan credit was executed. It took the form of an agreement by Morgan's (N.Y.) and 109 other American banks to purchase British Government dollar Treasury Bills in amounts of $10 m or multiples thereof for periods of 30, 60 or 90 days, thus providing the British with an available war chest of $200 m (£40 m) with which to protect sterling.[20]

That the credit was arranged as expeditiously as possible and for an amount which made it the largest inter-war era credit provided by Morgan's shows two things. The first is that the New York house still retained a great deal of influence over the American banking community, particularly in the Northeast. The second is that the participants, although no doubt partially drawn into the trans-action by Morgan's (N.Y.) pressure, also obviously believed in the importance of both the gold standard and the maintenance of sterling's stability. At a time when a record number of American banks were failing and with German exposure far in excess of that of British banks American financial institu-tions were willing to enter into the British credit on three days' notice. The German experience had shown that something besides high interest rates was needed to produce new money. That extra dimension appears to have been an American belief in the importance of the British battle to the U.S. This consciousness of solidarity was to be one of the casualties of the British defeat.

Morgan's believed the signing had not come a moment too soon for the political waters remained troubled. On 26 August, the Labour Party had issued a manifesto announcing its opposition to the National Government and its proposed budget cuts and proposing to substitute for reductions in the unemployment benefit the taxation of fixed interest-bearing securities and a decrease in the interest

paid in respect of war debts.[21]   Together with the
virtually unanimous rejection by the Labour Party of
MacDonald, the result was foreign skepticism as to
the ability of the National Government to carry out
its stated mission.   Clearly concerned, Morgan's
(N.Y.) immediately cabled Morgan Grenfell to ascertain, among other things, whether an Associated
Press prediction that the Government would not have
a working majority in the House of Commons was
true.[22]   Morgan's, in company with the American
Government, was also not pleased that the Labour
Party's explanation of the fall of the late Government placed great weight on the allegation that a
bankers' ramp led by George Harrison had been
primarily responsible for its demise.   While Morgan's could and did take comfort in the fact that
it was not mentioned either by name or implication,
Acting Secretary of State Castle personally expressed his indignation to the British Charge
d'Affairs in Washington.[23]
    The Bank of England immediately made plans to
draw under the American credits, convening for this
purpose a meeting of the Committee of Treasury on 29
August.[24]   The British Government prepared for the
special session of the House of Commons scheduled to
begin on 8 September whose purpose was to debate the
Government's economy plan.   To aid in this task H.D.
Henderson prepared a memorandum which attempted to
anticipate Labour Party strategy.   He speculated
that a class attack would be most likely and
stressed the importance of emphasizing that 'had the
pound been allowed to go during the present crisis
it would not have been a matter of a depreciation of
10% or 20%, but a real 'degringolade.'   Henderson,
in passing, made a further point which was in the
event as interesting as his main thesis:

> It is well to remember that the
> controversy over the return to the gold
> standard in 1925 is more familiar to most
> of the British public than the experience
> of continental inflation and that the
> critics of the return to gold are fairly
> held to have been justified by the event.
> To many reasonable minds, accordingly, the
> idea of the depreciation of sterling
> conveys no more serious suggestion than
> that of a reversal of the dubious policy
> of six years ago.[25]

The reaction of the British public after 21 September would prove the prescience of this remark.

Also prepared for MacDonald was an analysis which showed that the National Government's proposed economies differed only marginally from those which were acceptable to the late Labour Government. The Prime Minister, obviously distressed at the events of the previous week, spent much time responding to the numerous angry or sad letters he had received from Labour Party members explaining their decision not to support him. For example, John Baker said the bankers knew at the time of the 1920 Brussels Conference that their policy would involve massive unemployment yet they persisted anyway and R.S. Young, M.P., while stressing his sorrow at the turn of events, concluded that: 'the international bankers will have to face up to the fact that democracy will simply not tolerate poverty in the midst of plenty.'[26] MacDonald tried to justify his actions, telling his constituency party that the crisis facing the government was of such magnitude that it could have brought the country to an industrial standstill causing wages to fall drastically, unemployment pay to disappear and costing the working classes millions of pounds. The Prime Minister also took the opportunity of pointing out to Herbert Morrison that:

> When the necessary legislation is passed, the Party will be able to discuss things in a house still standing and not from the top of heaps of ruins, so whatever you may say or do, I have the credit of saving the Party.[27]

The credits having been obtained, sterling appeared firmer on 29 August as the pound traded at $4.86, up one-eighth from the previous day. However, because the exchange rate was being supported by the Bank of England which had obtained American and French bridge loans for this purpose, it did not accurately reflect the true position of sterling which would remain shaky unless and until the budgetary proposals became reality.[28] The concern over the pound was universal; Dr. G. Vissering of the Netherlands' Central Bank called Harvey to request that Dutch gold held by the Bank of England be earmarked. Harvey huffily refused, saying that the Dutch could either take their gold back to Amsterdam or keep it in London but if they chose the latter course they would not be placed in the position of a preferred creditor. To assuage Vissering's fears Harvey wrote him about the credits and stressed the total commitment of the National Government to the maintenance of the gold standard.[29] Austen Chamberlain, now at the Admiralty, was concerned enough at the possible effect of Labour propaganda to suggest to R.H. Brand that the latter write a series of columns for The Times to explain the August crisis and the necessity for staying on the gold standard, Chamberlain adding that the tone should be along the lines of 'if Napoleon had won at Waterloo.'[30] Such a series of articles was tailor-made to respond to the cable sent by Lamont to Grenfell on 29 August, which stressed Lamont's view that it was crucial for the new Government to remember how vital the restoration of American confidence in Britain was, especially as, in Lamont's opinion, the American financial community now shared the City's distrust of the drift of British political affairs.[31] Grenfell was worried enough to read this cable to the Committee of Treasury and, together with Harvey, authorized Peacock to discuss it privately with Neville Chamberlain.[32]

Lamont's message was followed on Monday, 31 August by a cable from Morgan's (N.Y.) to Grenfell. Its purpose was to highlight the New York house's concern at what it viewed as the poor handling of the sterling exchange, a symptom of which was the frequent breaks in the value of sterling in the New York market after the London market had closed. Morgan's (N.Y.) suggested better liaison between the Bank of England, the Bank of France and the FRBNY so that the credits would become an offensive weapon rather than a sitting duck for rapacious financiers. Having been left by his New York partners to decide whether to divulge the contents of this message to the Bank of England, Grenfell showed it only to Peacock who agreed that he and Harvey would take up the exchange question with Sir Robert Kindersley, head of the Committee of Treasury's Exchange Committee, but without revealing the source of the concern.[33] While Harvey pondered this problem, he also worried over what he saw as the Government's lack of progress in turning words into deeds. Thus to Herbert Samuel he wrote that the Bank was very concerned about the delay in announcement of the Government's programme as this hesitancy had led to doubts being expressed both domestically and abroad. Two days later, on 31 August, he wrote to Francis Rodd that improvement in the currency situation

would surely come if only the Government would make
a satisfactory announcement of its agenda and then
back it by appropriate propaganda throughout the
nation.[34]

Harvey had indeed taken to heart Morgan's criticisms about the method of utilization of the
credits with the result that the Committee of
Treasury agreed on the last day of August to autho-
rise the expansion of the Bank's current arrangements for handling foreign exchange operations.[35]
Yet Morgan's (N.Y.) remained concerned about the
sterling exchange, sending their London partners on
1 September an analysis of the New York and London
markets with a particular emphasis on the weakness
and lack of depth of the forward market.[36] The
attention of the New York partners was not solely
concentrated on this subject; Leffingwell, as was
usual for him, reflected on the broader British
situation. In a wide-ranging letter sent to Lamont,
he placed a great weight on Keynes' attitude as a
destabilizing force in the situation, attributing
the economist's animosity to the principles Leffingwell viewed as sacred to Keynes's perverse and
Puckish personality and to resentment that the
Macmillan Report, on which Keynes had laboured hard,
had been eclipsed by the May Report.[37]

Morgan's (N.Y.) continuing concern over the
British situation was echoed by the FRBNY. Harrison
shared the New York partners' belief that the
credits were being mishandled and on 3 September
cabled Harvey to say that in his opinion the British
decision to peg sterling at $4.86 to $4.86 1/8, a
rate considerably above the gold point, only encouraged sales of sterling. Harrison's solution was to
allow sterling to fluctuate just slightly above the
gold point.[38] Harvey replied that while he was in
general agreement with these sentiments this was not
the time to change tactics.[39]

Thus matters stood while the Government
attempted to make its contribution to the battle.
The Cabinet knew that the eyes of the world's
financial leaders were focussed upon it yet they
were anything but united. MacDonald, mirroring the
feelings of his colleagues, wrote Stanley Baldwin to
ask: 'How long can this Government continue?' The
Prime Minister's answer to his rhetorical question
was 'not very long.'[40] Matters were not made
easier by the advice rendered by Harvey and Peacock
who were called to the Cabinet meeting of 3 September. The Deputy Governor stated that although the
formation of the present Government had somewhat

improved the position, causing withdrawals of foreign exchange to decrease, they were still larger than the Bank cared to see. While Harvey admitted that he really did not know why the sterling drain was continuing, he was sure that 'the future course of events depended largely upon the attitude of the British public towards the Government's proposals.' Thus at the height of the currency crisis, the Bank of England, which in past years had exulted in its control over financial matters, was claiming that it could not be responsible for the fate of the pound; the Government and the British people would decide the issue. Interestingly, at this time Harvey did not seek to hold foreigners responsible; on the contrary he went out of his way to state that the Bank of England had found the FRBNY and the Bank of France to be most cooperative.

With the probable motive of reinforcing his comments, Harvey was very forthcoming with figures illustrating the position. Since the beginning of the crisis, the Bank had lost close to £130 m ($650 m), of which £35 m ($175 m) had been in gold. £50 m ($250 m) had been derived from the central bank credits, drawings had been made under the Morgan credit and the remainder came from the Bank's own reserves of foreign exchange. The last item must have come as a surprise to the Cabinet which would not have been aware that the Bank possessed such reserves.

As if this was not gloomy enough, Harvey stated that the agreements pertaining to the central bank credits provided that, failing other means of repayment, these borrowings would be repaid in gold. The Deputy Governor said that this 'amounted in effect to a lien on a portion of their existing gold holding and reduced their actual free holding to little more than £80 m or about the equivalent of the new Government credit.' This alarming exposition of the credit agreements was, however, seriously misleading. They did not provide for a lien on the Bank of England's gold or anything close to it. Rather they contained a gold payment clause which required repayment to be made in gold.[41] What this meant was clearly stated by Siepmann in an internal bank memorandum written less than three weeks later where he delineated the difference between the 'usual gold clause' and a negative pledge on gold with the former constituting a mere moral obligation on the debtor's part to provide gold for repayment. It is further clear from Siepmann's memorandum that he was not expounding a

new position but rather stating the accepted inter-
pretation.[42]   The Bank of England again displayed
a belief that ends justified means, to wit, that in
certain circumstances, mere facts should not stand
in the way of persuasiveness.

After debating the merits of disclosing to the
House of Commons the exact balance of payments
position (it was decided to use only general terms),
Harvey was then asked what the effect abroad of a
general election would be.   He replied that it might
not be harmful if the results indicated a country
united and determined to make major financial
readjustments, but, if this were not the case,
foreign opinion would be greatly disturbed.   Peacock
agreed, stating that the talk that the present
Government might remain in office for only a few
weeks had been troubling.   The discussion then moved
to the importance of correctly steering public
opinion and the meeting ended with the Prime Minister mentioning the attacks which had been made on
the Bank of England's handling of the situation and
the Government's role in bowing to bankers' pressure.   As MacDonald believed that this was caused by
ignorance, he suggested that when the crisis was
over, the Bank of England 'should be prepared to
meet these charges and to make some statement as to
the principles which had guided them in dealing with
the general financial situation.'[43]   Not only the
British public but future historians would have
profited had the Bank done as MacDonald requested.

As it was, both the Bank of England and the
Cabinet left this Cabinet session disquieted.
Harvey and Peacock believed it was vital for the
Government to put forth firmly an economy programme
and concentrate its efforts on enactment.   Instead
the Cabinet's chief concern appeared to be the
merits of an election, a question which the bankers
believed to be nothing if not ill-timed.   For their
part, the Ministers, who had been raised in an
atmosphere which held the Bank of England to be
financially omnipotent, saw that the Bank at its
time of ultimate testing was wanting.   Harvey and
Peacock had spent a good deal of August saying that
if the economy programme was agreed upon and new
credits obtained, all would be well.   The politicians had followed their lead yet the promised
results had not been delivered and to make matters
worse the bankers appeared to refuse any responsibility for the current state of events and even
declined to offer an explanation of why their
prescription of the previous month had not produced

123

a cure. No wonder Samuel Hoare for one later noted that he had been most unimpressed by the performance of the Bank and the City.[44]

The question facing the Government was whether it could handle the stern demands placed on it. These were not only internal in origin; Lamont writing on 4 September to Grenfell placed the responsibility for dealing with American public opinion on the British Government.[45] At the same time the BIS expressed the opinion that British finances were now the shakiest in Europe.[46] Certainly much had changed in the six weeks since the London Conference had convened to attempt to solve the German problem.

During this period Montagu Norman was recuperating in Canada. From Quebec, his initial destination, he had travelled to St. Andrews and then, on 4 September, to Digby, Nova Scotia. Although his departure from Great Britain had been caused by a physical and nervous breakdown, previous accounts of the crisis, notably those of Clay and Sayers, were not justified in concluding that the Governor was uninvolved in its dénouement.[47] On the contrary, the Governor, while in the New World, participated in the final stages of the battle he had for so long waged. Norman's first conversations were with Harrison on 22 and 23 August. During the first discussion, which had been previously arranged by cable with Norman and by telephone with Peacock, the hitherto undecided question of whether Norman would go to Bar Harbor as he desired was finally answered in the negative because of Harrison's belief that the British situation was too critical for Norman to take any action which could lead to unnecessary publicity and false rumours. In response to Norman's query as to the current state of events, Harrison described the budgetary programme but did not go into much detail because he was unsure of how well Norman was and did not want to trouble him unnecessarily. Norman, however, assured Harrison he was feeling much better and would telephone him on the next day.[48]

During the conversation of 23 August Harrison was more forthcoming. He told the British Governor that he had spent the day out at Glen Cove with the Morgan's (N.Y.) partners and that the Cabinet was now in session deliberating on the economy programme. Norman agreed with Harrison that the implication contained in some of the Government's messages that it would resign if either Morgan's (N.Y.) or the New York Governor thought the pro-

gramme inadequate placed an unfair burden on the
Americans. Harrison, by way of reiterating that the
proposals' merits could only be properly weighed in
London, stated that he had asked Harvey several
times for his opinion as to the programme's adequacy
and while the Deputy Governor generally implied that
it was satisfactory, he did not give a direct
answer. Norman, according to Harrison, intimated
that Harvey probably would not allow himself to be
pinned down but that he, Norman, believed that the
programme was inadequate, and as any inadequate
programme would cause trouble in a year or so the
correct approach would be to seize this opportunity
to force an economic adjustment encompassing a
reduction in the cost of production and in wages
drastic enough to make British goods competitive
again. Norman concluded by saying that if this were
done, the British crisis would be cured without the
need for further credits but conceded that Harrison's point as to the risky nature of placing total
weight on budgetary reform had some merit.[49]

Thus by the end of August, Norman had discarded
the non-participatory attitude he had demonstrated
during the earlier part of the month. However, it
is interesting to speculate on Norman's prior
intentions concerning his role during the August and
September crisis. During previous breakdowns it had
been his habit to go to South Africa yet this time
he refused to go there and instead chose North
America for his destination.[50] Perhaps the
Governor wanted to be able to return to Britain
relatively quickly. On the other hand, he may well
have intended to play a major role behind the
scenes, as it were, free from public scrutiny. His
relationship with Harrison and Morgan's (N.Y.) made
this feasible and there is much in Norman's character to suggest such a strategy. In either case, it
is clear that Norman retained his earlier assumptions and still believed that something drastic had
to be done to end the strained conditions under
which the Bank had been operating. In August his
solution was drastically to force down British costs
of production. During the following month a different solution would appear.

Harrison could not have been pleased to hear
Norman's negative opinion of the budgetary proposals. Yet he appears not to have mentioned his
conversations with the British Governor to anyone,
least of all Harvey. The Deputy Governor, left in
the dark as to his chief's whereabouts, in despera-
tion cabled Harrison to ask: 'Have you seen our

125

Governor? We have urgent messages for him.'
Harrison confined his answer to a simple statement
of Norman's current domicile and his present intention to sail from Halifax on 13 September. Harrison
then cabled Norman to tell him to expect to hear
from Harvey.[51]

No budget day was the focus of more attention
than that of 8 September 1931. MacDonald found it
an ordeal and reflected that 'Tories in the crowd
from the inside are even worse than from outside.'[52] Although the Government won its first
vote of confidence by a majority of 59, the Labour
Party persisted in its bitter opposition to the
National Government's proposals. The attitude of
Henderson and his followers was motivated in part by
the firm stance against the Government taken by the
TUC and in part by bitterness. This was a logical
response for a party that resented being labelled
unpatriotic yet found it next to impossible to make
substantive comments for it had supported most of
the proposals now being put forth by the National
Government. In delivering his budget message,
Snowden, for his part bitter at his rejection by the
Labour Party, did not hesitate to make this last
point abundantly clear. His speech, which ended
with the emotional quotation: 'Come the world
against her, England yet shall stand', was perhaps
the best of his career but it did not sway his
former colleagues. Nor did it produce anything
better than a mixed reaction from financial markets
which appeared undecided as to whether the budget
would prove sufficient to turn the tide of gold and
foreign currency towards Britain.[53]

Against this background Morgan's (N.Y.) continued to question the way the credits were being
handled. On 7 September they cabled Morgan Grenfell
to convey their concern at the rapid drawdowns under
the credit; within ten days, 40% of the American
tranche had been requested. They posed detailed
questions to ascertain the amount of reserves, the
status of the French credit and the timetable for
implementation of the budgetary changes. Finally
they asked:

> Are the British Treasury and the Bank of
> England satisfied that the present method
> of dealing with the sterling exchange is
> the best that can be devised? In this
> connection the question naturally arises
> as to why the Bank of England does not use
> the classic remedy of Bank Rate instead of
> apparently pegging the exchange.[54]

Obviously Harvey's efforts to alter the handling of foreign exchange had not assuaged their fears.

The next day Morgan Grenfell responded and, after giving the schedule for the closing of the French credits and a summary of the status of the Government's programme, said:

> It would be wrong to think that the Bank of England has in any way abandoned the use of the classic remedies of the Bank Rate, gold shipments etc. when in its judgement such action is desirable. If it is suggested that they appear to have refrained from using these remedies during the past few weeks it must be remembered that the whole situation is most unusual and those responsible have always to weigh the relative advantages that might be expected to accrue from these remedies against the possible disadvantages of taking any steps which might tend to further distance public confidence at home and abroad.[55]

As Morgan Grenfell did not point out which disadvantages had weighed against using the textbook methods, the fears of the New York partners were probably not assuaged. Harvey had to deal with the same concerns emanating from the FRBNY as Harrison also remained convinced that the credits were being wasted. On 8 September the Deputy Governor took the opportunity to tell Harrison that the French had concurred in his decision to continue to peg sterling.[56]

Simultaneously American Government officials were airing their opinions of the British predicament. Hoover, who had previously expressed his approval of the Morgan loan, took the opportunity of Stimson's return to Washington on 8 September to tell the Secretary of State that he anticipated that Britain would be unable to keep sterling at par and predicted it would fall by 20%. The President, whose involvement in European affairs had increased steadily since his decision to propose the Moratorium, then began speaking about reparations and war debts. He viewed the now universally admitted linkage between war debts and reparations as a significant problem because it forced the U.S. to treat all nations alike when he would prefer to be able to help Britain, who needed assistance without aiding France, who did not. Hoover, however, blamed

this on the Balfour Note and Annex 3 to the Young
Plan, not admitting that the link between two kinds
of payment obligations was not created by mercenary
Europeans but represented a clear factual relationship.[57]   Hoover's concern about the European
situation led him to tell Stimson four days later
that he was considering another gesture on reparations and war debts but first felt it was imperative
to get a plan and a war chest with which to fight
the domestic banking crisis whose dimensions were
growing daily.   However, the President attached
unrealistic preconditions to any new international
initiative; before any new American move both the
Balfour Note and Annex 3 of the Young Plan would
have to be abrogated and an agreement by France to
reconsider German capacity to pay achieved.[58]
     Atherton reported to Castle on 11 September
that Warren Fisher had attributed the now publicly
known adverse balance of payments to the financial
situation in Holland and Switzerland, an internal
flight of capital and the payment for foodstuffs.
The American diplomat himself added withdrawals from
the U.S. and France as further causes of the negative figure.   Atherton devoted much attention both
in this letter and in a subsequent missive to
Stimson to the possibility of a British tariff being
enacted.[59]   His comments reflected a pervasive
American worry that the National Government, in
accord with the views of most Conservatives, would
indeed impose a tariff.   Clearly the Americans,
although not at all dependent on foreign trade (it
composed about 10% of total U.S. trade), were
nonethe.ess unhappy at the prospect of the demise of
Britain's free trade policy.
     Thus by the end of the first two weeks of
September, much remained unsettled. However, the
French credit had been oversubscribed, bringing much
satisfaction to its French organizers and reassurance to the British.[60]   Further the British
Government, having disclosed its budget, could now
concentrate on the defense of sterling. Therefore
MacDonald wrote to the Cabinet on 10 September that to
better handle the financial situation he was proposing the creation of a Cabinet Subcommittee on the
Financial Situation (hereafter the 'Financial
Subcommittee') composed of himself, the Chancellor
of the Exchequer, the Foreign Secretary, Lord
Reading and the Minister of Health, Neville Chamberlain. Reading, a favourite of Morgan's due to their
close relationship during the First World War, was
the Cabinet Minister who showed the most initiative

during the crisis. He suggested to Snowden that the Treasury prepare for the first meeting an analysis of the method of mobilization of foreign securities used during the War, having previously urged Mac-Donald to have the Bank of England prepare detailed financial data for the Financial Subcommittee's consideration.[61] The mood at the Bank of England appeared more cheerful; Harvey, amongst other things, probably was relieved that he had made contact with Norman.[62] The latter cabled his deputy on 10 September that he was meeting Harrison somewhere and confided that his definite plan was to sail on 16 September on the Duchess of Bedford.[63] Perhaps Harvey hoped that the meeting of the two Bank Governors, for which Norman appears to have postponed his departure, would be as productive for Britain as those between Strong and Norman in previous years. In that event the position of sterling might become more secure for some time to come.

ii

Monday, 14 September, saw the first meeting of the Financial Subcommittee. Reading and Chamberlain were informed by Snowden that Fisher had reported that, according to Harvey, £20 m ($100 m) had been used which meant that at the present rate of expenditure, the borrowed funds would be exhausted in about a month. According to Fisher, Stimson had promised to do what he could to help the British including discussing the country's plight with American financiers. Therefore Fisher suggested that his close personal friend, American Counsellor Atherton, be approached to discuss the situation with Stimson.
    This led to a discussion orchestrated by Reading as to the origin of sterling sales. The Foreign Secretary pointed out that, as many sales appeared to be British inspired, the Committee ought to consider methods of curbing such transactions. Reading continued to dominate the meeting as it moved on to the question of the soundness of the American financial situation (the consensus was that its financial stability was overrated) and to the creation of a balance sheet reflecting British resources as at that date. The gloomy results produced by this exercise were still being assessed when Harvey joined the meeting. He gave an updated account of the British exchange position saying that heavy withdrawals had occurred at the end of the

previous week. As these were made to obtain francs,
there was some hope that this particular drain had
been triggered by a desire to take advantage of the
profitable opportunity presented by participation in
the French tranche of the British Government credits
(an eventuality which had been feared by British
officials). In reply to a question posed by
Reading, Harvey appeared pessimistic about the
ability of the Government or the Bank to stop
British capital flight and he further made the false
statement that the sale of sterling by British
citizens was not really an important problem.[64]
After exploring the immediate prospects for Britain,
the Deputy Governor turned to the last major issue
for discussion, the question of the use of gold. He
said that, while in recent weeks the Bank had not
resorted to the use of gold, the Bank continued to
anticipate allowing the export of gold to be resumed
when conditions had become more stable.[65] Harvey's comment illustrates the fact that in one sense
the battle for Britain's gold standard had been lost
during the first week of August when the Bank of
England, through its manipulation of the market at
the behest of their lenders/advisors in New York and
Paris, halted British sales of gold. To be sure
devices such as altering discount rules and open
market operations had diluted the impact of classi-
cal gold standard theory long before the summer of
1931. But quantity does at times betoken a change
in quality and the use of £120 m ($600 m) in foreign
exchange over a six week period was unprecedented
enough to suggest in itself that the era of the
traditional gold standard had come to an end.

More important than the subjects covered at the
first meeting of the Financial Subcommittee were the
matters not discussed. Morgan's had pointed out -
correctly - that for the pound to remain on gold, a
united and stable government was a key prerequisite.
Three things were imperilling this: the attitude of
Labour, the possibility of an election and the
question of a tariff. These were the factors which
would determine the pound's fate yet the conferees
did not begin to deal with them. However, the
latter two issues were the subject of much debate on
Monday, 14 September and Tuesday, 15 September.
MacDonald, writing to the King, cited the growing
feeling among politicians that the financial situation could only be straightened out by a Government
which had the support of an organized party in the
House of Commons.[66] A day later, on 15 September,
Morgan Grenfell cabled to its New York partners that

there was a difference of opinion as to whether the National Government should stay in office after the budget was balanced, a process which Grenfell estimated would take three weeks. If party opinion led by Conservatives in favor of an early dissolution should prevail, a general election might be expected around 15 October.[67] Not only Peacock but Henry Clay of the Bank of England worked ceaselessly for a tariff, the latter writing to Geoffrey Lloyd on 14 September that the only way the battle for the gold standard could be won was if Britain had a positive balance of payments and this was impossible in the absence of a tariff.[68] Clay also took the opportunity of exhorting his fellow citizens during a radio broadcast the following day not to wait for Parliament but immediately to reduce imports and insofar as was possible buy only British goods.[69]

Tuesday, 15 September, seemed destined to be dominated by the election question, MacDonald writing in his diary that he was being pressed to lead an immediate campaign.[70] Yet a morning message from Sir Austen Chamberlain, First Lord of the Admiralty, enclosing a telegram from the Admiral of the Atlantic Fleet soon pushed the election talk to the back of the politicians' minds. In response to a proposed cut in pay for experienced ratings (part of the economy scheme) about 500 men at Invergordon had assembled for mass meetings, ignoring orders to return to their ships until their protest was over. In response to this and to the sailors' continued insubordination, the Admiral announced the postponement of Atlantic Fleet manoeuvres.[71] It was this action which elevated what might have remained a small incident into a major occurrence. Headline news around the world (except in Britain where coverage was played down at the Government's request) the reports made alarming reading for two reasons.[72] The first was that still fresh in people's minds was the memory of the Russian and German revolutions which had been marked by mutinies of their respective fleets. This knowledge, together with the traditional belief in the solidity and reliability of the Royal Navy caused tremors to rock world money markets, a reaction exacerbated by fears that if protest had doomed one plank of the economy platform, this would inevitably lead to other parts being pried loose.

The latter fear was proved to be realistic when it was announced the next day that the grievances of the men would be considered and if possible redressed. The Cabinet had unhappily been backed into a corner by what appears to have been the weakness of Chamberlain and the Admiralty.[73] Attention then shifted back to the financial sphere. When MacDonald met with Harvey on Wednesday morning, 16 September, he was met with dismal news. For Harvey had been told the previous day that at the present rate of usage, the Bank's reserves of dollars and francs would last approximately a fortnight. The two alternatives were further foreign borrowings or an increase in Bank rate coupled with the sale of gold.[74] Yet Harvey, unbeknownst to MacDonald, was probably aware that further borrowing, at least from the U.S., was not possible. Harrison had spent Monday, 14 September and Tuesday, 15 September with Norman in Quebec and they obviously discussed the British situation.[75] During these discussions Harrison would have certainly told Norman that, mainly due to the increasing depth of American banking and financial problems and the precarious position of the many American foreign loans, the chances of a new American credit were virtually non-existent. Furthermore, given their fairly close relationship and the fact that the two Governors' discussions were in person rather than by cable or over the still distrusted telephone, Norman probably was far better informed of where Harrison stood than Harvey would have been. As Harvey and Norman had been in communication, it makes sense to assume that prior to his departure for England on 16 September Norman informed his deputy as to the outcome of his meetings with the New Yorker.[76] Thus it is quite likely that Harvey had a much better idea of the future than the Government, which had no reason to suspect that Norman had done anything in Canada other than recuperate.

Such a scenario would help explain why Cat-terns, Chief Cashier of the Bank, prepared a memorandum on 16 September detailing the ramifications of proceeding without further credits.[77] If Norman had indeed confirmed to Harvey that an appeal to the U.S. would be futile and perhaps also had opined that maintenance of the gold standard no longer seemed possible, Harvey's resultant actions and general attitude may have been what motivated the Treasury on 17 September, prior to the meeting of the Financial Subcommittee which had summoned Harvey and Peacock to a session at 4:00 p.m. on that day, to begin drafting the legislation necessary for a departure from the gold standard.[78] Although Norman had been the great exponent of a universal gold standard, an about-face by mid-September is certainly within the realm of possibility. No longer caught in the maelstrom, he was in a position to be able to view the situation dispassionately and probably realized that if sterling had not responded in the anticipated manner after both a change of government and the obtaining of £130 m ($650 m) in foreign credits, there was little likelihood of a sudden turnaround. Thus it would have been reasonable for Norman to conclude that there was not much point to expending the Bank of England's gold reserves in what would be a doomed cause. Rather the logical move, although perhaps not a noble one, was to jettison the gold standard as soon as practicable after losing a sufficient amount of gold to verify the depth of the crisis. Furthermore to maintain the status quo would require additional borrowings. Even if these were forthcoming, to Norman their price may have been too high; always jealous of the leading position of the Old Lady he surely shared the sentiments of The Times' City Editor who on 10 September wrote:

> It is humiliating for any country, especially a creditor country, to have to raise money abroad to support its currency and the better the budget is balanced, the sooner the credits can be repaid and the humiliation forgotten.[79]

Finally leaving the gold standard at this juncture would aid Norman's own position. Under attack all summer and, furthermore, having deserted his post in time of battle, he may reasonably have feared for his job. Indeed according to a Time magazine article of late August speculation was rife that he was to be replaced, an opinion shared by Cochran in Basle.[80] Renominations for Governor and Deputy Governor were scheduled for late autumn. It may well have been Norman's conclusion that, if the decision to leave the gold standard was inevitable, it would be better for him personally if it were taken when he was literally and apparently informatively at sea.

Norman's future relationship with Harvey and Peacock support this hypothesis. Harvey served as Deputy Governor until his retirement in 1936. Peacock and Norman continued their close friendship, Norman in 1932 specifically entrusting to his close friend secret missions because he believed Peacock the most trustworthy of his associates.[81] Given

Norman's exceedingly centralized management style, it being no exaggeration to say he believed that La Banque, c'est moi, it seems difficult to believe that Norman would approve of Harvey and Peacock taking a decision as major as leaving the gold standard without consulting him when they had the ability to do so and an awareness that he was conversant with the current situation. The intimacy of Norman's post 1931 relations with Harvey and Peacock would seem to indicate the Governor's approval of their activities during Norman's absence. Thus after taking into account Norman's personality and approach a very likely conclusion then is that he had been involved in a decision that, all things remaining equal, Britain should leave the gold standard.

A question which must be asked is whether, assuming that Norman was involved in the decision to leave the gold standard, his participation made a difference to the outcome of the crisis. It is true that Harvey and Peacock were well aware that their battle was not going well. However, given the fact that Britain possessed the resources to continue the fight for some time after the actual surrender and keeping mind the gravity of the decision that was made, it may well have been that Norman's concurrence, if that is what they indeed received, was the support Harvey and Peacock needed to be able to urge the Cabinet into a move that would by its timing alone in Sayers' words cause 'bitter complaints and resentment' among other central bankers whose respect Norman had worked so hard and so long to earn.[82]

That Harvey and Peacock may have personally come to the conclusion that the gold standard was at least temporarily doomed was not something they revealed on 17 September to either the Committee of the Treasury or the Financial Subcommittee. At the former meeting the main topic of discussion was the possibility of a General Election and the negative effect this would have on the position of sterling. The record of proceedings of the Financial Subcommittee shows that while Harvey was explicit about the increasingly large financial demands made on the Bank (the drain on Wednesday had been £5 m ($25 m), he did not convey a sense that the decision to depart from the gold standard might be taken within hours. Indeed neither Harvey and Peacock demurred during a discussion of the possibility of obtaining further credits from the U.S. and France and both concurred in the decision that the American and

French governments should be contacted. Again the
question of a general election and its possible
effects on the financial situation proved a topic of
great interest.[83]

The Cabinet indeed did not appreciate how
critical matters were for MacDonald made no move to
alter his weekend plans at Chequers.[84] Grenfell,
however, was under no such illusions, and on 17
September he asked J.P. Morgan, who was in Scotland,
to return to London.[85] Interestingly on 17
September Harvey refused to talk with Harrison.
C.P. Mahon on his behalf cabled to Harrison that:
'Deputy Governor wishes me to inform you that owing
to his engagements in meetings he is unable to speak
to you today but that at present he has nothing
special to say.'[86] As the two men had spoken or
cabled virtually daily since the beginning of
August, the most logical explanation for this
somewhat odd behavior is that Harvey, unable to
disclose the fact that a decision had been made to
leave the gold standard, wanted to avoid being in a
position to have to lie to the New York Governor.

18 September proved the day of surrender for
the British forces fighting the battle for the gold
standard. Gold losses Thursday having amounted to
over £10 m ($50 m), MacDonald was called at Chequers
and immediately returned to London.[87] At what
MacDonald called the most solemn conference ever
held at 10 Downing Street, Harvey, Peacock and
various Treasury officials discussed the situation.[88] The Deputy Governor made it clear that he
believed that the only course of action was for
Britain to leave the gold standard. He made it
appear that he had discussed the situation after
Friday's close of trading with Harrison which was
not in fact true.[89] Furthermore, Harvey, in
response to a question from MacDonald, said he did
not think it was worthwhile to raise even £100 m
($500 m) if people were only going to withdraw it.
At this time the Prime Minister seemed to accept the
unpalatable inevitability and the balance of the
meeting was devoted to the mechanics of this water-
shed decision.[90]

Although the Americans had received word that
MacDonald's message, authorised at the previous
day's Cabinet meeting, would arrive at 1:00 p.m.,
Eastern time on Friday, the addressee, Secretary of
State Stimson, did not in fact receive it until
5:45 p.m. He immediately took it to the White
House. That night the President and Stimson were
joined by Secretary Mellon, Commerce Secretary

Robert Lamont and Henry Robinson. After canvassing various possibilities they concluded that there was nothing they could do to ameliorate the admittedly serious British predicament. Neither the Federal Reserve Banks nor the private institutions were in a position to grant further credits and any government loan would need the consent of Congress. Yet to call a special Congressional session would be nothing short of disastrous because it would open the doors to a flood of domestic relief legislation which would drown any proposal to aid Britain. Finally a gesture on war debts would be unavailing for no money was payable by Britain until December 1932. Thus the meeting ended.[91]

The exact nature of the British plight was probably something of a surprise to the American government. It is true that fairly accurate reports of Harvey's meetings of 17 September had appeared in The New York Times on Friday morning but the Secretary of State of course relied to a great extent on the United States Embassy in London.[92] This turned out to be a mistake because not only did Atherton apparently never communicate Fisher's message (if indeed Fisher ever delivered it) but American Ambassador Charles Dawes was consistently wrong in his predictions of the future course of events in Britain. The reason for this was that Dawes relied heavily on informants in the National Government Cabinet and on the Court of Directors for the facts upon which he based his prognostications. Unfortunately for him, his Government source, J.H. Thomas, was not on the Financial Subcommittee and for this and other reasons was unaware of much that was going on. Dawes' financial contacts were Kindersley and McKenna and they suffered from the same lack of information as Thomas.[93] However, foreknowledge would not have altered Stimson's reply to British Chargé d'Affairs Osborne. Delivered late on the evening of 18 September it regretfully informed the British Government that the American Government could offer only sympathy.[94]

During the White House conference Hoover had telephoned Thomas Lamont for his views of the situation. This was probably not the first Morgan's (N.Y.) had heard of the decision as Lamont's diary records a meeting on the exchange position at 7:00 p.m.[95] Yet it was a matter of some embarrassment to Grenfell that his partners learned so late the depth of the crisis. It appears that the Deputy Governor either under the pressure of events or, out of embarrassment, did not call Harrison, who was to get in touch with Morgan's (N.Y.), until late Friday evening and when he did, Harvey indicated only that there was a possibility that Britain would leave the gold standard.[96] Actually Morgan's (N.Y.) could have been informed far earlier of the parlous state of the British gold standard for Grenfell, in his capacity as director of the Bank of England where he sat on the Committee of Treasury and as the influential Conservative Party M.P. for the City, obviously possessed detailed information about the Bank of England's hour-to-hour position. Grenfell had of course an unenviable role. His clear conflict of interest forced him to choose which loyalty was more important - that to his nation or that to his partners who were also his friends. King and country won out but at a price; Grenfell was conscience-stricken about the disadvantageous position he had placed the New York house in and would repeatedly apologise during the next year.[97]

Saturday, 19 September was taken up by the myriad of details, some larger than others, which the decision to leave the gold standard necessarily entailed. Harrison and Harvey spoke twice that day. The British decision which Harvey now confirmed as definite greatly shocked Harrison, who obviously had received no intimations of such an eventuality from Norman. Indeed, notwithstanding the fact that Friday's losses had exceeded £17 m ($85m), Harrison tried to see if there was any way the gold standard could be preserved but his attempt met the same fate as had MacDonald's the previous day.[98]

The British remained firm in their course of action despite the fact that the French, having received a message similar to that given Stimson, immediately offered a long-term loan of £15 m - £25 m ($75 m - $125 m) independent of action taken by any other market.[99] The French were clearly eager to do whatever they could to ensure that Britain remained on gold, Laval saying as much to British diplomat Ronald Campbell on Saturday morning.[100] This was not disinterested charity. The French, having begun September with high sterling reserves, had actually increased their holdings during the month and therefore stood to lose a great deal if the British left the gold standard. Furthermore there was concern over the repayment of French credits. Finally the French feared that the British departure from gold would destroy the gold standard system and with it their current financial hegemony.

However the British were not interested in a further French credit. This was clearly seen at the conference held at 10 Downing Street on Saturday afternoon. In attendance were MacDonald, Baldwin and Samuel, Harvey and Peacock, Fisher and Leith-Ross and Sir Robert Vansittart, Permanent Under-Secretary of State at the Foreign Office. Fisher said that the Treasury view on the subject of a fresh credit was that the French offer was insufficient to stem the tide. The conferees also discussed the mechanics to be put into place and received an update of the withdrawals from Harvey. [101]

On the same day, J.P. Morgan, accompanied by his son and partner Harry, returned to London. The elder Morgan went to the American Embassy where he conferred with Dawes and J.H. Thomas. According to the Ambassador, the financier first broke the news about the decision to leave the gold standard to Thomas and then the three discussed the question of a general election, Thomas predicting that the National Government would have 400 out of 600 members of the new Parliament. [102] In the meantime Lamont, at Peacock's request, prepared a draft public announcement for the British Government to release which Peacock sent to the Treasury. Lamont also drafted a press statement to be circulated to American newspapers which emphasized the temporary nature of the suspension and the fact that it would not affect any obligations payable in gold previously contracted by the British Government. (This was designed to prevent a massive dumping of British Government dollar denominated securities.) [103]

Yet Morgan's (N.Y.) was not resigned to the British decision. On 20 September they cabled Morgan Grenfell to ask whether it was not possible for sterling to remain on gold if the Bank rate were immediately raised and other methods of controlling the exchanges utilized. Their London partners somewhat testily replied that the Bank of England had of course considered raising Bank rate but had decided that with money so cheap in the U.S. this would simply exacerbate any panic instead of cure the widespread doubts. [104] With that the New York house had to rest content because the game was up. Sunday was spent completing the necessary chores and informing appropriate parties of what the next day would bring. Thus MacDonald invited Henderson to 10 Downing Street on Sunday evening and the Foreign Office sent cables to all embassies. The French, who had offered all possible assistance to the

138

British, agreed to suspend sterling trading although
they did not follow the British lead and completely
close the stock market.[105]

From Washington Osborne reported that during
his conversation with Stimson early on Saturday
morning the Secretary of State had taken the opportunity to say that the British debt funding terms
were the occasion of shameful regret to all right
thinking Americans but also emphasized that two main
difficulties stood in the way of revision, the
Balfour Note and Annex 3 of the Young Plan.[106]
Stimson, who was spending Sunday with the President
at his Camp Rapidan retreat spent part of the
morning reflecting on the ramifications of the
British decision to leave the gold standard, both
for Britain and for the world.[107]

At the Bank of England, most unusually for a
Sunday, all was activity. Meetings were held of
leading clearing bankers and representatives of
accepting houses and brokerage firms as plans were
worked out to cope with such items as a rise in Bank
rate to 6% effective simultaneously with the departure from gold and the closing of the Stock Market.
Harvey drafted and sent the famous cable to Norman
aboard the Duchess of Bedford which said: 'Sorry we
have to go off tomorrow and cannot wait to see you
before doing so.'[108] Hitherto interpreted as
Norman's first indication of the dénouement of the
crisis, it could equally have been the prearranged
notice that the eventuality envisaged during the
previous week had indeed come to pass.

A full Cabinet meeting was held at 4:30 p.m.
After the many uninformed Ministers learned of the
events of Friday and Saturday, the Cabinet approved
the various actions that had been taken and the text
of the necessary amendment to the Gold Standard
Act.[109] After further discussion which resulted,
most significantly, in the decision that Britain's
going off the gold standard would not affect the
Cabinet's decision to implement an economy programme, the meeting adjourned.[110] Clearly everyone was wondering, what came after the end of the
world?

NOTES

1.   The Times, 24 August 1931, p. 15.
2.   Morgan Grenfell, BG Credit 1931, Morgan
Grenfell to Morgan's (N.Y.), 31/4934, 24 August
1931; PRO 30/69/1753, MacDonald Diaries, 24 August
1931.

3. Morgan Grenfell, BG Loan in the USA-5A, Hopkins to C.F. Whigham, 24 August 1931; B/E, S73, Harvey to Hopkins, 24 August 1931.

4. Morgan Grenfell, BG Credit 1931, Morgan Grenfell to Morgan's (N.Y.), 31/4934, 24 August 1931; Memorandum of telephone conversation between Morgan and Grenfell (London) and Lamont & C. Whitney (New York), 25 August 1931 (noted as shown to Deputy Governor, 25 August 1931); B/E, MB53, C/T Minutes, 26 August 1931.

5. B/E, S73, Siepmann Note of conversation with Moret at the Bank of France, 25 August 1931; Harrison Papers, Binder 59, Harrison Memorandum, 25 August 1931, concerning telephone conversation with Lacour-Gayet, 25 August 1931.

6. The New York Times, 25 August 1931, p. 1.

7. Whaley-Eaton Service, 'Foreign Letter No. 645', 25 August 1931.

8. Morgan Grenfell, BG Credit 1931, Internal Memorandum (undated) on the Crisis (hereafter M.G. Memorandum), p. 8, Morgan's (N.Y.) to Morgan Grenfell, 31/2386, 25 August 1931; FRBNY, Crane Trip, Crane to Harrison, 18, 27 August 1931.

9. Stimson Diaries, Reel 3, Vol. 17, Memorandum of Conversation with MacDonald, 27 August 1931; Memorandum of Conversation with Morgan, 27 August 1931.

10. Morgan Grenfell, BG Credit 1931, Morgan's (N.Y.) to Morgan Grenfell, 31/2410, 29 August 1931.

11. The Times, 17 September 1931, p. 17.

12. B/E, C43/298, Note of Conversation at the Ministry of Finance, France, 6:30 p.m., 26 August 1931.

13. F.W. Leith-Ross, Money Talks: Fifty Years of International Finance, (Hutchinson & Co., London, 1968), p. 138.

14. NA, RG59, 751.62/153, Marriner to Secretary of State, 25 August 1931.

15. B/E, C43/248, Note of Conversation at the Bank of France, 5:00 p.m., 26 August 1931, Note of Conversation at the Ministry of Finance, 6:30 p.m. 26 August 1931; Harrison Papers, Binder 59, Harrison Memorandum, 27 August 1931, of telephone conversation with Lacour-Gayet, 26 August 1931.

16. By having the British Consul-General in Paris endorse the bills in blank, they could be considered a domestic issue and thus not subject to the onerous tax applicable to foreign issues.

17. B/E, C43/298, Note of Conversation at the Ministry of Finance, 6:30 p.m., 26 August 1931.

18. B/E, C43/298, Note of Conversation in Paris, 27 August 1931.

19. Morgan Grenfell, BG Credit 1931, Morgan's (N.Y.) to J.P. Morgan, 31/2401, 27 August 1931.

20. Morgan Grenfell, BG Credit 1931, Morgan's (N.Y.) to Chancellor of Exchequer, 28 August 1931, concerning credit opened by Morgan's (N.Y.) and other U.S. Banks on behalf of His Majesty's Government.

21. Dalton, op. cit., pp. 274-7.

22. Morgan Grenfell, BG Credit 1931, Morgan's (N.Y.) to Morgan Grenfell, 31/2393, 27 August 1931.

23. Lamont Papers, 96-14, 27 August 1931; PRO, FO371/15679, Osborne to Foreign Office, 26 August 1931.

24. Morgan Grenfell, BG Credit 1931, MG Memorandum, p. 11.

25. PRO 30/69/260, Henderson, Notes on the Economy Issue', 27 August 1931.

26. PRO 30/69/1315, J. Baker to MacDonald, 26 August 1931; R.S. Young to MacDonald, 28 August 1931.

27. PRO 30/69/1314, MacDonald to W. Caxon, 25 August 1931; MacDonald to H. Morrison, 27 August 1931.

28. The New York Times, 30 August 1931, p. 5; FRBNY, Crane Trip, Crane to A. Sproul, 22, 28 August 1931.

29. B/E, G3/210, Harvey to G. Vissering, 27 August 1931.

30. Brand Papers, Box 115, Chamberlain to Brand, 28 August 1931.

31. Lamont Papers, 111-23, Lamont to Grenfell, 31/2413, 29 August 1931.

32. Morgan Grenfell, BG Credit 1931, Morgan's (N.Y.) to Grenfell, 31/2417, 31 August 1931.

33. Morgan Grenfell, BG Credit 1931, Morgan's (N.Y.) to Grenfell, 31/2417, 31 August 1931, penned notation.

34. B/E, G3/210, Harvey to H. Samuel, 29 August 1931; Harvey to Rodd, 31 August 1931.

35. B/E, MB 53, C/T Minutes, 31 August 1931.

36. Morgan Grenfell, BG Credit 1931, Morgan's (N.Y.) to Morgan Grenfell, 31/2418, 1 September 1931.

37. Leffingwell Papers, Leffingwell to Lamont, 29 August 1931.

38. FRBNY, C261, Harrison to Harvey, 334/31, 3 September 1931.

39. FRBNY, C261, Harvey to Harrison, 402/31, 4 September 1931.

40. PRO 30/69/1314, MacDonald to S. Baldwin, 5 September 1931.

41. For example, the agreement with Morgan's (N.Y.) provided that, 'we [Morgan's (N.Y.)] will upon demand purchase from it [the British Treasury] British Government Dollar Treasury Bills in amounts of $10,000,000 nominal or multiples thereof. The Bills ... are to be payable at our office in the City of New York in gold coin of the United States of America of the present standard of weight and fineness without deduction for any British taxes and shall so state.' Morgan Grenfell, BG Credit 1931, Morgan's (N.Y.) to Chancellor of Exchequer, 28 August 1931, concerning credit opened by Morgan's (N.Y.) and other U.S. Banks on behalf of His Majesty's Government.

42. B/E, OV4/105, Siepmann Memorandum, 'Semi-Pledged Gold', 16 September 1931.

43. PRO, T172/1756, 'Secretary's Note of a Conversation Between Sir Ernest Harvey and Mr. Peacock and Members of the Cabinet,' 3 September 1931.

44. Templewood Papers, Box VII-1, Templewood Memorandum: 'The First National Government', undated.

45. Morgan Grenfell, BG Credit 1931, Lamont to Grenfell, 31/2428, 4 September 1931.

46. NA, RG39, Box 104, Cochran to Castle, 3 September 1931.

47. Clay, op. cit., p. 399. It is interesting that while Sayers concludes that Norman did not 'personally share in the responsibilities of these last hectic weeks' (Sayers, op. cit., p. 415) he does provide evidence to the contrary by noting that Harrison told Harvey that he had seen Norman. (Ibid., p. 407, n.1.).

48. FRBNY, Harrison Papers, 3115.2, Harrison Memorandum, 24 August 1931, concerning telephone conversation with Norman, 22 August 1931.

49. Harrison Papers, Binder 59, Harrison Memorandum, 24 August 1931, concerning telephone conversation with Norman, 23 August 1931.

50. Morgan Grenfell, BG Credit 1931, Grenfell to Morgan, 18 August 1931.

51. B/E, S40/1, Harvey to Harrison, 404/31, 5 September 1931, Harrison to Harvey, 304/34, 5 September 1931.

52. PRO 30/69/1753, MacDonald Diaries, 8 September 1931.

53. The New York Times, 11 September 1931, p. 1.

54. Morgan Grenfell, BG Credit 1931, Morgan's (N.Y.) to Morgan Grenfell, 31/2473, 7 September 1931. The bankers used the term 'pegging the pound'

to indicate direct buying and selling of sterling in order to keep it at par. Raising the Bank rate in order to accomplish the same goal would not have been considered 'pegging'.

55. Morgan Grenfell, BG Credit 1931, Morgan Grenfell to Morgan's (N.Y.) 31/4987, 31/4988, 8 September 1931.

56. FRBNY, C261.1, Harvey to Harrison, 411/31, 8 September 1931.

57. Stimson Diaries, Reel 3, Vol. 18, 8 September 1931.

58. Stimson Diaries, Reel 3, Vol. 18, 12 September 1931.

59. HHPL, Castle Papers, Atherton to Castle, 11 September 1931; NA, RG59, 841.51/965, Atherton to Stimson, 11 September 1931.

60. Morgan Grenfell, BG Credit 1931, Morgan et Cie. to Morgan's (N.Y.) 87.652, 10 September 1931. The French credit was divided into two parts with half taking the same form as the American tranche and the other half being issued as an invitation for a public subscription for franc-denominated British Treasury Bills.

61. Cambridge University Library, Cambridge, Stanley Baldwin Papers, volume 44, MacDonald to Cabinet, 10 September 1931; PRO, PREM 1/97, Lord Reading to MacDonald, 10 September 1931; PRO, T172/1746, Reading to Snowden, 11 September 1931.

62. FRBNY, Crane Trip, Crane to Harrison, 9 September 1931.

63. B/E, S40/1, Norman to Harvey, 10 September 1931.

64. Harvey had been sufficiently alarmed about British sales of sterling to write to various culprits such as Lord Bradbury to ask them not to continue to purchase dollars. Also Fisher had told Atherton that internal capital flight was one of the causes of Britain's problems. As the Bank of England not the Treasury kept track of currency movements, Fisher could only have known this if the Bank so informed him.

65. PRO, Cab 27/462, Minutes of Meeting, Committee on the Financial Situation, 14 September 1931.

66. PRO 30/69/1314, MacDonald to King George V, 14 September 1931.

67. Morgan Grenfell, Gold Standard 1931 - Bundle 233, Morgan Grenfell to Morgan's (N.Y.), 31/4999, 15 September 1931.

68. B/E, SMT 5/3, Clay to Peacock, 15 September 1931; SMT 5/3, Clay to Godfrey Lloyd, 14 September 1931.

69. B/E, SMT 5/60, Clay Speech, 15 September 1931. The general effect of this appeal is unclear but at least advertising copywriters were rapidly benefitted, for within the week advertisements of major retailers pointed out with monotonous regularity that the illustrated goods were British in origin and thus their purchase would be a patriotic act beneficial for the British economy.

70. PRO 30/69/1753, MacDonald Diaries, 15 September 1931.

71. PRO 30/69/1314, A. Chamberlain to MacDonald, 15 September 1931.

72. The New York Times, 16 September 1931, p. 10.

73. The New York Times, 17 September 1931, p. 1; D. Dutton, Austen Chamberlain: Gentleman in Politics (Ross Anderson, London, 1985) pp. 303-5.

74. PRO 30/69/1753, MacDonald Diaries, 16 September 1931; B/E, S74, Catterns to Harvey, 15 September 1931.

75. B/E, S40/1, Norman to Harvey, 12 September 1931.

76. Evidence of their communication may well be seen in a letter from Grenfell to Morgan dated 17 September 1931 in which Grenfell stated that Norman had sailed for England and briefed Morgan on the Governor's condition. Grenfell clearly received this information from Harvey who in turn learned it from either Harrison, Norman or from both men. (Morgan Grenfell, BG Credit 1931).

77. B/E, S74, Catterns to Harvey, 16 September 1931.

78. B/E, S74, F. Phillips Memorandum, 17 September 1931.

79. The Times, 10 September 1931, p. 17.

80. Time, 24 August 1931, p. 16; NA, RG39, Box 104, Cochran to Castle, 3 September 1931.

81. B/E, S31/2, Norman to Peacock, 17 December 1931.

82. Sayers, op. cit., p. 415.

83. B/E, MB 53, C/T Minutes, 17 September 1931; PRO, Cab 27/462, Minutes of Meeting, Cabinet Committee on the Financial Situation, 17 September 1931.

84. PRO 30/69/1753, MacDonald Diaries, 18 September 1931.

85. Morgan Grenfell, BG Credit 1931, Grenfell to Morgan, 17 September 1931.

86. FRBNY, C261, C.P. Mahon to Harrison, 17 September 1931.

87. Whether this was cause or effect is unclear as the Bank had taken the position that it was advisable to lose gold before announcing the departure from the gold standard.

88. PRO 30/69/1753, MacDonald Diaries, 18 September 1931.

89. See pp. 136-7 infra.

90. PRO, PREM 1/97, Notes of a Meeting on 18 September 1931.

91. PRO, T188/30, MacDonald to Stimson, 5:00 p.m. and 8:30 p.m., 18 September 1931; Stimson Diaries, Reel 3, Vol. 18, 18 September 1931.

92. The New York Times, 18 September 1931, p. 1.

93. Examples of Dawes' use of the information provided by his sources is provided in his cables to Stimson of 15, 17 and 18 September 1931, respectively NA, RG59, 841.51/964, 841.00/1169 and 841.00/1170.

94. NA, RG59, 841.51/971A, Stimson to Dawes, 19 September 1931; PRO, T188/30; Osborne to Mac-Donald, 576, 19 September 1931; PRO, FO371/15681, Osborne to Reading, 25 September 1931.

95. Lamont Papers, 173-1 Lamont Diaries, 18 September 1931.

96. Morgan Grenfell, BG Credit 1931, MG Memorandum, p. 16.

97. See, e.g., Morgan Grenfell, BG Credit 1931, Grenfell to Lamont, 16 March 1932.

98. Harrison Papers, Binder 59, Harrison Memorandum dated 19 September 1931, concerning telephone conversations with Harvey at 6:30 a.m. and 8:35 a.m., 19 September 1931.

99. PRO, T188/30, MacDonald to Flandin, 5:00 p.m. and 8:30 p.m., 18 September 1931; B/E, OV 45/4, Bank of France Proposals to Bank of England, 19 September 1931; PRO, FO371/15681, Campbell to Reading, 26 September 1931.

100. PRO, T188/30, Campbell to Snowden, 19 September 1931.

101. PRO, PREM 1/97, Note of a Conference held on 19 September 1931.

102. NA, R659, 841.51/975, Dawes to Stimson, 19 September 1931.

103. B/E, Gold Standard - Gold, Grenfell to Peacock, 19 September 1931; Lamont Papers, 196-14, 'Statement', 19 September 1931; Morgan Grenfell, Gold Standard-Bundle 233, Morgan's (N.Y.) to Morgan Grenfell, 31/2454, 19 September 1931 (noted as sent to Peacock).

104. Morgan Grenfell, Gold Standard-Bundle 233, Morgan's (N.Y.) to Morgan Grenfell, 31/2461, 20 September 1931, Morgan Grenfell to Morgan's (N.Y.), 31/5012, 20 September 1931.

105. PRO 30/69/1753, MacDonald Diaries, 20 September 1930; T188/30, Foreign Office to Dominion and Foreign Governments, 20 September 1931; Foreign Office to Campbell, 4:35 p.m. and 7:00 p.m., 20 September 1931.

106. PRO, T188/30, Osborne to Foreign Office, 578, 20 September 1931.

107. Stimson Diaries, Reel 3, Vol. 18, 20 September 1931.

108. B/E, S40/1, Harvey to Norman, 20 September 1931.

109. See Appendix below.

110. PRO, Cab 23/68, 20 September 1931.

Chapter Six

REVELATION

September 1931 - December
1932

'This step [Great Britain's
departure from the gold
standard] seems to me to be
the second necessary stage
in the work of the National
Government, the first being
the balancing of the
Budget. The completion of
the new Government's work
will be the restoration of
trade in this country.
    This being the case,
it seems to me a hopeful
and not discouraging event
and one which brings the
great work of the Govern-
ment much nearer to completion.'

Statement given by J.P.
Morgan to the Associ-
ated Press, 21 Sep-
tember 1931

The Monday morning Prime Minister MacDonald had
surely been dreading was replete with news and
speculation devoted to Great Britain's departure
from the gold standard. In New York the first page
of The New York Times contained an extended report
from London and also reported on American and world
reactions to this monumental event.[1] Much was
made of J.P. Morgan's statement quoted above for it
was only the second public announcement he had made
in his entire career; Owen Young writing to Morgan
said: 'your reserves of silence accumulated through
many years make your statement extraordinarily
effective here and everywhere in the world.'[2] In
London The Times' leader struck a note which would
be heard often during the next few months:

A suspension of gold payments by a Socialist Government would have been one thing.
But suspension by the National Government
committed to retrenchment and reform is

another. The Socialist Government would have had to go off the gold standard with an unbalanced Budget and might never have returned to it. The National Government has been compelled to go off the gold standard with a balanced Budget though with an unbalanced trade account. When that account too has been balanced, as it will be, this country will return to the gold standard. And that it is determined to do when the conditions are propitious. It may be said emphatically that there is not cause for alarm in the decision which the Government has reached. On the contrary, the action will inure to the benefit not only of this country, but also of the whole world. [3]

The worst having happened, Dawson obviously felt an obligation to make the best of it but his approach was disparaged by many who had believed strongly in the gold standard. Siepmann for one complained that the public was being misled by those who were lauding the departure from gold. [4] This ambivalent view of the demise of the gold standard remained apparent as the Bank, the Treasury and the Cabinet during the succeeding weeks and months discussed the future direction of monetary policy.

They were starting with a clean slate as no real planning had been done on financial policy should Britain go off the gold standard. During the last week of September with sterling below $4.00 the Bank was largely occupied with the technicalities inherent in this change. Norman, who had arrived in Liverpool on 23 September and returned to the Bank of England on 28 September, together with Harvey, took care of such melancholy matters as officially informing other central banks of the British decision and sending them for their reference the relevant legislation which had been immediately approved by Parliament and assented to by the King. It appears that to Norman the most painful letters were those to central banks such as that of Denmark and Sweden which in the wake of the British decision followed suit immediately. [5]

The Scandinavian countries were not alone; within four weeks eighteen countries had departed from the gold standard. It thus seemed that the vindictive desire of many British to leave the U.S. and France high and dry upon their vast gold stocks was nearing reality. Certainly the U.S. rapidly felt the strain as it lost $180 m gold[6] during the week ending 26 September[7]. Much of this gold drain originated in Paris for the French had lost billions of francs on their sterling deposits. Determined never again to be caught in such a position, they immediately began converting their large dollar holdings into gold. Lacour-Gayet told Harrison that, in addition, as the French feared their sterling losses would cause a lack of confidence in French financial stability they believed that increasing metallic reserves while at the same time reducing the possibility of a future similar problem was the best way to assuage any doubts.[8] Accordingly the spirit of monetary cooperation between the big three of interwar finance began to disintegrate, replaced by an attitude of sauve qui peut.

However, the U.S. was not only facing French demands. Other central banks similarly burned by the dénouement of the British crisis sought assurances from the United States that their dollar-based assets would not meet a similar fate. Replying to a BIS cable, Harrison firmly refused McGarrah's request that a central bank or the BIS be allowed to keep its deposits in earmarked gold without foregoing the interest payment which would have been earned had the deposits remained in dollars.[9] The response to Harrison's negation of this proposal was rapid - by 28 October, when the drain stopped, the U.S. had lost $728 m gold.[10] British withdrawals contributed to this total, in part as a result of the not unexpected return of British capital which had fled its home port during the crisis. But it appeared to some Americans in Britain that their erstwhile ally was also pursuing a policy of beggar thy neighbor. Both Morgan and Harrison found themselves deluged with requests to counter rumours about the soundness of major American money-centre banks and, according to Atherton, Norman was deliberately impugning the strength of the American economy.[11] Whatever the truth in these particular reports, it is clear that a major change in Anglo-American relations spawned by the fall of the pound off the gold standard was beginning to make itself felt. Not only was the solidarity between the Bank of England and FRBNY broken but the former's need for American help, both potential and actual, was greatly diminished. Undoubtedly the defeat the British had suffered also increased anti-American sentiment which had been exacerbated by British resentment at what was viewed as insufficient Ameri-

149

can cooperation during the battle for Britain's gold standard. Most importantly, the decision to leave the gold standard altered the focus of Anglo-American financial relations. The maintenance of sterling on gold as a primary concern was replaced by the questions of reparations and war debts and by the generally problematic world economic conditions. That on these issues American and British interests diverged in important ways would become increasingly clear in the months ahead. Further, with respect to questions of monetary policy, the change in the pound's status created important differences in priorities for the two countries. To the U.S., the gold standard still reigned supreme and, not surprisingly, Americans wanted Britain to return to the gold standard as soon as possible both in order to reinforce it and also to minimize the trading advantage the demise of Britain's gold standard had brought her.[12] For their part, the British increasingly viewed a return to gold as a step to be taken only when the problems to which they attributed sterling's fall, e.g., sterilization of gold, the U.S. tariff, the world economic crisis, were solved.[13]

However, political not financial affairs were the focus of British attention during the first month after the departure from gold. The decision announced on 21 September had solved neither the problem of when an election should be held nor settled the vexatious tariff question. Between 21 September and the dissolution of Parliament on 7 October MacDonald and his Cabinet colleagues debated the terms upon which an election could be fought. Finally Neville Chamberlain hit upon a formula whereby each party represented in the governing coalition would write its own manifesto and on that innovative basis a vicious campaign was fought which resulted in a landslide victory on 28 October for the National Government which emerged with a triumphant majority of 497 seats.[14]

As the reconstituted Cabinet, together with the Treasury and the Bank of England, debated currency matters, it was the French and Americans who were at the centre of international attention. At the invitation of the American government (probably issued at his own prompting), Premier Laval visited the U.S. during the last week of October.[15] His arrival was preceded by that of Charles Farnier and Robert Lacour-Gayet of the Bank of France who sailed to New York on 8 October to confer with Harrison about the international financial situation.[16] In addition the French voiced their concern that the U.S. was moving towards an inflationary policy. The immediate cause of their alarm was the formation by private bankers during the previous week of the National Credit Corporation. Although none of the banks whispered about in London was in trouble, the American domestic banking situation had deteriorated with 305 banks failing during September. Indeed, President Hoover was more and more convinced that the U.S. was in deep financial trouble, a sentiment which was echoed by other observers. For example, on 5 October, one financial commentator attributed the recent fall in American stock prices to domestic not foreign causes.[17] The deteriorating American economic picture had two important effects on international financial relations. First, as Hoover told Stimson, it would be increasingly difficult if not impossible to get the American people to approve of any more sacrifices in Europe unless they were linked to a plan to alleviate distress in the U.S.[18] Secondly, the President increasingly accepted the need for government intervention to ameliorate the crisis. Specifically he proposed the formation of a corporation whose capital in an amount of $500 m subscribed by banks would be used to make liquidity advances against security not available for use at Federal Reserve Banks. Browbeaten by the President at a meeting at Secretary Mellon's house, leading New York bankers finally agreed to participate in the plan.[19]

To conservative Europeans, on the other hand, the NCC (and other similar steps which were taken later) appeared to be nothing more than gift wrapped inflation, especially to the French who adhered to a philosophy of deflation à l'outrance.[20] That the FRBNY raised its discount rate on 8 October from $1\frac{1}{2}$% to $2\frac{1}{2}$% did not comfort the French nor did J.P. Morgan's visit to the Bank of France on 7 October. Persistent and well publicized rumours continued to sap French faith in the dollar's soundness.[21] The tone of French newspaper articles did not go unnoticed by the Americans who were preparing for Laval's visit. Stimson noted that the President thought the French were deliberately trying to drive the U.S. off the gold standard.[22] Morgan's (N.Y.) was sufficiently concerned to send a cable to Morgan Grenfell intended to reassure the London partners and 'enquiring friends' that the American position was improving and not inclining towards unsound finance while Morgan urged Dawes to suggest to Hoover that at the conclusion of Laval's visit a joint statement affirming mutual adherence to the gold standard be issued.[23]

In anticipation of Laval's visit Lamont prepared a memorandum for Hoover's use. It started from the premise that France, although now the dominant power in Europe, was quite insecure both politically and financially. France needed reassurance in both areas: that its security needs vis-à-vis Germany would be recognized and that the U.S. was determined to safeguard the gold standard.[24] Lamont's plea for understanding was mirrored by that of Flandin who called on the American Ambassador to France on 20 October to explain that both the French Government and the Bank of France had done all they could to contain the raid on the dollar.[25]

Further preparations for the Hoover-Laval meeting (which was regarded as vitally important, particularly by Europeans), included a conference hosted by Harrison at the FRBNY's headquarters on 19 October. Present were not only Eugene Meyer and S. Parker Gilbert but Ogden Mills and various State Department representatives. The consensus was that the French sought publicly to establish Franco-American solidarity and that, within limits, the Americans should assist them. While the conferees believed that a revision of reparations and war debts was of great importance and should be supported, they felt it must be emphasized to the French that the American attitude on the debt question depended not only on financial arrangements but on other European questions, particularly disarmament. The link between war debts and reparations on the one hand and disarmament on the other reflected a long-standing American belief (not always shared by those across the Atlantic) that if Europeans decreased their spending on weapons, war debts would present less of a problem and reparations diminish in importance.

Four days later the meeting between the French and American leaders took place. In the course of their conversations, Hoover outlined what he labelled the general American viewpoint of the European crisis:

> [The President] said that the American would sum up the situation in this wise. We had started with a hundred fifty years of isolation from Europe. Fifteen years ago we were dragged by Europe into the war for the first time. And he would sum up the results of the following fifteen years

as follows: that it had cost the lives of
some 75,000 men and disabled over 200,000
more. We had spent in loans, or war
payments, something like $40 billion; and
that as a result Europe was now more
unstable than it was in 1914.[26]

This statement reveals the perspective which, in
large part, shaped American thinking throughout the
next 14 months. Understandably, Europeans did not
share this outlook; unfortunately few seemed to even
understand it.

On the subject of reparations, it was agreed,
in the words of the joint communique issued several
days later:

Insofar as intergovernmental obligations
are concerned we recognize that prior to
the expiration of the Hoover year of postponement, some agreement regarding them
may be necessary covering the period of
business depression...The initiative in
this regard should be taken by the
European powers principally concerned
within the framework of the agreements
existing prior to July 1, 1931.

By this pledge Hoover assuaged any French fears that
the U.S. would propose any further initiatives on
reparations; there would not be a second Hoover
Moratorium. In response to Laval's question as to
whether the U.S. would cooperate if the French and
British agreed to a reduction in reparations, the
Americans answered in the affirmative, subject to
caveats concerning the course of the depression and
the effect of any Congressional action. Although it
went virtually unremarked at the time, the President
had made thereby a major concession in his new
willingness to link war debts with reparations.
Regrettably his change of heart, significant as it
may have been, was, in terms of European-American
relations, a case of too little, too late.

To assert that the discussion on reparations
would haunt the conferees is no understatement. The
French as well as the British interpreted the
Hoover-Laval discussions and the resulting communi-
qué to imply an American agreement both to allow
Europeans to settle the reparations question as they
liked and then to match any reduction with comparable cuts in war debts. However, while Hoover sincerely intended to recommend war debts' revision to

Congress if reparations were reduced, he could not
and furthermore had no desire to eliminate them in
whole or in major part.[27] As specifics replaced
generalities, the chasm which separated the American
view on war debts and reparations from that of the
French and British would become increasingly
apparent.

As November succeeded October the moving finger
passed back to Germany. The German financial
situation had worsened steadily during the autumn;
as Dr. Vocke, an official of the Reichsbank, stated
in October, things were going from bad to worse.[28]
When the hope that the Hoover-Laval meeting might
change the situation proved false, the German
Government felt compelled to invoke Article 119 of
the Young Plan on 19 November and applied to the BIS
asking for the appointment of a special advisory
committee to investigate Germany's capacity to pay
reparations. The British were very concerned
about the deterioration in German finances because
so many of the City's acceptance lines were tied
down by the Standstill Agreement. This Agreement
aided Germany both by easing her liquidity crisis
and also by increasing her bargaining power - in
essence many London houses found themselves hostages
to Germany's fortune. As the leading bankers J.
Beaumont Pease and W.H.N. Goschen wrote to Norman:

> A breakdown of the Standstill Agreement or
> a failure to renew it in some satisfactory
> form would entail...in all probability
> another run on foreign balances.

They believed that the only way to protect the
Standstill Agreement was to prevent the resurrection
of reparations payments.[29]

The bankers' view was echoed by Stanley Baldwin
who, in a speech to the House of Commons on 19
November, emphasized the importance of commercial
debts over reparations although this represented a
sharp break with the French position which was based
on assumption that reparations had a first priority
over all other German obligations.[30] There is no
question that, from mid-November on, the British
Government, partly as a result of pressure from the
City, took the approach that reparations were to a
considerable extent responsible for, among other
things, the severe damage to Anglo-German trade and
the vast U.S. and French gold stocks. Thus the
British goal, as expressed in a Treasury memorandum
of 14 November, was to achieve a final settlement of

reparations embodying at the least a temporary total suspension and no resumption of payments without protection against possible transfer problems.[31]

The British attitude was largely responsible for the thrust of the report produced by the Beneduce Committee which began deliberating in Basle on 7 December in response to the German request. Its conclusion was:

> The adjustment of all governmental debts (reparations and other War debts) to the existing troubled situation of the world- and this adjustment should take place without a delay if new disasters are to be avoided - is the only lasting step capable of reestablishing confidence which is the very condition of economic stability and peace.[32]

The injunction as to war debts certainly fell on unresponsive ears when the 72nd U.S. Congress, having also convened on 7 December, began its consideration of the Hoover Moratorium. Due to the archaic system provided for in the Constitution, this was the first meeting of a legislative body which had been elected in November 1930. It was largely hostile to the President and far more concerned with domestic rather than foreign problems. Although this was not surprising given the increasingly parlous state of the American economy, Hoover and Stimson despaired of the future of the Hoover Moratorium.[33] The issue was not whether the Moratorium per se would be approved, because the President had in June received pledges of support from a majority of legislators in each House, but the form in which it would be passed. Even before Congressional hearings began, it was obvious that the Moratorium and the Administration's proposal to revive the World War Debt Funding Commission would meet stiff opposition. Because it was clear that the Moratorium would not be ratified prior to the 15 December due date for war debt payments, various countries sought reassurance from the State Department that they could in good faith omit to make the required payments. Yet Stimson's affirmative response ignited the wrath of Representative Louis McFadden, Chairman of the House Committee on Banking and Currency.[34] Stimson, called to testify by the House Ways and Means Committee, emphasized two points: that the French per capita monetary sacrifice exceeded the American and that

155

the Moratorium, rather than being, as had been
alleged, a device to help bankers get their money
out of Germany, instead convinced them to leave
their funds there.[35] The next day Stimson
switched his guns to the Senate and called upon the
influential Senator David Reed who had been upset by
Prime Minister MacDonald's statement that the
Moratorium marked the end of war debts.[36] Mac-
Donald was in fact sufficiently concerned by the
various reports reaching him to the effect that the
Congressional Resolution would circumscribe future
similar Presidential initiatives to write to Stimson on
16 December that, as the situation in Europe had
deteriorated since the summer, more rather than less
American help was called for. His fears were echoed
by Harrison who told Stimson that the Europeans
would probably link concessions on reparations to
similar steps on war debts.[37] The Secretary of
State, however, was mainly anxious to contain the
damage to his program which Stimson feared would
accrue from what he termed an atmosphere of general
bitterness triggered by the severe financial and
economic crisis. Thus he responded immediately to
MacDonald's letter urging him to keep his fears to
himself because interference might have dire
results, going so far as to suggest that the Senate
could refuse to ratify the Moratorium.[38]

Stimson's reading of the mood of Congress was
accurate. Although the Moratorium was ratified, the
President's proposal to resurrect the World War Debt
Funding Commission was given short shrift and
attached to the ratification Resolution was a rider
which stated:

> It is hereby declared to be against the
> policy of Congress that any of the
> indebtedness of the foregoing countries to
> the United States should be in any manner
> concealed or reduced and nothing in this
> joint resolution shall be construed as
> indicatory or contrary policy, or as
> implying that favourable consideration
> will be given at any time to a change in
> the policy hereby declared.[39]

Stimson explained to the very perturbed British
Ambassador Sir Ronald Lindsay that what had happened
simply illustrated the difficulties facing any
American President who ventured into the realm of
foreign affairs and that, just as the President had
indicated after his meetings with Laval, it was up

to European countries to take the initiative. Yet the Secretary of State was unable to assuage Lindsay's fears that the rider meant that the Americans would not do anything until the world was bankrupt.[40]

The British Ambassador was not the only European upset by Congress' action. Continental newspapers bitterly reported comments made by various American politicians. U.S. legislators had given them plenty of ammunition; for example, Representative Martin Dies said:

> I am disgusted with that maudlin sentiment that is continually urging us to save Europe. It seems to me that it is high time for us to save America. For the past fifteen years we have been engaged in the business of saving Europe; we have poured billions of dollars into the treasuries of Europe and enabled them to build up their industries and agriculture at the expense of the American people.[41]

Statements like this illustrate both the force of the isolationism that would exercise such dominance over the American political scene during the later 1930's and the dilemma faced by the executive branch of the American Government caught in the middle between the position it believed in, namely that war debts and reparations must be scaled down and what Stimson termed, 'the present, irreconcilable attitude of Congress.'[42]

The President and his advisors spent the week between Christmas and New Year pondering whether a response ought to be made to the Beneduce Report (in the end deciding not to do so) and formulating the proper attitude to be taken to the forthcoming international conference on reparations scheduled to convene on 18 January in Lausanne. Lindsay, writing to the Foreign Secretary, Sir John Simon, said:

> The American year is closing in an atmosphere of unrelieved gloom in which the dark and menacing clouds are illuminated only by flashes of panic apprehension.[43]

Norman contented himself with telling Harrison that he hoped 1932 would be happier than 1931.[44] Certainly the Governor was not alone in his sentiments.

As the New Year began, the formulation of monetary policy continued to be a problem for the British. After falling to $3.82 by 29 September, the pound remained firm for the next eight weeks, aided in large part by considerable sums of gold 'unhoarded' from India both because of distress selling and as a result of the one-third increase in the rupee value of gold caused by the depreciation of sterling.[45] During that period the questions of the level at which the pound should be stabilized and whether it should be returned to a gold basis were under consideration. A related issue was who should decide and administer British monetary policy. Matters were quite different from 1918 when the Cunliffe Committee's report reflected a consensus that Britain should return to gold at the pre-war parity as soon as possible. Such unanimity of opinion made it unnecessary to delineate lines of responsibility. However, the wide divergence of opinion and belief that was apparent after 21 September, meant that the identity of the decision makers would have a great influence on the final decision.

The end of the era during which the leadership of the Bank and its allies in the City concerning currency questions was accepted almost without question was anticipated as early as 23 September when MacDonald wrote to Baldwin:

> What are we now going to aim for? A return to gold, a return to currency values, a managed currency -- we cannot be mere spectators, with the City the active agents. We must keep a controlling hand....[46]

Immediately after the departure from gold the Bank of England indeed trod cautiously because of its highly tuned instinct and out of genuine uncertainty. In response to a query from MacDonald on 28 September as to the Bank's view on general financial policy Harvey declined to suggest any definite line of policy and indeed was wary of predicting the future course of events.[47] During the next two months the debate over formal stabilization continued although for most of October it was supplanted in politicians' minds by other considerations.

The Bank had more than enough to do. It was deluged with requests from central banks who wanted their sterling losses made good by the Bank of England. The Bank of the Netherlands, whose President had lost his job because of the losses sustained on Dutch sterling deposits, was particularly adamant. The Dutch had believed that the British would never leave the gold standard until most if not all of the Bank's gold reserves were spent; that the opposite had occurred seemed to them a great betrayal.[48] The Bank of France, similarly aggrieved, felt that, having spared no effort during the battle for Britain's gold standard, it ill behoved their ertswhile allies to damage French financial interests. That the Bank of France had been rendered technically insolvent by its losses on sterling no doubt aided the eloquence with which it pleaded its cause.[49] Finally the BIS was adamant that it should not suffer any loss on its sterling holdings. McGarrah cited in support of this proposition Article X of the BIS statutes. This provided immunity for the assets of the BIS from any measure such as seizure, confiscation, prohibition or restriction of gold or currency export or import.

It was a departure from past practice for the Bank of England to discuss with the Treasury the proper answer to these petitions for the reserves in question were owned by the Bank not the Government. A decision was reached to refuse all requests save that from the BIS which, after long consideration, was made whole.[50] Simultaneously Norman, partly at the instigation of Morgan's (N.Y.), faced the question of how to accumulate the foreign exchange and/or gold to repay the central bank and Government credits. It is an understatement to say that the New York house was embarrassed and distressed over the outcome of the British crisis. In an unprecedented move, Lamont and fellow partner Charles Steele wrote Morgan on 25 September that not only had the handling of credits been badly bungled but:

> The point that we must make to you ... is to have you know fully the unfortunate position in which the New York firm has been placed before the whole world and the public generally. What the banks here, without exception, fail to understand is why this enormous credit operation should have been permitted to blow up in our faces over night so to speak.[51]

In a cable sent four days later to the London house the New York partners enlarged on these thoughts. They began by observing that the collapse of sterling after borrowing $650 m seemed to thoughtful people 'to reflect on the judgement of the British Treasury and the Bank not to mention their Bankers.' Greatly concerned that having dissipated the borrowed funds the British would be unable to accumulate the necessary monies to repay the credits, the New York partners suggested that they be given the authority to accumulate foreign currency by selling sterling whenever it reached an agreed level.[52] They expanded upon this idea on 2 October and on the same day Morgan together with Grenfell saw Norman who gave the plan his blessing.[53] However, as it was thought appropriate that the account should be under the aegis of the Treasury, final authority was not obtained until 10 October.[54] The operation was very successful and a comfortable cushion of foreign currency was accumulated before the pound began its late autumn slide.

This favourable outcome also allowed the Treasury, now under Neville Chamberlain, and the Bank increased freedom to consider the future level of the pound. Opinions varied widely: Frederick Phillips initially favoured $4.00, then shifted to $3.65 and later to $3.40. H.D. Henderson suggested $3.90 as did Hopkins at first but then he plumped for $3.60-3.70. Leith-Ross kept to $4.00-4.25 and Hawtrey and Keynes advocated $3.40. Lord Bradbury was the most daring as he speculated on the merits of $1.00.[55] Francis Rodd summed up the prevailing sentiment when he wrote to Per Jacobssen, an economist at the BIS, that while there was much to be said for finding a new parity, it was most difficult to know what that parity should be.[56] Views also varied on what attitude the British should take on the subject of international monetary cooperation. Rather than being grateful, the British appeared increasingly angry at their former allies whom they seemed to blame for the gold standard's demise. It was in this spirit that Leith-Ross asked Keynes and Henderson to prepare a memorandum on the rules of the gold standard game highlighting any American or French violations.[57] Another development was that monetary policy was increasingly regarded by the Treasury, the Bank and other interest groups not as an isolated matter but as an integral part of the government's economic policy. Thus Clay wrote to Siepmann that the pound would not recover any stability as long as the disequilibrium in world trade persisted.[58]

It was not unexpected that the pound would start falling in November when the run on the dollar had temporarily subsided. Sharing the British surprise that sterling had stayed as firm as it had (indeed speculation was rife that the British had pegged the pound), many investors decided to get out at what they perceived to be the top with the result that sterling fell to $3.23 at the beginning of December.[59] The Bank of England was in a good position at the beginning of this period, having reduced the central bank credits as of 1 November to $150 m from $250 m.[60] Yet great attention was paid to the drop in sterling's value with meetings of the Bank's Foreign Exchange Committee, meetings of the Prime Minister's Committee on Financial Questions and continuous liaison between Norman and the Treasury.[61] The decision to stand firm, neither lowering nor raising Bank rate, proved the correct one and sterling recovered to $3.40 within four weeks.

Norman's chief concern in January was to decide how to handle the central bank and Government credits. As he explained to Harrison, his alternatives were to repay both credits by using virtually the whole of the Bank's currency reserves or to repay either the central bank or the Government credits thus allowing the Bank to conserve its assets.[62] Simultaneously Morgan's (N.Y.) considered the same question and came to the not surprising conclusion that their credit should be at least partially paid down.[63] Harrison disagreed and Norman decided to follow his advice and repay the central bank credits in full on 1 February.[64] Morgan's (N.Y.) was very disturbed by this development because they had promised their participants that the British Government credits would never be used to pay down the central banks' credits yet that was precisely what appeared to have happened. Furthermore many of the bank participants were sceptical of the British Government's ability to repay the borrowings and this decision did little to assuage their fears. Lamont went to see Harrison whilst Thomas Cochran, another Morgan partner, met with Norman but, albeit with fulsome regrets, the Governor declined to alter his decision.[65]

By this time, late January 1932, it had been tacitly accepted by most influential British that there would be no return to gold in the forseeable future and this, together with other developments,

made it highly improbable that Britain would seek
new bank credits. Therefore the Bank of England and
the Government needed Morgan's (N.Y.) less than the
New York house needed them and could behave accordingly.[66] Indeed the summer of 1931 marked the
apogee of the House of Morgan's influence. In part
this resulted from the total dearth of new business
with not one foreign issue being offered in the U.S.
during the first six months of 1932.[67] Another
factor which contributed to the decline in influence
of this financial institution was the usurpation of
many of its functions by government agencies. The
Treasury and, on its behalf, the BIS increasingly
did directly what Morgan's previously did for them
indirectly. Finally, investigations and hearings
before the Senate Committee on Banking and Currency
in 1932-1933 resulted in revelations which tarnished
Morgan's reputation even though its misdeeds (no
worse than those of any other bank) were in the
domestic not the foreign sphere.

Simultaneously with the debate over the appropriate value for the pound, the Treasury devoted
considerable energy to the problem of reparations
and the interrelated issue of war debts. During
December 1931 the British and French exchanged notes
and then met in Paris in preparation for the scheduled January conference with the Germans. The
French insisted on maintaining both the framework of
the Young Plan and the French 'solde' and would not
agree to giving commercial debts priority over
reparations. The British sought to make the market
safer for commercial debts and implied that the only
way that British funds would stay in Germany was if
the reparations issue was permanently diffused.

It was at this time that the Treasury also
prepared a draft of arguments to be used to justify
a British default on war debts.[68] The British
were well aware that the French intended to stop
making payments to the U.S. if reparations were
terminated. Therefore any pressure exerted on the
French in the direction of ending reparations would
also push them towards a default on war debts.
Furthermore the French sought a united front against
the U.S. It was thus increasingly clear that the
British were going to have to choose between the
U.S. and France - indeed Chamberlain stated that:

> the first question to be decided is
> whether we work for ourselves with the
> U.S.A. or with the French. I agree that
> the attitude of the U.S.A. Chambers makes

the first impossible and therefore there is really now only one course open.[69]

With another Anglo-French meeting set for early January, the British drafted various proposals. For Leith-Ross the line had to be that Germany was not able to pay anything; if France and other countries renounced their 'soldes', the British would suspend or renounce their own claims for inter-allied debts and take the approach that all the debtors were entitled to inform the U.S. that they would cease making payments in respect of war debts.[70] As it turned out, this was exactly the approach which was taken. Unfortunately Leith-Ross' belief, shared by Sir Ronald Lindsay, that this would lead to the acquiescence by the U.S. in a further moratorium through the election period and interregnum did not come to pass, in part because the British misunderstood American psychology - the U.S. had no intention of bowing to a fait accompli presented by her ertswhile allies. That this was the case was made abundantly clear in an aide memoire prepared by Stimson on 29 December for the French Ambassador but given to Lindsay as well. The key points made by this document were:

Only after the extent of Germany's capacity or incapacity to pay has been fairly determined and the manner and extent in which the resulting sacrifice will be borne by the nations who are entitled to receive reparations is also determined, would it be possible to bring such a question before the people of this country with anything but a certainty of failure. Then and only then could it be proposed that the situation of each of the nations which have obligations to the United States be examined individually in the light of the present temporary depression and the then existing international situation both as regards themselves and as regards the United States. This historic attitude of this country in keeping the question of the debts owed to it by the Allied nations entirely separate from the reparations owed by Germany is not based upon caprice or selfishness. Having at the close of the war relinquished to its allies all claims to any participation in war reparations, whether

163

in territory or money, this country was
unwilling thereafter to permit itself to
be drawn into a situation which would
inevitably result in it being represented
as the recipient of such reparations.
Under these circumstances it is only
natural that any method of relief to
Germany which on its face would show the
American taxpayers to be paying Germany
reparations would have no possibility of
acceptance here.[71]

It was true that the Americans considered that
changes in the reparations and war debts arrangements previously entered into were appropriate but
equally they envisaged limited not total revision,
to be determined by reference both to European and
American economic and political realities. Furthermore just as the British and French felt they could
morally justify a default, the Americans believed
that they were morally entitled to at least partial
repayment. That these diametrically opposite
perceptions would inevitably cause a conflict should
have been clear to both sides but, perhaps because
the diplomats knew that they were facing irreconcilable differences, each side refused to draw the
logical conclusions from the evidence at hand until
they had no other choice.

The increasingly anti-American tendency displayed by the British did not go unnoticed in
Washington. Walter Stewart, the American representative on the Beneduce Committee, having visited the
Treasury en route home, met with Mills and Stimson
on 11 January. He reported that he found considerable sympathy at the Treasury for joining the French
against the U.S. which would make default or even
repudiation inevitable.[72] When Undersecretary of
State Castle met with Lindsay three days later,
Stewart's words were reinforced as the British
Ambassador reported that talk of repudiation was
becoming widespread in London.[73]

However the British and the Americans were
spared an immediate confrontation over war debts
because as January progressed it became increasingly
obvious that both French and German political
exigencies demanded a postponement of the Conference. As new French elections were to be held in
May and the 'Hoover Year' expired in July, the
negotiations were scheduled for June. During the
next six months Britain followed a policy intended

164

to achieve victory for her proposals at the reparations conference, while in Washington Stimson worked
to try to lessen the chances of Great Britain
'going off with a touring party with the French and
against us.' In a letter to MacDonald, the Secretary of State stressed his desire and that of the
President to increase cooperation between Anglo-
Saxons. Interestingly Stimson, not alone, thought
that Norman was in great part responsible for the
hard line the British were taking on reparations,
while in reality the Treasury's position was both
more adamant and more influential. Echoing his
department's views (which he shared), Neville Chamberlain announced in the House of Commons that the
new budget did not make provision for either war
debts or reparations, thus illustrating the perils
which lay ahead for Anglo-American friendship.[74]

This budget also revealed one of the most
innovative financial devices to come out of the
inter-war period. This was the Exchange Equilisa-
tion Account, made public on 19 April and scheduled
to begin official operations on 1 July 1932. The
brain child of Frederick Phillips, it was empowered
to cause the issuance of Treasury bills and use the
proceeds to buy foreign exchange in order to control
the value of the pound. With $167 m with which to
begin operations, the Bank, which acted as agent,
and the Treasury, under whose aegis the EEA was
placed, had ample funds for their intended purpose.[75] Clearly British monetary policy had moved
swiftly in the six months since the departure from
the gold standard; such blatant market manipulation
was clearly not within the realm of either classical
gold standard theory or the version Norman had
followed prior to September 1931. Furthermore the
establishment and operation of the EEA illustrates
the power shift which had occurred between the Bank
of England and the Treasury. No longer was the Bank
largely deciding monetary policy in splendid isola-
tion. The Treasury, having originated the scheme,
remained actively involved in its implementation.
This is not to say the Bank of England was at once
rendered powerless - far from it. Yet a change,
indeed noted by Norman in October 1931, had taken
place and the days when the Bank and its Governor
reigned supreme over sterling were no more.[76]

During the first half of 1932 another lynch pin
of British monetary policy during the 1930's was
devised: the cheap money policy. This resulted in
Bank rate, at 6% since September, being reduced in a
series of six increments to 2% on 30 June 1932. It

remained at this level until 24 August 1939. 30 June also marked the launching of the massive war debt conversion operation. A vast success, it helped ensure the permanence of the cheap money policy.

Both the creation of the EEA and the conversion operation illustrated another development which had occurred over the past nine months - the erosion of the hitherto very close relationship between Norman and Harrison. The latter was neither consulted on nor informed about the EEA until the publication of the Budget and was not told about the conversion scheme until 30 June - one day before it began.[77] This was in marked contrast to the situation a year earlier when the two men discussed such matters, including specifically a conversion operation, well in advance of fruition. The increasing distance between the two men and their respective institutions, a movement initiated by the British, was an outgrowth of the changed circumstances which now applied to the British, determined as they were not to link the pound to gold until the economic climate was far more propitious and was also reflective of the decline in importance of Norman's role which had taken place.

At this time, however, Harrison was occupied by a second gold drain which hit the U.S. at the end of May, resulting in a loss of $401 m in the two month period 1 May - 30 June 1932.[78] Interestingly, the Bank of England ascribed this in part to the British abandonment of gold which it concluded had caused the demise of the gold exchange standard.[79] The French decision taken in April to resume earmarking gold played a part in this movement as did both renewed fears that the Federal Reserve Banks, which were actively conducting open market operations, were following an inflationary policy and the failure of the White House and Capitol Hill to agree on a balanced budget.[80] Although the vast majority of gold shipments went to France and Holland, England also was a recipient of U.S. gold; the Bank of England concluding that its share of the flow indicated a widespread fear that the U.S. would soon leave the gold standard.[81] In fact, the gold drain ended by the middle of June and, after an announcement that the French had withdrawn their last gold stocks in the U.S., the dollar rose on the New York market.[82] Thus attention focused once more on Europe, Lausanne specifically, where on 16 June what would be the last conference on reparations was officially opened.

iii

The British had continued their planning for the Lausanne Conference during its six months' postponement. During that time opinion had, if anything, hardened in favour of the elimination of reparations with the Treasury singlemindedly emphasizing the need to procure a lasting settlement in June. The British were well aware that more than ever the probable quid pro quo for a French agreement on reparations would be a common approach on war debts and greeted this prospect with varying degrees of distaste.[83] The Prime Minister, for one, heartily regretted having to make common cause with the French. Returning from the Geneva Conference on disarmament which was in session during April, he recorded that he 'always felt uncomfortable with [the French]; they never seemed straight.'[84]

Stimson was also present at the Geneva Conference and MacDonald took the opportunity to discuss with him the subjects of reparations and war debts 'off the record'. The Secretary of State reiterated that no approach to the U.S. on debt revision would succeed unless prior thereto the European powers undertook an adjustment of reparations and emphasized that to him such a settlement would include German agreement to a realistic payment schedule.[85]

Lamont, while visiting Europe during the spring of 1932, was also considering the coming Conference and made the suggestion (transmitted in a letter to Grenfell) that 'our good friend E.R. Peacock' (the same Peacock who had played such a large role during the battle to save Britain's gold standard) be appointed as a delegate to Lausanne. MacDonald invited Lamont to prepare a memorandum for him on the subject of reparations and while the banker in the end decided not to send the resulting document, he did write the Prime Minister urging him to push for a settlement which would provide for an extended moratorium but fall far short of a complete termination of reparations because:

> Americans feel generally, I think, that while Germany can pay nothing today, she has by no means undertaken her share of the enormous public debt created as a result of the War and now resting, with staggering weight, on Great Britain, France, Italy and even the United States.[86]

Revelation

When Lamont returned to the U.S. at the end of
May 1932, he both met with the President and Odgen
Mills and, for the benefit of Stimson, who was not
present, sent the Secretary of State a summary of
his European impressions. Having conferred with
British Treasury representatives as well as Norman,
Lamont informed the U.S. Government that both the
Treasury and the Bank of England advocated the
complete cancellation of reparations in order to
avoid a general German moratorium on all public and
private debts, a justification which he felt was
unsound. Lamont believed that the best way to avoid
implementation of the British programme at Lausanne
was for Hoover to take a new initiative on war
debts.[87] What the banker did not realize was that
the President was far too preoccupied with domestic
problems to devote much attention to foreign
affairs.[88] Thus, as far as the American government was concerned, the Europeans would be left to
their own devices.
Prior to the opening of the formal Lausanne
Conference, the British and French delegates met for
bilateral discussions. The consistency of position
displayed by the British was not mirrored by the
French who had been affected by two major changes
since January. The first was that the May elections
had produced a leftward swing, bringing with it a
new government headed by Eduoard Herriot who was
more likely to be persuaded towards the British
position by thoughts of a Franco-German rapproache-
ment. Secondly, notwithstanding her increased gold
stocks, the French economy had significantly
deteriorated. This left the French more susceptible
to both British pressure and German siren songs of
increased economic cooperation.[89] MacDonald came
to these bilateral meetings feeling that:

it would probably be necessary for the
British Government to lay before the
Lausanne Conference its conception of how
the reparations question should be
settled, and then try to secure action .
along those lines.[90]

The plan he brought with him was, if nothing else,
very simple: the slate must be wiped clean.[91] The
British were well aware that the Americans were not
in favour of a complete cancellation of war debts
for Stimson had previously told Lindsay that only a
plan involving everyone's 'joint sacrifice' would
have a chance of convincing Congress to agree to an

adjustment of war debts.[92] But the British believed that although a breach with the U.S. over war debts would be regrettable, only a complete cancellation could avoid a European financial collapse. MacDonald, however, was worried that Stimson might have felt that he had let the Secretary down. Therefore, he contacted American diplomat Hugh Gibson to explain to him that as the situation had rapidly changed since April, the British Government had no choice but to proceed in the manner the Treasury had envisaged from the beginning.[93]

As the Republicans gathered in Chicago to renominate Hoover, the French and British met the German delegation led by the new German Chancellor, Franz von Papen. Not surprisingly he had adopted the previously announced German position that they could not pay any reparations. Thus it was left to MacDonald and the British to find a way to reconcile the still present French desire for some reparations with the hard and fast German position.

The Geneva Conference had resumed its deliberations simultaneously with the convocation of Lausanne. This not only created an opportunity for the British, especially MacDonald, to meet with the Americans, but represented a personification of the linkage in American minds between the subjects of reparations and rearmament. The President particularly believed that armaments were a much larger burden than reparations and therefore suggested on 22 June sweeping across the board arms reductions of almost one-third. He hoped that this cut would both make a reduction in war debts a suitably palatable quid pro quo for the American taxpayer and enable Europeans to effect war debts' payments with increased ease.[94]

MacDonald, for his part, pressured by his Cabinet and the French to form a common front on war debts, sought to elicit from the U.S. some reassurance on the matter. To his dismay he was told that no promises concerning American reductions of war debts would be forthcoming. Notwithstanding this MacDonald and the British forged ahead, in the belief that 'if the Europeans came to an agreement which contained a promise to bring Germany back into the full life of the world...[MacDonald] did not believe that America would say she would prevent that agreement coming into effect.'[95] After nearly two weeks' work a settlement was achieved which very nearly approximated British and German goals. Bowing to Herriot's need to bring home something tangible, the Germans agreed to make a last reparations' payment of 3 milliard RM ($714 m). But this was to take the form of German long-term bonds whose issuance was hedged with so many caveats as to make their sale problematic at best. That the British view had so completely triumphed was a formidable achievement whose future potential for enhancing the chances for an economic recovery was greeted by American enthusiasm. However, this quickly dissipated when the so-called 'Gentlemen's Agreement' among the British, French, Belgians and Italians was revealed. It declared that the Lausanne Agreement would not be ratified by the signatory powers until they themselves had reached satisfactory settlements with their own creditors.[96] Thus the Americans, who had viewed Lausanne as an idealistic contribution to world economic recovery, quickly came to the conclusion that they were being asked to foot the bill for their erstwhile allies' generosity. The result was that while Hoover did not revoke his pledge made at the time of the Hoover Moratorium to reconsider war debts on the basis of capacity to pay, he did not take any initiative on debts (as he had been urged to do by Morgan's among others) but instead had the State Department issue a statement that the American Government's position on war debts had not changed. In fact it took a substantial effort to prevent Hoover from announcing that the war debts must be paid.[97] The Gentlemen's Agreement, together with a statement by Chamberlain that the U.S. had been consulted on the reparations issue, also inflamed Senate leaders. They were irritated yet further by the text of the Anglo-French 'Accord of Confidence' which provided for the signatories to 'exchange visits with one another with complete candor concerning...any questions coming to their notice similar to that now so happily settled at Lausanne' and therefore seemingly brought an Anglo-French démarche on war debts nearer to reality. The response from Hoover was not long in coming; the President made public a letter to Senator William Borah which stated:

> While I do not assume it to be the purpose of any of these agreements to effect combined action of our debtors, if it shall be so interpreted, then I do not propose that the American people shall be pressed into any line of action or that our policies shall be in any way influ-

enced by such a combination, either open or
implied.[98]

.s Treasury Secretary Mills, in part for political
reasons (the Presidential campaign was in full
swing), urged the President to do nothing on war
debts and the Hearst Press publicized its proprie-
tor's views on 'The Debt Cancellation Conspiracy',
it was clear that little progress on this issue
could be expected until after the American Presidential election.[99]

iv

Americans and the world arose on 9 November to
the news that the Democrats had swept both the
Presidential and Congressional elections. But with
war debts' payments due on 15 December and
President-elect Franklin D. Roosevelt not scheduled
to take office until 4 March, it was clear that the
outgoing Republican administration would have to
bear the brunt of dealing with this problem. And a
problem it was certain to be. The U.S. and Britain
had worked on totally different assumptions. The
Americans believed that reparations and war debts
although related, were not mirror images of each
other. Thus Stimson (one of the most internationally minded figures in the Administration) had felt
perfectly comfortable encouraging Europeans drastically to reduce reparations without in any way
intending to imply a dollar for dollar reduction in
debts. But the debtors thought it unjust, to say
the least, that the Americans should ask them to tax
their citizens to pay the U.S. The British also
overestimated the importance to Americans of the
good will of Europe and the importance of foreign
affairs in domestic politics. They saw more desire
for compromise than there actually was, especially
given the fact that the U.S. economic upturn of the
summer months had reversed course causing the
American economy to plunge ever more steadily
downwards.[100]
A British Note on the subject of war debts was
handed to the Secretary of State promptly on 10
November. It quoted the Hoover-Laval communique of
26 October 1931 on which it was maintained, reliance
had been placed in order to reach the Lausanne
Agreement. Then the British requested a postponement of the 15 December installment and the
commencement of discussions on the whole subject.

ic to the British position as they were conscious
that the British funding agreement was the most
onerous of the nine such agreements that the U.S.
had signed and further that, as the pound was
trading at its lowest level since September 1931,
the $95 m due the U.S. would cost the British 33%
more than the comparable payment had in 1930.
Indeed the President had proposed in late October a
scheme whereby the British would receive a certain
amount of credit against their war debt obligations
for U.S. imports accepted into Britain.[101] The
ticklish problems facing the Administration were how
to aid the British without similarly aiding the
French (who few in Washington wished to excuse from
their obligations) and how to circumvent the ever
growing Congressional opposition to any compromise.[102] It was hoped that Roosevelt, who had
agreed to meet with Hoover, would cooperate to make
possible some American concessions.

Lamont was sufficiently concerned to call
Stimson in order to share his fears that a failure
to agree to a postponement of the 15 December
payment would have harmful effects on the American
and world economies. The banker did not believe
Roosevelt would take any initiative himself but
thought that, if Hoover took any action, Roosevelt
would back him.[103] In the event, Lamont's
prediction about Roosevelt's disinclination to take
any responsibility for this problem was borne out by
the meeting between Roosevelt and Hoover which took
place on 22 November. Roosevelt's understandable
reluctance to take responsibility without power and
his refusal to support Hoover's plan for a revival
of the World War Foreign Debt Commission increased
Hoover's bitterness against Roosevelt and left the
Republican lame ducks with the burden of answering
the British and other Notes. After explaining its
approach to Congressional leaders, in the process
urging that a particularly conciliatory approach be
taken towards the British, the Administration
prepared its replies. As Stimson was very sympathetic to the British, (notwithstanding differences
with Sir John Simon over Manchuria), he had already
softened the President's language. But when he
handed the American Note to Lindsay on 23 November,
the latter's shocked reaction motivated him to
soften it again. The American Note as finally
delivered stressed the fact that a Congress not in
favour of postponement had full charge of the matter
and that the executive branch could only recommend
not implement changes. Yet it held out hope for the

delivered stressed the fact that a Congress not in favour of postponement had full charge of the matter and that the executive branch could only recommend not implement changes. Yet it held out hope for the future by pointing out that the President was in favour of a country by country review of the existing debt agreements and ended by saying that the payment of the December installment would increase the chances of a satisfactory settle-ment.[104]

Lamont ascribed the unfavourable British reac-tion to the American Note in part to the way in which it was written. The three Morgan houses had been working tirelessly to try to avoid a breach between the U.S., Britain and France. The partners in New York and London discussed developments daily, with each side trying to explain its government's stand and smooth ruffled feathers. But their intervention had only limited effect not least because in Britain it became clear that Whitehall wished to handle the problem by itself.[105]

While the Americans attempted to help the British find a compromise, MacDonald endeavoured to limit cooperation with the French. Much depended on American reaction to the British Note delivered to Stimson on 1 December. It emphasized the negative effect on the world economic situation any payment would have and added that if payment were to be made, it would be done by means of a shipment of gold thus emphasizing the sacrifice which such a payment would entail.[106] Interestingly, the British Ambassador advised Stimson in person on 1 December that his Government was concerned about the possible ramifications if Britain and France received different treatment.[107] Obviously francophile elements in the Foreign Office had become concerned at jeopardising the seemingly closer Anglo-French relationship. The question which remains is whether Britain could have achieved a better settlement by taking an independent approach towards the U.S. The answer is that in all probability a solitary initiative would have been fruitless because of the adamant Congressional opposition to debt revision exacerbated by the lame duck status of Hoover and Stimson. Therefore the decision to balance between the Americans and the French, attempting to alienate both as little as possible, was the correct one under the circum-stances.

At the same meeting, Lindsay also raised what Stimson labelled a British proposal to postpone the

capital portion of the installment ($30m) and pay
the interest portion ($65m) by means of serial
bonds.[108] According to MacDonald this idea was
first mooted by Norman who had been secretly contacted by Ogden Mills. Yet as archival sources
do not reflect any such Mills approach it may well
be that Norman had once again put his words into the
mouths of others. The Americans were receptive to
the British proposal but emphasized that the bonds
must be marketable, a caveat which the Foreign
Office rejected.[109] During the next five days the
two sides attempted to find some room for manoeuvre.
MacDonald was clearly dismayed at the breach between
the Americans and the British, telling American
diplomat Norman Davis that:

> the question which had been nearest his
> heart and for which he had worked hardest
> was the maintenance of the closest friend-
> ship and understanding between the United
> States and England ... and now he sees the
> danger of the success of his efforts being
> thwarted by an unfortunate and unjustifia-
> ble ill feeling and misunderstanding
> developing over this question of debts.

Yet notwithstanding MacDonald's genuine regret
at the situation, the gulf between the U.S. and
various European powers was bound to widen because,
as Davis perceptively noted:

> [the Europeans] have so completely per-
> suaded themselves that we have a moral
> obligation to be most lenient, that they
> overlook their own obligations as well as
> our rights and political difficulties and
> feel resentful over our reluctance to
> extend December 15 payments.[110]

The problem was that, as the two sides looked
at the war debts' issue from different ends of a
telescope, they understandably saw different images.
Looking at war debts as an independent or quasi-
independent contractual obligation justified an
attitude quite removed from viewing them as part of
a system which by definition encompassed reparations
as well.
As the British and French met in Paris to
discuss the situation, the Americans worked on a
reply to the British Note. Delivered on 8 December
and more conciliatory than previous notes, it con-

tained an offer to cooperate with Great Britain in a reexamination of the whole situation, always assuming the British would pay the 15 December installment. Thus the British now had to choose whether to make the required payment. On 12 December the decision was revealed; the British offered to tender the payment in gold on condition that it was regarded not as a resumption of the annual payments contemplated by the original funding agreement but as a capital payment to be taken into account when a new, final settlement was entered into. The Americans were very annoyed at what they viewed as an 'inept and clumsy' statement and immediately shot back a reply to the effect that the U.S. Government had no authority to accept a conditional payment.[111] Notwithstanding the British reservation, the Americans did accept the $95m gold tendered by the British through the Bank of England and FRBNY on 15 December. Stimson, looking back at the previous six weeks of negotiations, felt that Hoover should have shown more magnanimity and proposed an extension of the Moratorium irrespective of whether Congress would have passed it. To the Secretary of State the most heroic leader was Herriot who, having staked his office on his decision that France should make its payment, had lost.[112]

Although Hoover could have easily left the debt question alone, with Stimson's total support he now proposed to select an executive commission which would reexamine the war debts of countries which had made the 15 December payments.[113] Hoover further hoped that Roosevelt would not only support this suggestion but help select the Commission members. But Roosevelt declined to do either and his negative response put paid to any new initiative in 1932.[114] By June 1933, when the next installment was due, other events had worked to widen further the divide between the British and the Americans.

NOTES

1. The New York Times, 21 September 1931, p. 1.
2. Morgan Papers, O.D. Young to Morgan, 21 September 1931.
3. The Times, 21 September 1931, p. 13.
4. PRO, T175/56, Siepmann Memorandum, 23 September 1931.
5. B/E, G3/198, Norman to N. Rygg (President, Central Bank of Norway), 28 September 1931, Norman

to I. Rooth, (Governor, Central Bank of Sweden), 28 September 1931; see also G3/210, Harvey to heads of various central banks, 28 September 1931.

6.   Due to the floating value of the pound, pound/dollar equivalents will no longer be given.

7.   W. Lippmann et al., The United States in World Affairs - 1932 (Harper & Brothers, New York, 1933), p. 110.

8.   Harrison Papers, Binders 29, Lacour-Gayet to Harrison, 154, 21 September 1931.

9.   Harrison Papers, Binder 2, Memorandum of Executive Committee, 'Guarantee of Foreign Bank Deposits with this Bank', 28 September 1931; McGarrah to Harrison, 565, 1 October 1931; Harrison to McGarrah, 406, 2 October 1931.

10.   FRBNY, 'Gold Movements 1931'.

11.   Harrison Papers, Binder 59, Memorandum concerning telephone conversation with Norman and Harvey, 2 October 1931; HHPL, Presidential Papers - FA-F, Dawes to Stimson, 394, 2 October 1931; Castle Papers, Castle to Mills, 29 October 1931; Morgan Grenfell, JPM Miscellaneous 18/1, Leffingwell to Cochran, 21/2544, 9 October 1931.

12.   NA, RG59, 841.51/1076, A. Halstead, 'Probable Future Monetary Policy of Great Britain,' 29 February 1932.

13.   The severing of the pound from the gold standard also had the effect of freeing Britain from the need to cooperate on monetary matters with the French as well as with the Americans.

14.   C. Mowat, Britain Between the Wars 1918-1940 (Beacon Press, Boston, 1955), pp. 406-12.

15.   For an interesting account of the origins and background of the Hoover-Laval meeting see HHPL, Post Pres. Ind. - Stimson, H.L., Hoover to Stimson, 9 November 1943.

16.   The New York Times, 9 October 1931, p. 1.

17.   Whaley - Eaton Service, 'Foreign Letter No. 651', 5 October 1931.

18.   Stimson Diaries, Reel 3, Vol. 18, 29 September 1931.

19.   Stimson Diaries, Reel 3, Vol. 18, 5 October 1931; Morgan Grenfell, JPM Miscellaneous 18/1, Morgan's (N.Y.) to Morgan Grenfell, 31/2530, 8 October 1931.

20.   Morgan Grenfell, JPM Miscellaneous 18/1, Morgan's (N.Y.) to T. Cochran, 31/2544, 9 October 1931.

21.   The New York Times, 11 October 1931, p. 1.

22.   Stimson Diaries, Reel 3, Vol. 18, 13 October 1931.

23. Morgan Grenfell, JPM Miscellaneous 18/1, Morgan's (N.Y.) to Morgan Grenfell, 31/2571, 17 October 1931; HHPL, Pres. - Special Subjects - Financial Matters, Gold and Silver, Dawes to Stimson, 19 October 1931.

24. HHPL, Presidential Individuals - Lamont, T.W., Lamont, 'Memorandum for the President Concerning Laval Visit', 20 October 1931.

25. HHPL, Presidential Papers - FA-F, Edge to Stimson, 673, 21 October 1931.

26. Stimson Diaries, Reel 3, Vol. 18, 23 October 1931.

27. NA, RG 59, H/DP 033.51 Laval, Pierre/217, Memorandum, 20 October 1931, of Exchange of Views at Meeting in FRBNY, 19 October 1931, 462.00/R 296A/1, Stimson to Sackett, 27 October 1931; Stimson Diaries, Reel 3, Vol. 18, 23 October 1931; H.L. Stimson and M. Bundy, On Active Service in Peace and War (Harper & Brothers, New York, 1947), pp. 207-11.

28. B/E, OV 34/81, Siepmann Memorandum concerning telephone conversation with Dr. Vocke, 1 October 1931.

29. PRO, T160/438, J.B. Pease and W.H.N. Goschen to Norman, 10 November 1931, Leith-Ross to Hopkins, 9 December 1931.

30. NA, RG 59, 462.00/R 296A/29, Atherton to Stimson, 19 November 1931.

31. B/E, OV 34/112, British Treasury Memorandum, 'German Reparations,' 15 November 1931.

32. Cmd 3995, Report of the Special Advisory Committee Convened Under the Agreement with Germany Concluded at the House on 20 January 1930, quoted in James, op. cit, p. 229. (The Committee was known as the Beneduce Committee after its Chairman, Italian Alberto Beneduce).

33. For example, total farm income had declined 25% in the year ended December 1931, 2298 banks failed during 1931 and monetary circulation between August and December increased by $664 m which provided evidence for the existence of extensive hoarding.

34. NA, RG 59, 462.00/R 296/5350, L. McFadden to Stimson, 12 December 1931, RG 59, 462.00/R 296/354, Castle Memorandum of Conversation with Lindsay, 11 December 1931.

35. Stimson Diaries, Reel 4, Vol. 19, 16 December 1931; Stimson Papers, Reel 82, Stimson to J.W. Collier, (Chairman, House Ways and Means Committee), 16 December 1931.

36. Stimson Diaries, Reel 4, Vol. 19, 17 December 1931.

37. HHPL, Presidential Papers - FA-F, Dawes to Stimson, 463, 16 December 1931; Memorandum of Telephone Conversation between Stimson and Harrison, 17 December 1931.

38. HHPL, Presidential Papers - FA-F, Stimson to Dawes, 341, 18 December 1931.

39. Lippman, op. cit., p. 12.

40. HHPL, Presidential Papers - FA-F, Memorandum Concerning Conversation between Stimson and Sir R. Lindsay, 24 December 1931.

41. Morgan Grenfell, War Debts Moratorium 1, Morgan's (N.Y.) to Morgan Grenfell, 31/2779, 29 December 1931; Lippmann, op. cit., p. 9. Dies was later to win notoriety as the instigator of the House Un-American Activities Subcommittee.

42. Stimson Diaries, Reel 4, Vol. 19, 26 December 1931.

43. B/E, OV31/21, Lindsay to Sir J. Simon, 31 December 1931.

44. FRBNY, C261.1, 3/32, Norman to Harrison, 4 January 1932.

45. See, e.g., B/E, OV56/1, R.M. Kershaw, 'Export of Gold From India', 23 December 1931, Memorandum, unsigned, 31 December 1931.

46. Baldwin Papers, Vol. 44, MacDonald to Baldwin, 23 September 1931.

47. B/E, G3/210, Harvey to MacDonald, 28 September 1931.

48. NA, RG 59, 841.51/996, Swenson (Ambassador to Netherlands) to Stimson, 23 September 1931; PRO, T160/429, L.J.A. Trip (Governor, Bank of the Netherlands) to Norman, 27 October 1931.

49. PRO, T188/21, Moret to Flandin, cc. Leith-Ross, 6 October 1931; B/E, OV 45/5, R. Warren, 'The French Balances', 30 November 1931.

50. NA, RG39, Box 104, Cochran to Castle, 24 September 1931; PRO T175/56, Hopkins Memorandum concerning BIS sterling balances, 9 December 1931.

51. Lamont Papers, 108-16, Lamont and C. Steele to Morgan, 25 September 1931.

52. Morgan Grenfell, BG Credit 1931, Morgan's (N.Y.) to J.P. Morgan, 31/2491, 29 September 1931.

53. Morgan Papers, Morgan's (N.Y.) to J.P. Morgan, 31/2509, 2 October 1931; B/E, ADM 20/20, Norman Diaries, 2 October 1931.

54. Morgan Papers, Morgan to Morgan's (N.Y.), 31/5079, 3 October 1931.

55. Howson, p. 84; Churchill College, Cambridge University, Cambridge, R.G. Hawtrey Papers 1/48, Hawtrey to Hopkins, 'Pegging the Pound', 25 September 1931; PRO, T188/28, Henderson to Leith-

Ross, 25 September 1931; PRO T175/56, Siepmann Memorandum of a conversation between Siepmann and Lord Bradbury, 24 September 1931.

56. B/E, OV4/105, Rodd to P. Jacobssen, 19 December 1931.

57. PRO, T188/28, Leith-Ross to Keynes and H.D. Henderson, 13 October 1931.

58. B/E, SMT 5/3, Clay to Siepmann, 30 September 1931.

59. NA, RG59, 841.51/997, Dawes to Stimson, 5 October 1931.

60. FRBNY, C261.1, Harvey to Harrison, 544/31, 28 October 1931.

61. The existence of the Prime Minister's Committee greatly irritated Norman who considered that it represented a threat to his power. See B/E, Colleagues Si-T, J. Stamp to Norman, 3 December 1931.

62. FRBNY, C261.1, Norman to Harrison, 3/32, 4 January 1932.

63. Morgan Grenfell, BG Credit 1931, Morgan's (N.Y.) to Cochran, c.c. Morgan et Cie, 70.67, 332, 7 January 1932.

64. FRBNY, C261.1, Harrison to Norman, 16/32, 15 January 1932.

65. Morgan Grenfell, BG Credit 1931, Morgan Grenfell to Morgan's (N.Y.) 32/4529, 19 January 1932, Morgan's (N.Y.) to Morgan Grenfell, 32/2035, 22 January 1932.

66. The British Government credits were paid back as follows: The American credit was repaid $150 m on 4 March, $30 m on 29 March and $20 m on 5 April 1932. The French credit was repaid in increments between 6 February and 9 March 1932 and the French public issue was paid off at maturity on 7 September 1932.

67. Lippmann, op. cit., p. 78.

68. B/E, OV34/112, Treasury Memorandum, 'German Reparations and War Debts: February 1932', 15 February 1932.

69. PRO, T160/450, Chamberlain to Leith-Ross, 12 December 1931; T160/450, Leith-Ross to Chamberlain, 20 December 1931.

70. PRO, T160/450, Leith-Ross to Fisher and Chamberlain, 28 December 1931; Documents On British Foreign Policy, Series III, No. 3, Lindsay to Simon, 767, 29 December 1931.

71. NA, RG 59, 462.00/R 296 A1/1, Stimson Aide Memoire, 29 December 1931.

72. NA, RG 59, 800.51 W89 Great Britain/281-1/2, P.D. Boal Memorandum, 11 January 1932.

73. NA, RG 59, 462.00/R296/5448, Castle Memorandum concerning conversation with the British Ambassador, 14 January 1932.

74. Stimson Diaries, Reel 4, Vol. 20, 24 January 1932; Stimson Papers, Reel 82, Stimson to MacDonald, 27 January 1932; NA, RG 59, 841.51/1089, Atherton to Stimson, 20 April 1932.

75. Howson, op. cit., p. 87; Sayers, pp. 425-30.

76. B/E, MB 53, C/T Minutes, 7 October 1931.

77. Harrison Papers, Binder 21, Harrison to Norman, 148/32, 21 April 1932, Binder 46, Harrison Memorandum concerning telephone conversation with Norman, 29 June 1932, Harrison Memorandum concerning telephone conversation with Norman, 30 June 1932.

78. B/E, OV/32, Harvey to Harrison, 195/32, 31 May 1932; Lippman, op. cit., pp. 113-22.

79. B/E, OV 31/21, Memorandum, 'Gold Withdrawals From the United States', 30 July 1932.

80. Harrison Papers, Binder 69, Crane Memorandum concerning telephone conversation with Lacour-Gayet, 21 April 1932; Lippmann, op. cit., pp. 115-21.

81. Harrison Papers, Binder 60, Harrison Memorandum, 2 June 1932, concerning telephone conversation with Harvey, 30 May 1932; Harrison to Fancher, 8 June 1932.

82. The New York Times, 15 June 1932, p. 1.

83. See, e.g., PRO, T188/42, Note, 29 April 1932, of Meeting held in the Prime Minister's Room at the Hotel Beau Rivage, 29 April 1932; T160/440/F12800/01, Simon Note on Reparations Policy, 31 May 1932.

84. PRO 30/69/1753, MacDonald Diaries, 1 May 1932.

85. Stimson Diaries, Reel 4, Vol. 21, 29 April 1932.

86. Morgan Grenfell, War Debts Moratorium 1, Lamont to Grenfell, 13 May 1932, Lamont to MacDonald, 13 May 1932.

87. NA, RG 59, 462.00/R296 A1/154 1/2, Lamont to Stimson, 23 May 1932.,

88. Stimson Diaries, Reel 4, Vol. 22, 17 May and 30 May 1932.

89. For a discussion of German strategy at Lausanne, see James, op. cit., pp. 245-51.

90. NA, RG 59, 462.00/R296/5649, Mellon to Stimson, 13 May 1932.

91. DBFP, op. cit., No. 134, 'Notes of Meeting Held at the British Embassy, Paris,' 11 June 1932.

92. Stimson Diaries, Reel 4, Vol. 22, 31 May 1932; DBFP, op. cit., No. 117, Lindsay to Simon, 246, 1 June 1932.

93. NA, RG 59, 462.00/R296/1124, Gibson to Stimson, 14 June 1932.

94. The New York Times, 23 June 1932 p. 1., Stimson Diaries, Reel 4, Vol. 22, 19 June 1932.

95. NA, RG 59, 462.00/R 296 A1/179, Gibson to Stimson, 20 June 1932, DBFP, op. cit., No. 152, 'Meeting Among Representatives of Great Britain, France and Germany,' 29 June 1932.

96. Cmd. 3993, Final Act of the Lausanne Conference, 9 July 1932.

97. Morgan Grenfell, War Debts Moratorium 1, Leffingwell to Lamont, 32/4755, 27 June 1932; Stimson Diaries, Reel 4, Vol. 22, 28 June 1932; The New York Times, 10 July 1932.

98. Stimson Diaries, Reel 4, Vol. 23., 11 July, 13 July and 14 July 1932; PRO, T160/441, Lindsay to Foreign Office, 14 July 1932, T160/441/ F128108, Lindsay to Foreign Office, 13 July 1932; NA, RG 59, 462.00/R 296 A1/1248, Stimson Memorandum of Conversation with Lindsay, 14 July 1932; The New York Times, 12 July 1932, p. 1., 14 July 1932, p. 1., 15 July 1932, p. 1.

99. Stimson Diaries, Reel 4, Vol. 23, 17 July 1932; The New York American, 17 July 1932.

100. See, e.g., The Times, 7 November 1932, p. 15.

101. NA, RG 59, 800.51 W89 Great Britain/336, Stimson Memorandum, 10 November 1932, concerning conversation with Lindsay; RG59, 800.51 W89 Great Britain/ 338, Hoover to Stimson, 13 November 1932; RG59, 800.51 W89 Great Britain/336-1/2, Memorandum concerning telephone conversation among Stimson, Mills and Mellon, 31 October 1932; Stimson Diaries, Reel, 5, Vol. 24, 13 November, and 18 November 1932.

102. The New York Times, 15 November 1932, p. 1, 17 November 1932, p. 1.

103. NA, RG 59, 800.51 W89 Great Britain/588-1/2, Stimson Memorandum concerning telephone conversation with Lamont, 17 November 1932.

104. Stimson Diaries, Reel 5, Vol. 24, 23 November 1932; NA, RG 59, 800.51 W89 Great Britain/ 352, United States No. 3 (1932) Note to Great Britain, 23 November 1932.

105. Morgan Grenfell, War Debts Moratorium, Grenfell to A.J.H. Smith, 23 November 1932; See, e.g., Series of letters and memoranda between Morgan's (N.Y.) and Morgan Grenfell, 21 November to 2 December 1932; B/E, ADM 20/21, Norman Diaries, 30

November 1932, 1 December, 3 December, and 5 December 1932; Stimson Diaries, Reel 5, Vol. 24, 28 November 1932.

106. PRO 30/69/1753, MacDonald Diaries, 27 November 1932; Cmd. 4210, United States No. 4, 'Further Note Addressed to the United States Government', 1 December 1932.

107. NA, RG 59, 800.51 W89 Great Britain/361, Stimson Memorandum, 2 December 1932, concerning conversation with Lindsay, 1 December 1932.

108. The original funding agreement provided that Britain could upon delivery of appropriate notice obtain a postponement of the principal portion of the payment due. Although the notice period had long passed, the Americans acted as if the British had not waived this right.

109. PRO 30/69/1753, MacDonald Diaries, 27 November 1932; T188/41, F.O. to Lindsay, 2 December 1932; Stimson Diaries, 1 December, 2 December, and 3 December 1932; NA, RG 59, 800.51 W/89 Great Britain/362, Stimson Memorandum, 3 December 1932, concerning conversation with Lindsay, 2 December 1932.

110. NA, RG 59, 800.51 W89 Great Britain/347, Davis to Stimson, 4 December 1932.

111. The New York Times, 9 December 1932, p. 1; Stimson Diaries, Reel 5, Vol. 24, 11 December 1932; NA, RG 59, 800.51 W89 Great Britain/365, Stimson Memorandum, 12 December 1932, concerning conversation with Lindsay, 11 December 1932; RG 59, 800.51 W89 Great Britain/1369, Stimson Memorandum, 12 December 1932, concerning conversation with Lindsay, 12 December 1932.

112. Stimson Diaries, Reel 4, Vol. 24, 15 December 1932. Herriot's government was defeated on 15 December over the question of the payment of the war debt installment. However, in the words of one recent work on the subject, 'if he had not fallen honourably on the debt, he would have fallen dishonourably on the budget.' J. Jackson, The Politics of Depression in France: 1932-1936 (Cambridge University Press, Cambridge, 1985), p. 62.

113. The American Government intended both that Britain be the principal beneficiary of this proposal and that France and Belgium, neither of whom had tendered payments, not benefit at all.

114. The New York Times, 20 December 1932, p. 1, 21 December 1932, p. 1, 23 December 1932, p. 1.

CONCLUSION

BUT WHAT GOOD CAME OF IT?

> 'Your leadership in mone-
> tary reconstruction gave
> the world the best chance
> it had after the First
> World War for peace and law
> and order.'
>
> Russell Leffingwell to
> Montagu Norman
> 19 April 1944

Having unaccustomed free time during the Second World War, Russell Leffingwell and Montagu Norman corresponded regularly. Their letters were in large part devoted to reminiscences of that brief era spanning the fifteen years between 1918 and 1933 when central bankers and their merchant bank allies played a major part in the rehabilitation and running of the world's monetary systems. Not surprisingly both men believed that their cause had been a just one. They had sought to establish a system of global monetary stability and, as Leffing-well said: 'it was well worthwhile for both of us to keep our promises.'[1] Knowing that their views were out of favour, Leffingwell and Norman hoped that in the future more dispassionate assessments of the inter-war period would bring the vindication of both their underlying philosophy and subsequent actions. It is not the historian's role to convict or to exculpate: a distanced examination of the fight for the British gold standard has been the goal of this monograph. Having described the campaign in some detail, it is now possible to attempt to answer the questions set forth in the Introduction; were the tactics used during the last phase of the battle the correct ones, what was the effect on Britain of the loss of the battle; and finally, little Peterkin's query - what was the use of it, anyway?

i

There is no question that severe underlying problems caused the guardians of the pound's stabil-ity ever-increasing difficulties from the moment sterling was returned to the gold standard in April 1925. Already feeling the effects of Britain's declining industrial position, the nation's economy was hit by the global economic depression. This contributed to the further deterioration of the British balance of payments and caused other countries to seek ever greater liquidity, a quest bound to damage London's financial standing. Yet the existence of these and other contributory causes did not necessarily ensure that defeat would come when and in the way it did. That September 1931 marked the end of Britain's battle for the gold standard owed much to the uniquely unfavourable circumstances of 1931, chief among them the economic collapse of Central Europe, but its ending was also affected by the tactics used during the final campaign.

The key weapon used in the battle was the war chest of £130 m ($650 m) raised by borrowings in the U.S. and in France. This represented a turning away from the classic gold standard defensive weapons of rises in Bank rate combined with the sale of gold. Was the Bank of England correct to renounce the use of these traditional weapons? The answer is that while their use might have made a difference, it would have been difficult for the Bank, given the domestic and foreign pressures present during the summer of 1931, particularly during August, to have made full use of Bank rate or to have allowed gold to leave Great Britain.

The Americans and the French were adamantly opposed to a rise in Bank rate and/or a loss of gold. The British knew they needed allies both to provide credits and to form a united front behind which to fight off the attack. Needing these allies, the British had little choice but to take their advice which was motivated by Harrison and Moret's belief that given the prevailing investment climate either a large rise in Bank rate or a loss of gold would be interpreted as a sign of panic. To have ignored the counsel of the FRBNY and the Bank of France would have been difficult and impolitic for the Bank of England, whose room to manoeuvre was further limited by the lack of domestic support for the drastic Bank rate rises coupled with exchange controls which possibly might have stemmed the tide of sterling. With investors already discounting the pound, a Bank rate approaching German levels during June and July (i.e., 8-15%) would have been necessary to have been effective. Yet this was simply not a viable option. With business already very depressed, neither management nor labour nor their representatives in Parliament were willing to pay the price which such a high Bank rate would exact.

Although the return to gold was largely welcomed and most influential British supported the struggle in July and August, a consensus in favour of making major sacrifices for this battle of Britain did not exist. Yet without such a consensus or, in the alternative, a dictatorial regime which could render public opinion largely irrelevant, a drastic program on the scale necessary to be effective could not be mounted.

This being said, three points need to be made. First during July Norman clearly acted in a manner ill-calculated to achieve victory. Suffering badly from battle fatigue, the Governor projected a negative attitude at the worst possible moment. Perception plays a very large part in financial affairs and Norman's panicked attitude, particularly during the height of the German crisis, encouraged speculators to pounce and investors to flee the pound at a time when, notwithstanding the Macmillan and May Reports, they could well have first turned their attention to the U.S. whose budget deficit and German exposure both exceeded that of the British. Indeed in September and October the U.S. faced a gold drain larger in amount than that suffered by Britain during the summer. Second, both Harrison and Morgan's (N.Y.) criticized the British handling of the credits because they believed that the obvious pegging of sterling simply encouraged speculators to sell the pound while they were assured of receiving the highest possible rate. These criticisms were probably right in that holding the pound at the gold point rather than at or close to parity might actually have encouraged those with sterling deposits to adopt a wait and see attitude. Such a tactic might have proved beneficial because time could have been on Britain's side. With the U.S. financial position deteriorating, and given that foreign dollar holdings exceeded foreign sterling holdings, it would not necessarily have taken Britain's departure from the gold standard for the speculative fever to leap across the Atlantic. But by the middle of September the British will to continue to fight had been lost. Having been under constant strain for years, Norman and his colleagues had concluded that the battle was futile. This attitude made a continuance of the fight unlikely, though Harrison suggested it on 19 September as did Morgan's (N.Y.) the next day, particularly since it would probably have been necessary to use gold as ammunition.

But What Good Came of It?

This leads to the third point. The British reluctance to use gold was initially a response to external pressure; by early September this was no longer the case. Yet the British never let gold go in the quantities many contemporaries expected, and later commentators regretted this.[2] The explanation may well have to do with the increasingly defeatist tone exhibited from mid-August by certain officials at the Bank of England. Whether out of increasing xenophobia, expressed in a desire to allow the U.S. and France to wither away behind their gold barricades, or out of a sense of futility, men like Henry Clay, H.A. Siepmann and Francis Rodd appeared increasingly less wedded to the gold standard. Assuming that their attitude was shared by more senior officials at the Bank and elsewhere, it was quite sensible to spend French and American funds while retaining the British gold reserves not least because, if Britain went off the gold standard, it would be very difficult to accumulate comparable ones. This was not quite in the spirit that Norman and the Bank of England had been projecting for the past thirteen years but, at a transitional time when international monetary cooperation was breaking down, and when the British believed that it was the violation of the rules of the gold standard game by others which had greatly contributed to if not largely caused their problems, it was not a wholly unexpected attitude to take.

That Britain did not remain on the gold standard while simultaneously devaluing the pound was in part due to the increasing acceptance by influential British opinion of the respectability and even desirability of a British departure from the gold standard. Nevertheless, several other factors were probably more important. Given the German inflation of 1919-1923, there was a real fear that any change in the gold value of the pound would inexorably lead to a series of drastic devaluations. Consequently there was an overwhelming reluctance to take the responsibility for such a decision. Contributing to this attitude was a total lack of consensus - indeed even of prior consideration as to what level was appropriate for the pound in such an event.

Another important cause was the consistent inclination of the Bank of England and its various allies when faced with a threat to sterling to opt for cuts in government spending rather then devaluation. This was the result of several factors. That most bankers were philosophically opposed to in-

186

creased government spending, especially for social service benefits, played a large part. A related motivation was the honest belief of most bankers that unbalanced budgets both verged on the immoral (it being wrong to live beyond one's means) and were indicative of an untrustworthy hence uncreditworthy borrower. Thus not only did they exert themselves to prevent such an eventuality but Morgan's and other merchant bankers would not participate in support operations if they thought their purpose was to obviate the need for budget cuts. Also, the Bank of England took its role as the guardian of the gold standard very seriously. Therefore opting for devaluation when there was any alternative would have seemed a derogation of duty.

Finally making an unmistakable choice to leave the gold standard would have been psychologically very difficult for those in authority in 1931. As we shall see it was easier to wait until the decision, for that is what it was, could be portrayed by those who made it both to themselves and to others as an inevitability thrust upon Great Britain by forces beyond her control.

ii

The loss of the battle for the gold standard had consequences both expected and unexpected for Great Britain. In the international sphere, the British decision to go their own way put paid to Norman's theories of international monetary cooperation. Furthermore, on all sides the dénouement of the crisis produced bitterness and ill feeling. Whether out of guilt, a new found freedom, or from justifiable anger at French and American gold sterilization, the British were increasingly anti-American and anti-French. For their part the French were surprised by the sudden British surrender and aghast at the huge losses they had sustained in connection with the defense of sterling. The U.S. was deeply troubled over the gold drain affecting New York after 21 September and also by Britain's increasingly isolationist approach to monetary affairs. The result was the triumph of competition over cooperation. Increasingly an attitude of autarchy dominated the sphere of international monetary relations.

The domestic effects of the British departure from the gold standard were rather more unexpected. Even as astute an observer as Keynes believed at the end of August that the British public would not

favour devaluation.[3]   In the event, the fear of
leaving the gold standard proved far worse than the
actuality which, in certain respects, was liber-
ating.[4]   The burden of protecting the gold
standard appeared to have had an inhibiting effect
on British financial and economic policies.   The
absence of a gold standard contributed to the
innovative financial policies of the 1930's such as
the establishment of the Exchange Equalisation
Account and the provision of cheap money.[5]   Two
factors were chiefly responsible for this.   The
first was that Britain's departure from the gold
standard was successfully portrayed as a bowing to
the inevitable which left the British without any
guilt over what they had done.   In contemporary
documents one reads that Britain was 'forced' to
leave or was 'pushed off' the gold standard.   This
was simply not true.   Although it can be argued that
the result was foredoomed, its manner and timing
were not.   By choosing to portray the demise of the
gold standard in this fashion, the British were
freed from the psychological burden of having taken
what might otherwise have appeared as the coward's
path.
     The second factor was that by their actions the
British partially succeeded in destroying the
international nature of the gold standard.   With
virtually the whole of the British Empire and the
Scandinavian countries off the gold standard within
a matter of weeks after the British decision, the
gold standard in the traditionally accepted sense no
longer existed.   Furthermore, this string of devaluations meant that the British devaluation did not
have the usual effect of a full scale increase in
the cost of British imports.   The development of the
sterling bloc subsequently served many of the same
purposes as the gold standard and at first proved
easier for Britain to live with.
     The departure from gold also had a significant
effect on the administration of Britain's economic
and financial affairs.   It caused a major decline in
the power of the Bank of England.   Having wrested
back control over monetary matters after the Treasury's encroachments during the First World War,
Norman's reign as chief arbiter of the pound's fate
lasted a mere eleven years.   It would be an exaggeration to say that the events of September 1931 were
solely responsible for this change but the battle
and subsequent defeat certainly accelerated the
process.   It left the Cabinet and the Treasury
determined to have an increased voice in determining

188

currency matters. Their attitude was partly the
result of a not unreasonable feeling that the Bank
of England had failed to live up to its reputation.
There was also a growing realization, prompted by
the fall of the Labour Government, that not only was
Norman's portrayal of currency questions as an
objective and apolitical science untrue but, by
abdicating jurisdiction over monetary affairs, the
Government was necessarily surrendering a great deal
of power in other spheres. Finally, by admitting in
July 1931 that the German crisis was too big for
central banks to handle, Norman himself contributed
to the diminution of his power. The Governor's
request for limited Government intervention in
financial affairs led to the exacerbation of an
already unstable situation in which the authority
over monetary matters was increasingly split between
the Bank of England and the Government. It could
not last; that the result was an increase in government power at the expense of the Bank of England is
not surprising in a century which has seen a
general, massive enlargement of governmental power.
In this, as in so many other things, Britain was
first off the mark. In both the U.S. and France the
departure from the gold standard brought with it the
demise of the independent power previously exercised
by the FRBNY and the Bank of France, respectively.
The bankers had fallen short of their own or their
countries' expectations and it was now the turn of
others.

iii

The final issue simply put is: was there a
point to a battle that cost Great Britain much pain
and suffering and within a relatively short time
proved to be futile? To answer this question, one
must examine the facts without looking backwards.
Remembering how the world financial situation
appeared in the aftermath of the First World War,
the British response made great sense. It was
increasingly clear that the exports on which Britain
had relied for her financial supremacy no longer
produced the income they had before 1914. It then
followed that invisible exports must be protected
and encouraged to grow. The best way to do this
seemed to be to return the pound to gold at the rate
which would produce the maximum confidence and
certainty; that is, at the pre-war dollar parity,
notwithstanding the possibility of inflicting some
hardship on the British economy for a transitional

189

period. In so doing the Bank of England and the
British Government heeded not only their financial
experts and representatives of industry but also the
pleas of most other countries. As it happened the
period of adjustment never ended, not least because
Britain was to be the only European country to re-
establish pre-war parity and also because almost all
the predictions made prior to 1925 about the future
course of monetary affairs proved wrong. But as it
would have taken extraordinary prescience to anticipate the unprecedented financial events of this
period, it may be said that the path taken in 1925
was far more sensible than would appear later.

Moreover, the decision to return to gold, which
was, after all, made right after the war's end, was
a product of its time, reflecting two important
intellectual currents present in 1918-1920. The
first of these was the desire to set the clock back,
ignoring the fact that the First World War had
produced major structural alterations in global
financial relationships. With this as a goal the
only possible course of action was to return Britain
to gold at its previous parity. Connected with this
response was the belief that the ghastly conflict
had to have a purpose; hence the slogan 'the War to
end all Wars.' While no one would have claimed that
British soldiers died to protect $4.86 5/8, a
failure to return to it could have seemed to have
been in a sense a negation of their sacrifice.

Second, Montagu Norman's determination to
return Britain to the gold standard and his
proselytizing approach to international monetary
cooperation and to the gold standard as a global
goal reveals him as a spiritual comrade of Woodrow
Wilson. Just as the American President believed
that the League of Nations would end future
conflicts, Norman believed that the adherence to the
gold standard by independent, apolitical central
banks would ensure world financial stability. His
goal of international financial cooperation built
upon the gold standard was a laudable one. That it
was not attained does not make the attempt any less
worthwhile.

One may fault the Bank and the Government for
unquestioningly accepting the return to gold itself,
particularly given our experience of floating
exchange rates. Unfortunately a smoothly func-
tioning system such as the pre-war international
gold standard is rarely questioned; thus the battle
for Britain's gold standard had to be fought and
lost before its raison d'être could be transformed
from an assumption to a debatable issue.

190

The waging of this battle achieved a second result which was to establish the two prerequisites necessary for the abandonment of the gold standard: its discrediting and the emergence of viable alternatives. As it was the traumatic experiences of the British economy from 1925 to 1931 which made possible the development of both preconditions, it is not surprising that the decision to abandon the gold standard was not made earlier. Thus one may conclude that, if nothing else, the battle for Britain's gold standard in 1931 contributed to the evolution of monetary policy which produced the economic progress of the 1930's and the post-war era. That, in itself, was no small achievement.

NOTES

1. Leffingwell Papers, I/6/133, Leffingwell to Norman, 31 July 1944.
2. See, e.g., B/E, G 14/316, Niemeyer Memorandum, 21 September 1931.
3. Keynes, op. cit., p. 596.
4. In this connection, an article by Dr. Hjalmar Schacht is instructive. Written for the Deutsche Allgemeine Zeitung on 25 September 1931, Schacht's theme was that the British departure from the gold standard was a masterful stroke which showed that the real spirit of England was still alive. He went on to credit Britain with having chosen to effect her recovery by her own will rather than allowing a slow bleeding to death and advocating that Germany follow the lead of her fellow Saxons.
5. This is not to say definitively that the departure from the gold standard either alone or in conjunction with other decisions taken with respect to monetary matters was responsible for Britain's rapid recovery from the slump during the 1930's. For a discussion of the various factors which influenced Britain's economic progress, see, e.g., D.H. Aldcroft and H.W. Richardson, The British Economy, 1919-1939 (Batsford, London, 1969), B.B. Gilbert, British Social Policy 1914-1939 (Batsford, London, 1970), and Howson, op. cit.

[21 & 22 Geo.5.]   Gold Standard   [Ch. 46.]
                  (Amendment) Act, 1931,

CHAPTER 46

An Act to suspend the operation of sub-   A.D.1931
    section (2) of section one of the Gold
    Standard Act, 1925, and for purposes
    connected therewith.
                        [21st Stepmber 1931.]

Be it enacted by the King's most Excellent
Majesty, by and with the advice and consent
of the Lords Spiritual and Temporal and
Commons, in this present Parliament
assembled, and by the authority of the
same, as follows:

    1. --(1) Unless and until His Majesty   Suspension
by Proclamation otherwise directs, sub-   of right
section (2) of section one of the Gold   to pur-
Standard Act, 1925, shall cease to have   chase gold
effect, notwithstanding that subsection   bullion.
(1) of the said section remains in force.   15 & 16
                                              Geo.5.c.
                                              29.

    (2) The Bank of England are hereby
discharged from all liabilities in respect
of anything done by the Bank in contraven-
tion of the provision of the said subsection (2) at any time after the eighteenth
day of September, nineteen hundred and
thirty-one, and no proceedings whatsoever
shall be instituted against the Bank or any
other person in respect of anything so done
as aforesaid.

    (3) It shall be lawful for the Treasury
to make, and from time to time vary, orders
authorising the taking of such measures in
relation to the exchanges and otherwise as
they may consider expedient for meeting
difficulties in connection with the suspension of the gold standard.

This subsection shall continue in force for a period of six months from the passing of this Act.

2. This Act may be cited as the Gold Standard (Amendment) Act, 1931.

SELECTED BIBLIOGRAPHY

I   Manuscript Sources

A   Great Britain

1.   Bank of England, London

            General Archives
            Henry Clay Papers
            Sir Ernest Harvey Papers
            Lord Norman Papers

2.   Public Records Office, Kew

            Cabinet Papers: 23, 24, 27
            Foreign Office: FO 371
            PREM: 1/96, 1/97
            Treasury: T160, 171, 172, 175, 176, 177,
                  200, 208
            Ramsay MacDonald Papers

3.   Morgan Grenfell & Co., Limited, London

            General Archives

4.   Private Papers

            Lord Baldwin Papers, Cambridge University
                  Library, Cambridge.
            Ernest L. Bevin Papers, Churchill College
                  Library, Cambridge.
            R.H. Brand Papers, Bodleian Library, Ox-
                  ford.
            Austen   Chamberlain   Papers,   Birmingham
                  University Library, Birmingham.
            Neville Chamberlain Papers, Birmingham
                  University Library, Birmingham.
            Geoffrey Dawson Papers, Bodleian Library,
                  Oxford.
            Paul Einzig Papers, Churchill College,
                  Cambridge.
            R.H. Hawtrey Papers, Churchill College,
                  Cambridge.
            Lord Swinton Papers, Churchill College,
                  Cambridge.
            Lord   Templewood   Papers,   Cambridge
                  University Library, Cambridge.

B   United States of America

1.   Federal Reserve Bank of New York,
        New York, N.Y.

     General Archives
     George L. Harrison Papers

2.   Herbert Hoover Presidential Library, West
        Branch, Iowa

     Herbert Hoover Presidential Papers
     Herbert Hoover Post-Presidential Papers
     William R. Castle Papers

3.   National Archives, Washington, D.C.

     Department of Treasury: RG 39
     Department of State: RG 59

4.   Private Papers

     George L. Harrison Papers, Butler Library,
        Columbia University, New York, N.Y.
     Thomas W. Lamont Papers, Baker Library,
        Harvard University, Cambridge, Mass.
     Russell C. Leffingwell Papers, Sterling
        Library, Yale University, New Haven,
        Conn.
     Thomas H. McKittrick Papers, Baker
        Library, Harvard University,
        Cambridge, Mass.
     Eugene Meyer Papers, Library of Congress,
        Washington, D.C.
     Eugene Meyer Oral History, Butler Library,
        Columbia University, New York, N.Y.
     Ogden L. Mills Papers, Library of
        Congress, Washington, D.C.
     J.P. Morgan Papers, Morgan Library, New
        York, N.Y.
     Jackson Reynolds Oral History, Butler
        Library, Columbia University, New
        York, N.Y.
     Henry L. Stimson Papers, Sterling Library,
        Yale University, New Haven, Conn.

C   Federal Republic of Germany

     Bundesarchiv, Koblenz

Bankers Trust Company, Berlin Branch: R111

II   Printed Sources

A   Official Publications

1.   Great Britain

Documents on British Foreign Policy, 1918-1939, Series 1A (edited by W.N. Medlicott, D.A. Dakin, M.E. Lambert), 7 Vols. London, 1966-1975, Series 2 (edited by E.L. Woodward and Rohan Butler and others), 13 vols., London, 1946-1960.

Command Papers

Cmd
3897 Report of the Committee on Finance and Industry, London, June 1931.
3995 Report of the Special Advisory Committee convened under the Agreement with Germany concluded at the Hague on 20 January 1930, Basle, December 22, 1932.
4126 Final Act of the Lausanne Conference, July 1932.
4210 United States No. 4, Further Note Addressed to the United States Government, 1 December 1931.

2.   United States of America

Department of State, Papers Relating to the Foreign Relations of the United States 1924-1933, Washington, D.C., 1939-1950.

B   Newspapers and Periodicals

1.   Great Britain

The Times
The Economist

2.   United States of America

The Commercial and Financial Chronicle
The Herald Tribune
The New York Times
Time

C   Secondary Sources

Aldcroft, D.H., <u>The Inter-War Economy: Britain</u>
    <u>1919-1939</u>, London, Batsford, 1975.

Aldcroft, D.H. and Richardson, H.W., <u>The</u>
    <u>British   Economy   1870-1939</u>,   London,
    Macmillan, 1969.

Barnett, C., <u>The Collapse of British Power</u>,
    London, Eyre Methuen, 1972.

Bassett, R., <u>1931</u>, London, Macmillan, 1958.

Becker, W.H. and Wells, S.F. Jr., eds.,
    <u>Economics and World Power</u>, New York,
    Columbia University Press, 1984.

Bennett, E.W., <u>Germany and the Diplomacy of the</u>
    <u>Financial Crisis - 1931</u>, Cambridge,
    Harvard University Press, 1962.

Bernard, P. and Dubiel, H., <u>The Decline of the</u>
    <u>Third   Republic</u>,   Cambridge,   Cambridge
    University Press, 1985.

Blake, R., <u>The Conservative Party from Peel to</u>
    <u>Churchill</u>, London, Eyre and Spottiswoode,
    1970.

Bloomfield, A.I., <u>Monetary Policy Under the</u>
    <u>International Gold Standard: 1880-1914</u>,
    New York, Federal Reserve Bank of New
    York, 1959.

Boyle, A., <u>Montagu Norman</u>, London, Cassell,
    1967.

Bullock, A., <u>The Life and Times of Ernest</u>
    <u>Bevin, Volume I</u>, London, William Heinemann
    Ltd., 1960.

Burk, K. ed., <u>War and the State</u>, London, George
    Allen and Unwin, 1983.

Burk, K., <u>Britain, America and the Sinews of</u>
    <u>War</u>, London, George Allen and Unwin, 1985.

Cairncross, A. and Eichengreen B., <u>Sterling in</u>
    <u>Decline</u>, Oxford, Basil Blackwell, 1984.

Selected Bibliography

Chandler, L., <u>Benjamin Strong: Central Banker</u>,
   Washington, Brookings Institution, 1958.

Clarke, S.V.O., <u>Central Bank Cooperation</u>, New
   York, Federal Reserve Bank of New York,
   1967.

Clay, H., <u>Lord Norman</u>, New York, Macmillan,
   1957.

Clifford, A.J., <u>The Independence of the Federal
   Reserve System</u>, Philadelphia, University
   of Pennsylvania Press, 1965.

Dam, K.W., <u>The Rules of the Game</u>, Chicago,
   University of Chicago Press, 1982.

Dalton, Hugh, <u>Call Back Yesterday</u>, London,
   Frederick Muller, 1953.

Dilks, D., <u>Neville Chamberlain</u>, Cambridge,
   Cambridge University Press, 1984.

Dutton D., <u>Austen Chamberlain: Gentleman In
   Politics</u>, London, Ross Anderson, 1985.

Feiling, K., <u>Neville Chamberlain</u>, London,
   Macmillan, 1946.

Feis, H., <u>The Diplomacy of the Dollar - the
   First Era</u>, Baltimore, Johns Hopkins
   University Press, 1950.

Feis, H., <u>1933: Characters in Crisis</u>, Boston,
   Little Brown and Company, 1966.

Forbes, J.D., <u>J.P. Morgan, Jr.</u>, Charlottes-
   ville, University Press of Virginia, 1946.

Friedman, M. and Schwartz, A.S., <u>A Monetary
   History of the United States</u>, Princeton,
   Princeton University Press, 1963.

Gilbert, B.B., <u>British Social Policy 1914-1939</u>,
   London, Batsford, 1970.

Gilbert, M., <u>Winston Spencer Churchill, Volume
   V,</u>, London, Heinemann, 1976. Companion:
   <u>The Exchequer Years: 1923-1929</u>, London,
   Heinemann, 1976.

Hoover, H., *The Memoirs of Herbert Hoover*, New York, Macmillan, 1952.

Howson, S., *Domestic Monetary Management In Britain 1919-1938*, Cambridge, Cambridge University Press, 1975.

Howson, S. and Winch, D., *The Economic Advisory Council, 1930-1939*, Cambridge, Cambridge University Press, 1977.

Jackson, J., *The Politics of Depression in France: 1932-1936*, Cambridge, Cambridge University Press, 1985.

James, H., *The Reichsbank and Public Finance in Germany, 1924-1933: A Study of the Politics of Economics during the Great Depression*, Frankfurt, Fritz Knapp Verlag, 1985.

Keynes, J.M., *The Collected Writings of John Maynard Keynes, Volume XX - Activities 1929-1931*, Cambridge, Cambridge University Press for the Royal Economic Society, 1981.

Kennedy, S.C., *The Banking Crisis of 1933*, Lexington, University Press of Kentucky, 1972.

Kindleberger, C.P., *The World in Depression*, London, Allen Lane, 1973.

Kindleberger, C.P., *A Financial History of Western Europe*, London, George Allen and Unwin, 1984.

Leffler, M.P., *The Elusive Quest; America's Pursuit of European Stability and French Security, 1919-1933*, Chapel Hill, University of North Carolina Press, 1978.

Leith-Ross, Sir F.W., *Money Talks*, London, Hutchinson and Co., 1968.

Lippman, W. and Scroggs, W.O., *The United States In World Affairs - 1931*, New York, Harper & Brothers, 1932.

Selected Bibliography

Lippman, W., et al., The United States in World Affairs - 1932, New York, Harper & Brothers, 1933.

Lippman, W. et al., The United States in World Affairs - 1933, New York, Harper & Brothers, 1934.

McKercher, B.J.C., The Second Baldwin Government and the United States, 1924-1929, Cambridge, Cambridge University Press, 1984.

McKibbin, R.I., 'The Economic Policy of the Second Labour Government', Past and Present, lxviii, August 1975.

McKibbin, R.I., The Evolution of the Labour Party, Oxford, Oxford University Press, 1976.

Maier, C.S., Recasting Bourgeois Europe, Princeton, Princeton University Press, 1975.

Marquand, D., Ramsay MacDonald, London, Jonathan Cape, 1977.

Moggeridge, D.E., British Monetary Policy - 1924-1931, Cambridge, Cambridge University Press, 1972.

Moggeridge, D.E., 'The 1931 Financial Crisis - A New View', The Banker, cxx, 1970.

Moreau, E., Souvenirs d'un Governeur de la Banque de France, Paris, Editions M. Th. Genin, 1954.

Mowat, C., Britain Between the Wars 1918-1940, Boston, Beacon Press, 1955.

O'Halpin, E., Sir Warren Fisher of the Civil Service 1919-1939, Cambridge Ph.D., 1982.

Perrett, G., America In the Twenties, New York, Touchstone, Simon and Schuster, 1982.

Pollard, S., The Development of the British Economy 1914-1980, 3rd ed., London, Edward Arnold, 1984.

Redmond, J., 'The Sterling Overvaluation in 1925: A Multilateral Approach', Economic History Review, xxxvii, November 1984.

Rose, K., King George V, London, Weidenfeld and Nicolson, 1983.

Sayers, R.S., The Bank of England, 1891-1944, Cambridge, Cambridge University Press, 1976.

Schucker, S.A., The End of French Predominance In Europe, Chapel Hill, University of North Carolina Press, 1976.

Silverman, D.P., Reconstructing Europe After the Great War, Cambridge, Harvard University Press, 1982.

Sinclair, A., Corsair: The Life of J. Pierpont Morgan, Boston, Little Brown and Co., 1981.

Skidelsky, R., Politicians and the Slump, London, Macmillan, 1967.

Smith, R.N., An Uncommon Man - The Triumph of Herbert Hoover, New York, Simon and Schuster, 1984.

Snowden, P., An Autobiography, London, Ivor Nicholson and Watson, 1938.

Stimson, H.L. and Bundy, M., On Active Service In Peace and War, New York, Harper and Brothers, 1947.

Trachtenberg, M., Reparations In World Politics, New York, Columbia University Press, 1980.

Williams, D., 'London and the 1931 Financial Crisis', Economic History Review, xv, April 1963.

Williamson, P., 'Financiers, the Gold Standard and British Politics, 1925-1931' in Turner, J., ed., Businessmen and Politics, London, Heinemann, 1984.

Williamson, P., 'A Bankers' Ramp? Financiers and the British Political Crisis of August 1931', <u>English Historical Review</u>, xcix, October 1984.

Wilson, J.H., <u>American Business and Foreign Policy 1920-1933</u>, Boston, Beacon Press, 1973.

Wilson, J.H., <u>Herbert Hoover: Forgotten Progessive</u>, Boston, Little Brown and Co., 1975.

Young, G.M., <u>Stanley Baldwin</u>, London, Rupert Hart Davis, 1952.

For Product Safety Concerns and Information please contact our
EU representative GPSR@taylorandfrancis.com Taylor & Francis
Verlag GmbH, Kaufingerstraße 24, 80331 München, Germany